American

COMPOSERS

EDWARD STRICKLAND

American

COMPOSERS

Dialogues on Contemporary Music

INDIANA UNIVERSITY PRESS
Bloomington and Indianapolis

Earlier versions of each of the interviews except for the conversation
with Ingram Marshall have appeared in *Fanfare*.

The paper used in this publication meets the minimum requirements of
American National Standard for Information Sciences—Permanence of
Paper for Printed Library Materials, ANSI Z39.48-1984.

 ™

Manufactured in the United States of America

Library of Congress Cataloging-in-Publication Data
Strickland, Edward.
    American composers : dialogues on contemporary music / Edward
Strickland.
        p.   cm.
    Includes bibliographical references.
    Includes index.
    ISBN 0-253-35498-6 (alk. paper). — ISBN 0-253-20643-X (pbk. :
alk. paper)
    1. Composers—United States—Interviews. 2. Music—United
States—20th century—History and criticism. I. Title. II. Title:
Eleven composers.
M ML390.S942   1991
    780'.92'273—dc20   90-46787

1   2   3   4   5   95   94   93   92   91

for J. O. and Catherine Strickland
Peter and Margaret Duffy

And these the Labours of the Sons of Los in Allamanda:
And in the City of Golgonooza: & in Luban: & around
The Lake of Udan-Adan, in the Forests of Entuthon Benython
Where Souls incessant wail, being piteous Passions & Desires
With neither lineament nor form but like to watry clouds
The Passions & Desires descend upon the hungry winds
For such alone Sleepers remain meer passion & appetite;
The Sons of Los clothe them & feed & provide houses & fields

—Blake, *Milton*, Plate 26

Contents

In the 1970s, when I was a graduate student and then a professor, the musicians I listened to most frequently, almost daily for months at a time, were the pianists Glenn Gould and Keith Jarrett. Beyond surface mannerisms the two had little in common but excellence, so I suppose I gravitated to one or the other depending on whether my musical mood called for incisiveness or expansiveness, a sense of absolute control or utter exposure.

By the end of the decade I was writing for *Fanfare* magazine, mainly on Baroque music, and in July 1982 I phoned CBS Masterworks for information on Gould's forthcoming re-recording of Bach's Goldberg Variations. I was asked if I would like to set up an interview with Gould, but I declined, largely because I was submerged in the practical as well as the emotional repercussions of the deaths of my parents in March and May. I had never interviewed anyone about anything in my life, and the moment did not seem propitious, but I promised to call back to discuss the possibility of an interview during my Christmas vacation.

When I phoned back in October, it was to check the facts in a memorial article on Gould I had been asked to write.

Four years later I was invited to interview Keith Jarrett. Though daunted by my still complete inexperience and his reputation as volatile and difficult, I accepted immediately. At noon two months later, recovering from a severe flu, I drove across New Jersey through the sporadically freezing rain, expecting to talk for perhaps an hour. We ended up conversing, to our mutual surprise, into the evening. When I belatedly reached my dinner date, she told me she was about to request a dredging of the Jersey lakes.

In the meantime I had been invited to interview Steve Reich, another musician whose work had intrigued me for years. I did so two weeks later at the end of a five-mile walk through Manhattan to digest the extensive notes I had organized in self-defense after reading an interview that began, "I could tell Steve Reich thought I was a jerk."

Reich, like Jarrett, proved extremely gracious and cooperative both during the interview and afterwards.

When not merely constitutional, the perceived arrogance or egomania of interviewees arises from a context which *demands* they talk about themselves in detail that would be considered shameless elsewhere, an exigency few of their critics, professional or otherwise, have ever confronted. Furthermore, the composer usually does not know the interviewer from Adam (or Eve), while, more unfortunately, the interviewer on today's assignment from the local paper often does not know the composer from Magister Leoninus (or Hildegard of Bingen). Interviews are normally arranged by the record company, opera company, or whatever company has cash on the line, and they generally reflect the uncomplicated aspirations of these corporate entities— i.e., to familiarize potential consumers with the artist's name and current project. After a hundred or a thousand such interviews ("Well, Mr. Jarrett, they tell me you play the piano"; "So what's all this about repetition, Mr. Reich?"), it is no wonder if the artist withdraws defensively, shifts to automatic pilot, or even vents understandable frustration. Interviewers have themselves been known to do the same when today's column rather than a life's work is in question.

Having enjoyed my conversations with both composers, I decided to contact others I admired, beginning three months later with La Monte Young, for what became an irregular series of magazine interviews. The conversations appear in chronological order in transcripts edited from two dozen cassette tapes. I have tried to convey not only the content but also the tone of each dialogue, within (and when it served that primary purpose, slightly beyond) the limits of conciseness. I was not interested in fabricating either the robotic Ping-Pong game of *Q* and *A* or the monologue-*cum*-filler-questions that still dominate the print interview genre. I was even less interested in an ostensibly unmediated tape transcription like Andy Warhol's '60s period piece, *a*.

Pure transcription from tape to print is, in fact, impossible. There is no way of accurately representing the overlapping of voices, the rhythm of the exchange, or, for that matter, the pace and inflection of the individual voice. One can italicize, capitalize, etc., to suggest nuances of dynamics or pitch, but what is left to the imagination are such essential elements as the laser-beam delivery of Steve Reich, the most virtuosic talker I have ever met, or the simultaneously courtly and homespun drawl of George Crumb; the vibrancy of Meredith Monk's voice (even when she is not singing), or the striking approximation of the additive-process structure of his music in occasional sentences of Philip Glass—stopping a thought, repeating it with an additional phrase, repeating all the preceding, and concluding the thought.

Body language is all but totally lost in print: Jarrett's expression modulating as surprisingly as his piano solos from pained intentness to unguarded hilarity; Terry Riley sitting on a mat by the wood-burning stove in contagious tranquility; La Monte Young one moment leaning back precariously on his chair with a slice of grapefruit and the next pacing the floor; Glass responding to alternate questions as if world peace hinged on his response and he was wondering what to have for dinner. (In fact, he probably was, since we parted at the local Korean greengrocer's.)

The nonintellectual adventures of the series included a short trip through space to concrete, courtesy of a subway grating, on the way to

Monk's loft, and a near-collision with a bottle thrown not at me but at the universe by a local derelict as I waited for Glass to arrive home. But the most curious event occurred two days before my interview with Riley in his Sierra Nevada home three hours northeast of San Francisco.

At noon the day after my arrival in the Bay Area, pressured by a social engagement, I walked to the nearest and by no means my favorite of the area's hundreds of Mexican restaurants for my ritual burrito. As I finished it, I looked up from the local paper to find diagonally across from me two boys flanking a man who bore a striking resemblance to photos of Riley. With some trepidation I walked over and launched what sounded to me like an absurdist game of Twenty Questions with "Excuse me, are you a composer?" Looking slightly astonished, the man answered yes, and I resisted the urge to continue with "Are you a composer of (tonal music, string quartets, tape loops etc.)?"—opting rather for the obvious question, which was also answered affirmatively.

Riley had driven down unexpectedly to visit a hospitalized relative. To augment the coincidence, he had first taken his sons to the vegetarian restaurant up the street, but they had overruled him, so that both he and I were there under social duress. "When you came out of nowhere asking me if I was a composer," Riley confirmed later, "I thought, 'Who *is* this, some kind of psychic?' " When I pulled up at his door two days later, his younger son announced, "Hey Dad, it's the guy from the taco place!"

I want to thank Terry and the other musicians for their participation, and for their support *Fanfare* publisher Joel Flegler, Ron Firman, Dennis Strickland, Adrien Kathryn Strickland, C.F.M., Virginia Pump, Ivonne Ramírez, Martin Drury, José Luis Torres, Joseph Wunderle, Jean Lodge, Jeff Petry, and Ileana (flor de las) Flores.

Chiang Mai, Thailand
September 1990

American

COMPOSERS

This book was not designed to present either a case or a "school" of composers but to offer informal dialogues with artists whose work intrigued me personally and represented some of the most important innovations in recent American music. If Minimalists appear to have a disproportionately maximal presence, that is due to the importance of the work of the quite individual composers so labeled, who find themselves progressively more procrustean bedfellows as their distinctive styles continue to evolve. While Minimalism is the first indigenous classical style created and shared by Americans, it may further serve, in historical context, as a metonym for the new American classical music in its two most important facets, the democratizing of genre and the globalizing of influence.

We are all weary of hearing the term "renaissance" applied instantly to the artistic trend of the week, but I believe we are witnessing the maturation after two centuries of nationhood of a distinctly American music, rooted in the European classical tradition in which all of these composers were trained, yet asserting its independent identity by embracing both the nonclassical music of its own culture and the musical riches of once-alien non-Western cultures. As opposed to the elitism of postwar Serialism and the academic hegemony (and to some extent the international incestuousness of avant-garde experimentalism), the new American music is inclusive rather than exclusive, merging what H. Wiley Hitchcock terms the "vernacular" and "cultivated" national traditions while incarnating more successfully than any other art form the supranational network of communication foretold by McLuhan.

Communication is a dangerous word for its implied reduction of art to information—e.g., literature courses catalogued under "Communication Arts." I use it, however, to suggest the revival of the concept of music as shared sound rather than printed score, performance rather than research science, act rather than theory. Examples of the two extremes are Keith Jarrett's description of his solo concerts as "a communion with the whole audience" and the now (in)famous title—not the composer's but his editors'—of Milton Babbitt's 1958 essay, "Who Cares If You Listen?"

To apply a distinction of literary theorist M. H. Abrams, the movement from academism represents a reorientation toward a more "pragmatic" (from Greek *pragma*, deed or action) theory of art as a means of affecting an audience and away from a predominantly "objective" theory of the artwork as a formally beautiful construct or artifact. Concomitant developments include explorations of nontraditional modes of performance (George Crumb's processions and rituals, the multimedia possibilities of Meredith Monk's sometimes movable musical feasts, or John Adams's *Christian Zeal and Activity*) and musical ensembles, often led by the composer-performer (La Monte Young's Theatre of Eternal Music, Steve Reich and Musicians, the Philip Glass Ensemble, Anthony Davis's Episteme or Group/Davis), along with open-ended forms amenable to spontaneous invention influenced by the specific concert audience or acoustic (Jarrett's and Terry Riley's solo keyboard concerts, John Zorn's game structures, Ingram Marshall's live/tape performances). The result has been music of greater vitality and distinctiveness than that of any period in our history.

Most recent surveys of American music emphasize the pluralism and hybridism that distinguish it, reflecting the diversity of cultural ingredients in the American melting pot. To a much greater extent than earlier, music has subsumed into a classical structure some of the richness of our nonclassical idioms, especially the very different musical languages of jazz and rock, which represent, with motion pictures, the most internationally recognized expressions of American culture.

This involves a second degree of coalescence, in a sense, since well before the commercial jazz-rock "fusion" music of the 1970s, jazz and rock were in their individual origins "fusion" musics, jazz deriving primarily from blues, ragtime, and marching-band music, rock integrating black blues (and its dance-oriented offshoot R&B) and white country music.

Allusions to the jazz tradition by European classical composers go back to Debussy's *Children's Corner Suite* and *Préludes* and Stravinsky's *Ragtime* and *Piano Rag Music*; while in America Charles Ives, who as a student frequented and may have spelled the pianist at the local vaudeville house, interpolated ragtime into the "Hawthorne" movement of his "Concord" Sonata. Though the sonata was not published until 1919 (and then privately), shortly after its composition other American composers began to make extensive use of—or, perhaps more accurately, reference to—the jazz tradition. Henry Gilbert's *Dances in Ragtime Rhythm* dates from 1915, Wallingford Riegger's *Triple Jazz* and Louis Gruenberg's First Violin Sonata from 1918. In the '20s George Gershwin is the prime example, but other notables include John Alden Carpenter (*Krazy Kat* and *Skyscrapers*), George Antheil (*Jazz Symphony* and *Ballet mécanique*), and Aaron Copland (the Organ Symphony, Piano Concerto, and *Music for the Theater*). The early '40s saw Randall Thompson's *Jazz Poem* and the jazzlike syncopations of William Schuman's *Symphony for Strings*, and in the next decade and later Gunther Schuller promoted "third-stream music" as a *rapprochement* of jazz and classical music. Artists such as Miles Davis, Gil Evans, and John Lewis incorporated classical elements into jazz; occasionally Bach fugues and other European compositions were jazzed up, to little purpose other than fun; and works were written for hybrid ensembles of jazz and string quartets.

In all of this the results resemble more closely a chemical mixture than a compound. The effort to span the void between two musical worlds is as audible as it is noble, the forced integration of styles a musical equivalent of busing. For the most part, for half a century American composers alluded to jazz and tried to adapt (or convert or co-opt) it to their purposes—see Langston Hughes's comments on blues symphonies in "Note on Commercial Theatre"—with all the self-consciousness of the subtitle to *American Life* bestowed by its creator, Adolph Weiss, in 1929: *Scherzoso Jazzoso*. Today's composers have had the advantage of experiencing those experiments and perhaps building upon them. More important, many of them have had active experience as jazz players. The result is a more cogent, less superficial cross-fertilization of genres.

Among the artists interviewed, Keith Jarrett is a musical amphibian both as interpreter and as composer, recording jazz and Baroque classics with equal success. Among the early Minimalists, La Monte Young, Terry Riley, and Steve Reich all helped support themselves playing bop, blues, or ragtime in their student days (and in the case of Riley afterwards). Anthony Davis and John Zorn both have extensive jazz experience, Zorn having recorded an album of Ornette Coleman compositions leading a combo on alto.

In his essay "On Poesy or Art" (c. 1818), Samuel Taylor Coleridge makes a distinction germane to this topic while redefining the mimetic concept of art in terms more congenial to the Romantic sensibility. Art imitates nature, he suggests, by copying not its sensuous data, which he calls *natura naturata*, but its "essence," *natura naturans*, the "co-instaneity of the plan and the execution" in natural growth, the creative principle itself. This is reflected, he says, in the organic rather than the mechanical structure of the artwork, for mimesis is ultimately a formal rather than a material principle. The artist does not select and recontextualize content but evolves it.

Analogously, the jazz influence in contemporary music is qualitatively different from earlier adaptations or expropriations of its musical vocabulary. Rather than snatches of blue notes, cameo appearances by wa-wa mutes, or obtrusive episodes of rag or swing rhythm, we now confront a wholesale adaptation of specific techniques (syncopation, scat, call-and-response), of a jazz-aligned and non-European sense of meter and rhythm, and, most important, of improvisation, the central tenet of the jazz faith, as a creative principle within (or without) composition.

While both Anthony Davis and John Adams point to Duke Ellington as a model for their arrangements and orchestrations, Davis proves the more formally eclectic in his consistent use of improvisational elements in his composed works. This represents an extension of the Charles Mingus–inspired experimentation begun in the early '70s by Anthony Braxton and others associated with AACM (Association for the Advancement of Creative

Musicians) and BAG (Black Artists Group). Their work rather than the electrified sound effects of their more popular jazz-rock contemporaries may come to be recognized as the real "fusion" music of the period, uniting art-music structures and the improvisation of jazz—"our persecuted chamber music," in Virgil Thomson's words. The technique of juxtaposing composition as a base and improvisation as a "creative sound-burst" (Braxton) also influenced the alternation of open and set improvisational modes in the work of Zorn, who learned from AACM and BAG firsthand in his early twenties. With the incorporation of improvisational structures within the compositional framework—also operative in the jazz Impressionism of Jarrett's earlier concerto-like works—the content as well as the duration of a given work changes from one performance to the next, through the addition/subtraction of melodic/harmonic/rhythmic motives. There is even broader durational, if not thematic, leeway in much of Minimalist ensemble work, as there is in Young's *The Well-Tuned Piano*, each realization of which is, with reason, separately entitled by date.

Meredith Monk mentions jazz singers Ella Fitzgerald and Mildred Bailey and "new thing" saxophonist Albert Ayler as influences in expanding her concept of vocal possibilities. The founder of "free jazz," Ornette Coleman, is a major structural influence on Zorn as well a stylistic influence on his alto playing. But the influence of modal jazz is most widespread, particularly in Minimalism, as the composers testify.

Pianist George Russell provided the theoretical basis for modal jazz with *The Lydian Chromatic Concept of Tonal Organization* and contributed a modal introduction to Dizzy Gillespie's "Cubano Be" as early as 1947. Miles Davis popularized the style in the title track from his 1958 *Milestones* and perfected it in the landmark *Kind of Blue* the following year. The modal style, entailing the rejection of harmonic progressions (chord changes—or just "changes," in musicians' parlance) for improvisation within scales (modes), often other than the conventional major and minor, was further advanced and Easternized with reference to Arabic *maqamat* and Indian *ragam* by Davis's former sideman, John Coltrane, from 1960 (*My Favorite Things*) through 1964 (*A Love Supreme*).

Apart from inspiring exploration of Western (classical and liturgical) as well as Eastern modes, modal jazz was an enormous structural influence on the harmonic movement of Minimalism: the three simple modulations of Riley's *In C* now seem like an extension of Davis's "So What"—a performance of which by Chet Baker Riley had set canonically with tape loops two years earlier in *Music for the Gift*. Perhaps most important, the adaptation of the harmonic freedom permitted by modality as a compositional technique led inevitably to a greater emphasis on the improvisational element essential not only to jazz but also to *maqam* (or the *dastgah, makam,* and *shashmaqam* of Iran, Turkey, and Uzbekistan) and raga. After fading from jazz popularity, modalism was taken up for its incantatory and hypnotic possibilities by acid-rockers later in the decade.

The style is revived, interestingly, in a recent jazz album by Keith Jarrett (another alumnus of Miles Davis bands), a series of modal improvisations punningly entitled *Changeless*. They are trio improvisations and thus necessarily only approximate the open-ended quality of his solo concerts, which take the fundamental jazz principle of improvisation to the limit—*creatio ex nihilo*—"nothing" begetting Chopinesque lyricism and post-Bachian chromatic counterpoint in tandem with blues, gospel, lullabyes, and musical evocations of every continent, including Antarctica. Though Jarrett has expressed no admiration for Minimalism other than for the work of the Estonian Arvo Pärt, both in *Changeless* and in a recent concert he has employed a technique reminiscent of La Monte Young's "clouds," in which lower-register notes are played so fast as to lose their individual identity and suggest a sustained roar.

Young avers that these "clouds," which now last several minutes, in earlier days might have lasted forty-five. The Idaho-born composer's sense of stasis derives less from modal jazz (his landmark *Trio for Strings* was composed before it became popular) than from a humbler indigenous source, the long-held harmonies of the two- and three-chord cowboy songs he heard daily as a child, combined in strange synthesis with, among other things, the American Indian music to which an Apache friend introduced him as a teenager. Despite its Oriental atemporality, Young notes that his music displays a peculiarly American sense of sounds suspended in time, an expansiveness that suggests the mythic West as much as the mystic East.

On two sides of the continent, Riley and Jarrett, living rurally on what was Indian land, note the influence of their environment in their work. John Zorn, the ultimate city musician, feels the greatest influence on his music of montage was growing up in the ethnic crazy quilt of New York; while George Crumb attributes his inner acoustic to his upbringing in a West Virginia valley near the junction of the Kanawha and Elk rivers. If Young's music in its theoretically infinite extension evokes the western sky, Crumb's alternately shocking and finely calibrated timbres may be the bequest of small-town peace in the valley, which transforms bird calls or cricket chirrups into "surround-sound" sonic events. The ambiental underscoring of acoustic phenomena by their emergence from silence to prolonged resonance is closely allied to the sense of both abruptness and temporal suspension in Crumb's work, which may explain Eric Salzman's calling Crumb "a Stravinskyite turned Minimalist."

Crumb avows, surprisingly to me, the influence of another branch of American music, indicating that the rock music his sons collected came to expand his ideas of vocal potential even further away from the *bel canto* tradition. The influence is somehow more obvious, possibly because less rhetorical, in the extended-vocal techniques of Meredith Monk, who briefly found herself alternating between *lieder* and lead-singing in a rock group.

In composers like Jarrett, Zorn, Laurie Anderson, Glenn Branca, Rhys Chatham, Paul Dresher, and Scott Johnson the rock influence is often explicit, but it is a significant if less obvious force in early Minimalism as well, since modal jazz was not the only native influence putting the brakes on Minimalist harmonic movement. Much of the rock'n'roll in the air in the early days of Minimalism was of the three-chord, blues-based variety or the inevitable tonic–relative minor–subdominant–dominant ballad progression.

The riff may be as important as the raga here. Reich alludes to "Shotgun," the 1965 hit by Junior Walker and the All Stars, which featured the leader's lounge-funk sax over a relentless eight-note organ/bass hook. A longer-lived fame was granted James Brown for his balletic and quasi-improvisational soul ariosos moaned and grunted over an endless collective riff with abrupt (melo)dramatic rests by the brass and electric guitars of the Famous Flames. Furthermore, while "Shotgun" observed the time limit of the 45-rpm disc, a Brown song might extend its single harmony to soap opera (or *Four Organs*) length onstage.

Ingram Marshall suggests that rock amplification is a subconscious influence on all contemporary composers, but it is an obvious one on Branca and Glass in particular, which may account in part for the latter's having achieved the most widespread popularity of the Minimalists. The hard-edged dynamic and rhythmic insistence of much of the music for the Philip Glass Ensemble is worlds away from the chimelike canonic buoyancy of Steve Reich and Musicians, attributed by drummer Reich in part to his emulation of bop drummer Kenny Clarke's brushwork. While Glass has collaborated with rock artists, Reich's ensemble has recently performed at the JVC Jazz Festival, bringing that wheel full circle. "Very strong but very subliminal" is baby-boomer John Adams's characterization of rock's influence on his pulsation and harmonic rhythm; perhaps more apparent non-classical presences in his work are spirituals (virtually ubiquitous in Marshall's work) and show music.

What may be, paradoxically, as American as native topographical and musical influences is the profound indebtedness of the new American music to musics of other cultures. Our classical music—like jazz and rock to a large extent—remains based in the European music to which it has had an intimate if often oppressive relationship. Barbara Tischler has argued recently that American music came of age in the 1920s not by defining itself parochially against European influence but by joining an international movement of what was then avant-gardism. My own feeling is that the achievement of a national musical identity, while undeniably advanced during the period in question, remains more problematic than Tischler seems to grant. Certainly the period represents a liberation of American music from the dessicated tone colors of the post-Romantic palette and an advance in structural as well as harmonic complexity. Nonetheless, there lingers in the let's-be-American obsession of the '20s and '30s ("I was anxious to write a work that would be immediately recognized as American in character," said Aaron Copland) something of the forced nationalism of the native-

American vogue at the turn of the century, or even the arbitrary program-matism of the '20s and '30s of the *previous* century. (Witness Bohemian-born Anthony Philip Heinrich, "the Beethoven of America," author of the *Barbecue Divertimento* and *Yankee Doodliad*—and the immortal subtitle, "There is no *da capo* in death.")

For some of us, there is more sense of the western frontier in ten minutes of La Monte Young than in the *Grand Canyon Suite* and all the transplanted cowboy themes of *Billy the Kid* and *Rodeo*, just as—to turn from the cowboys to the Indians—there is more of their world in sections of Jarrett's *Spirits* or Riley's *Cadenza on the Night Plain* than in all the heroic earnest-ness of Arthur Farwell's pioneering Wa-Wan Press.

Native Americans have been as misrepresented musically as politically, however well intentioned the efforts of American composers. Heinrich's *Pushmataha, a Venerable Chief of a Western Tribe of Indians* (1831) owes more to Chateaubriand than to the chief. None of the Indian operas of Charles Sanford Skilton, Victor Herbert, Charles Wakefield Cadman, Ar-thur Nevin, or Alberto Bimboni make any real attempt to assimilate the world they pillage for the quaint and pathetic. Arthur Foote, Charles Tom-linson Griffes, and even Edward MacDowell fare little better; the songs of the Iroquois, Kiowas, and Omahas that MacDowell discovered in a German songbook are painfully subordinated in *Indian Suite* to a (very) late-Roman-tic aesthetic. This is not to degrade the efforts of these composers, good or indifferent, but to suggest the inadequacy of the picturesque approach to an alien world, of the musical tourism that finally creates only Broadway buck-aroos and Impressionistic braves.

It may not be going too far to suggest that the skill and training of these artists work against them in this protoethnomusicological effort. In a later period, the very sophistication of the avant-garde techniques acquired by Copland in his European studies thwart, to my ears, his efforts to convey the spirit of a less-convoluted cultural milieu than Paris or Brooklyn. In the absence of an organic connection between method and content, a sense of disjunction or superimposition rather than efflorescence of style and form is unavoidable. While any effort to convey an alien culture or subculture is necessarily an approximation, there are degrees of success in evading the sense of "translation." Some insist *Hamlet* is better in German (and, con-ceivably, *Guys 'n' Dolls* in Czech), but just as the classical jazzbos of the '20s recall a folksinger I once heard introducing his courageous rendition of Bessie Smith's "Empty Bed Blues" with an Oxbridge accent, so the *ersatz* Indians of the past inevitably evoke not Crazy Horse but Tonto.

If the avant-gardism of the '20s and '30s represents the fulfilment of the quest for American musical identity, what became of that identity in the '40s and '50s? Is there anything distinguishably American about Serialism and its offshoots this side of the Atlantic, or doesn't the *a priori* neutrality of the style entail cultural (and with some exceptions, one might even argue, expressive) deracination? Is there an atonalist (or experimentalist) whose works reflect the reality of postwar American as opposed to European society, apart from its underlying and often rhetorically exaggerated Cold War anxiety?

The rigidity of Serialism may be by definition a stylization of what was an atonal style, which had more to do with world view than with establishing precompositional parameters as transcendental categories. Whether or not the tone row is a reaction-formation provoked by the anxiety attendant upon Schoenberg's "emancipation of dissonance," the restless energy of American society, particularly in the '60s, did not prove especially amenable to its strictures. Even if much of early Minimalism ends up as biographical footnotes, its radical reaction against academism in the dogged, maybe even boring, simplicity of its insistence on bare-bones tonality, modular structure, and rhythmic repetition (leaving aside relatively more complex questions of harmonic and dynamic stasis) was a cathartic prerequisite to its more sophisticated musical contributions.

Minimalism effected its liberation from "the dark-brown Angst of Vienna" (Reich) and the Parisian "wasteland, dominated by these maniacs, these creeps, who were trying to make everyone write this crazy creepy music" (Glass) only by allying itself with the non-Western world: India, Ghana, Bali, the Middle East, and elsewhere. In this it served as a model for later music, just as it was anticipated by such American explorers of non-Western music as John Cage, Henry Cowell, Lou Harrison, and Alan Hovhaness.

Indian music has had the most profound influence on recent American music. Notating Ravi Shankar's music for Western musicians transformed Glass's concept of musical structure, leading Glass to study with tabla master Alla Rakha and to visit India frequently to experience the music and Khatikali dance-drama *in situ*. La Monte Young and Terry Riley have studied North Indian Kirana singing with Pandit Pran Nath for two decades, which has transformed their entire careers, not to say lives. George Crumb's experience of the music of his Indian colleagues at the University of Pennsylvania had a profound effect on his concept of the function of the drone. The '60s association of Indian music with consciousness expansion through chemical or other means persists into the '80s in John Corigliano's imaginative montage of Indian microtonality with Stravinskian dissonance and a metamorphic "Rock of Ages" in the first hallucination sequence of his score for the film *Altered States*.

Steve Reich studied drumming in Ghana and Balinese music back home. African drumming (and hocket) pervade his *Drumming*, despite mild disclaimers by the composer. Pygmy influences are acknowledged by Jon Hassell, James Newton, and Paul Dresher and appear in sections of Jarrett's *Spirits* and the choral chant of Glass's *Einstein on the Beach*; while David Byrne Africanized tape looping and *musique concrète* with Brian Eno in *My Life in the Bush of Ghosts*. More broadly speaking, the rhythmic base and varied repetitiveness of African music, in part filtered through the cross-rhythms of jazz, are an essential influence on the ensemble work of the Minimalists and Anthony Davis.

Davis is one of many to have felt the influence of Indonesian music, in his case the *wayang* shadow-puppet theater that has inspired, and after which he has named, many of his works. Davis acknowledges the influence of the earlier exploration and adaptation of gamelan by Reich, and these two, along with Lou Harrison, have been most successful in internalizing that influence. It appeared in American music as early as Colin McPhee's 1936 *Tabuh-Tabuhan* and Cage's 1939 *First Construction (in Metal)*, for trans-Asian cymbals and gongs, etc., arranged in a modular rhythmic structure analogous to Indian *talam* (and was felt in his later prepared-piano pieces). Like McPhee, Ingram Marshall spent time in Indonesia; he has composed a gamelan piece entitled *Woodstone* and has made the long wooden Balinese flute, the gambuh, something of a trademark in his ethereal combination of primitive, or primal, woodwind with the electronic technology of synthesizer and tape.

Crumb's percussion is often gamelan-tinged, while Afro-Iberian flamenco underlies the extended vocals of his Lorca settings and the very different musical world of Reich's *Clapping Music*. Mongolian *hoomi* and Tibetan overtone (and chord) chanting have left their mark on Monk and especially on David Hykes, as soloist and leader of the Harmonic Choir. This music was regarded as almost extraterrestrial in the mid-'80s, but it has already been accepted into the mainstream musical vocabulary of film scores (*Dead Poets Society*). Crumb has been influenced by Chinese operatic techniques and the Japanese instrumentarium; Young by the shrill suspension of *gagaku*; and John Zorn by the Tokyo avant-garde—he is in fact a member of it and spends several months a year in his apartment in Tokyo. South American and Caribbean percussion add dramatic voices to Zorn's sonic collages. Marshall's work is known for its reproduction (and transformation through digital sampling) of ethnic music from Corsica, the Balkan states, Scandinavia, and the Soviet Union.

This internationalizing of American music would have been impossible at an earlier period, not only because international discs and tapes proliferated only relatively recently but also because of the insecurity of American composers particularly vis-à-vis their European brethren. Before looking beyond Europe, American music had to declare its independence, however self-consciously. From this perspective the American(istic) music of the '20s and '30s may be seen as a necessary preparation for a more instinctive, less calculated reclamation of domestic roots as well as the search for kinship with musics as distant as the other side of Earth.

The incorporation of planet-wide musical riches into our own heritage (McPhee, Harrison, Reich, and Davis, for example, represent four generations of Americanized gamelan) may illustrate to some a kind of musical imperialism, an exploitation of musical resources. From another perspective, imitation, as opposed to gratuitous borrowing, is the sincerest form of flattery, and the ever-growing respect in America for the diversity of world music may reflect the maturation of a nation of immigrants that invented itself by declaring universal equality.

The democratizing of genres and globalizing of influence, which I have suggested are the two most important trends in recent American music, seem now to possess an irresistible momentum, barring extramusical considerations, social or political, that might arise. Even the trappings of performance illustrate this democratizing, from casual dress (tuxedo suppliers are in a bear market) and cognomens (it is not "Terence Riley" or "S. Michael Reich") to the desegregation of composer and performers (in composer-led ensembles) and of performers and audience (Pauline Oliveros's participatory events, concerts in lofts, and light environments like Marian Zazeela's with first-come-first-serve seating on the floor). The relative deemphasis on both the solistic and the conductorial aristocracies of concerto form and traditional orchestral organization is a further instance of musical democratization.

One does not have to subscribe to any of the diverse eschatologies of Marx, McLuhan, or Teilhard, in or out of fashion, to sense the profound cultural and spiritual implications of musical globalization, if our artists are in any sense our antennae or, in Shelley's more Romantic words, "the hierophants of an unapprehended inspiration." This view of the artist, specifically the musician, as *vates* [prophet] has been endorsed from a Marxist perspective by Jacques Attali, who goes a step beyond the musico-cultural etiology and morphology of Max Weber and Theodor Adorno in arguing that music is not merely derivative or reflective of its culture but literally prefigurative: "Music is prophetic and social organization echoes it."

Then again, perhaps he and Shelley are wrong. And maybe the point of view expressed here suffers from an inevitable lack of temporal perspective.

It is plausible to interpret American music history as constructed of alternating periods of subservience to the European tradition and self-assertion; thus it is conceivable that our own *fin de siècle* may witness a return to European roots, and the movements we have been discussing (which in fact have parallels across Europe) will be seen as temporary aberrations, exotic detours. A reaction against rash syncretism might result in a resurgence of nationalistic music and/or a rigorously neoclassical typology of genres. A music historian of the future might lump together all the artists here, from the slow-motion Minimalist Young to the frenetic maximalist Zorn, in a chapter on "The Eclectics."

If so, I hope what follows helps clarify how they felt way back when. As one of them, George Crumb, notes below in another context, there is a nobility in purism as well as in eclecticism. Let's hope it sounds as interesting.

Select Bibliography

Jacques Attali. *Noise: The Political Economy of Music*. Translated by Brian Massumi. Minneapolis: University of Minnesota Press, 1985.

Gilbert Chase. *America's Music: From the Pilgrims to the Present*. 3d ed. Urbana: University of Illinois Press, 1987.

James Lincoln Collier. *The Making of Jazz: A Comprehensive History*. New York: Dell, 1978.

David Ewen. *American Composers: A Biographical Dictionary*. New York: Putnam, 1982.

Paul Griffiths. *Modern Music: The Avant Garde since 1945*. New York: Braziller, 1981.

————. *Encyclopaedia of 20th-Century Music*. London: Thames and Hudson, 1986.

Charles Hamm. *Music in the New World*. New York: Norton, 1983.

H. Wiley Hitchcock. *Music in the United States: A Historical Introduction*. 2d ed. Englewood Cliffs: Prentice-Hall, 1974.

————, ed. *The New Grove Dictionary of American Music*. New York: Grove's Dictionaries, 1986.

Daniel Klingman. *American Music: A Panorama*. New York: Schirmer, 1979.

Wilfrid Mellers. *Music in a New Found Land: Themes and Developments in the History of American Music*. New York: Knopf, 1965.

John Rockwell. *All American Music: Composition in the Late Twentieth Century*. New York: Knopf, 1983.

Eric Salzman. *Twentieth-Century Music: An Introduction*. 2d ed. Englewood Cliffs: Prentice-Hall, 1974.

John Schaefer. *New Sounds: A Listener's Guide to New Music*. New York: Harper and Row, 1987.

Barbara Tischler. *An American Music: The Search for an American Musical Identity*. New York: Oxford, 1986.

Peter Yates. *Twentieth-Century Music*. New York: Putnam, 1967.

Keith Jarrett

Photo by Susanne Stevens, courtesy ECM Records.

Keith Jarrett was born in Allentown, Pennsylvania, in 1945 and began playing piano and drums at age three. He took up other instruments, as well as composition and improvisation, while still in grade school, and at fifteen he gave a piano recital of his own work. After declining a scholarship to continue composition studies in Paris with Nadia Boulanger, he attended the Berklee School of Music in Boston for a year on another scholarship. He then abandoned formal classical training and "starved for about five months" in New York, "playing the drums, and getting all the neighbors mad" before attracting attention for his jazz pianism while he was still in his teens. By his mid-twenties, Jarrett had played in combos led by Art Blakey, Rahsaan Roland Kirk, Charles Lloyd, and Miles Davis and had recorded with his own trio and quartet.

From the mid-'70s Jarrett drew enormous acclaim for a series of improvised solo concerts, several released on Manfred Eicher's Munich-based ECM Records, including the ten-disc *Sun Bear Concerts*. The solo concerts continued until January 1984 and resumed at a less grueling pace three years later. By then Jarrett had recorded a number of jazz albums with American and Scandinavian quartets as well as more classically oriented compositions. They included eerie improvisations on half-stopped Baroque organ *(Hymns/Spheres)* and soprano saxophone *(Invocations)* and concerto-like works *(Arbour Zena, Luminessence)* for improvising piano, bass, and saxophone with arranged strings.

After abandoning the solo concerts in early 1984, Jarrett began releasing albums of jazz standards with Gary Peacock and Jack DeJohnette, with whom he continues touring and recording. For a year and a half he devoted himself primarily to performing classical recitals and concerts. In mid-1985, frustrated to the point of numbness, he canceled further engagements and recorded what became *Spirits* alone in his studio in a reconverted barn beside his home. He used only the instruments on hand and two cassette recorders, on which he overdubbed himself playing a family of Moeck recorders, tablas (the Indian drums that are his favorite instrument), soprano saxophone, other winds, plucked strings, percussion, and a bare minimum of piano.

Jarrett described the unpremeditated primitivism of *Spirits* as an intuitive rather than a calculated reaction to the speciousness of contemporary musical and other technology. Its twenty-six sections range from under two to eight minutes, some pristine in their lyricism, others pulsing with rhythm or unsettling in their desolation. Jarrett considers *Spirits* his most important composition to date, and subsequent conversations and correspondence, now five years after its inception, confirm it as a watershed work in its influence on both his interpretive and his compositional concerns.

As an interpreter Jarrett has released beautifully transparent recordings of Bach's *Well-Tempered Clavier* and Goldberg Variations. He has recorded a vibrant reading of the piano concerto written for him by Lou Harrison and, with Gidon Kremer, a taut account of Arvo Pärt's *Fratres*. He has performed concertos by Mozart, Bartók, Colin McPhee, Peggy Glanville-Hicks, and Alan Hovhaness, as well as his own, *The Celestial Hawk*. His solo repertoire includes composers from Scarlatti to Gurdjieff.

Jarrett has also written numerous chamber works, several of which were released on the two-disc *In the Light,* and a brooding piano piece called *Ritual,* recorded by Dennis Russell Davies. More recent works include *Sacred Ground* (showing American Indian influences), *Terra Cotta, Rem(a)inders, Movement for*

Violin and Piano, and *Piece for Oboe and Strings.* Perhaps his most impressive compositions for other musicians have been the Bachian-Bartókian *Suite for Solo Violin* and the moving *Elegy for Violin and String Orchestra,* occasioned by the death of his maternal grandmother, a Hungarian gypsy who spoke Wendish. He has continued writing for strings with a recent work for viola and orchestra.

If Bartók is Jarrett's major precursor in the string compositions, Asian-influenced Eastern European modalism is a prime force. Other presences in the sometimes-epic piano improvisations, the instant compositions for which Jarrett is best known, are the dark-hued Impressionism of Bill Evans and the right-hand spring of Bud Powell. While one might assume the creative principle here to be a search for musical ideas, Jarrett has described his task, rather, as attentiveness and a continual *rejection* of the more facile musical ideas offered by—he might say *to*—his remarkably fertile imagination. They represent a revival of classical rhapsodic form (perhaps another bequest of his Hungarian roots), to include, thematically, transglobal music and, technically, jazz improvisation within the extended episodic structure of the rhapsody. Jarrett has described the concerts, characteristically, in terms offhand ("This is a melody that happened in Germany") and arcane ("Death hovers around quite a bit at solo concerts").

His improvisations are not restricted to concerts, since studio albums like *Staircase* (on piano) and *Book of Ways* (on clavichords) document less-extended improvisational forays, often more successful in their compression than all but the finest solo concerts, if never as startling or as heralded.

Our conversation took place in the composer's studio on a dank afternoon in December 1986. In the course of four hours of conversation, we each rose from our chairs once, to replenish the supply of tissues.

STRICKLAND: Where did you get the title *The Sun Bear Concerts?* Does it mean anything in Japanese?

JARRETT: There *is* an animal called the sun bear that's found only in Asia. One day the recording engineer and Manfred [Eicher] and I went to the zoo. The engineer is a collector of stuffed animals, the most serious one I've ever met in my life—he'll fly halfway around the world for a certain panda or panther—and he said, "That's a sun bear" and told us if you walk up to it and irritate it, although it looked so gentle, small, and sweet-faced, it could hit you with its forepaw and knock you a block away. It had a strength used only when necessary. And there's sort of a marathon task in the ten-record set.

STRICKLAND: I'm wondering if that has anything to do with the way you were perceived by a lot of people at that time. You stopped playing, had run-ins with club owners and audiences, etc.

JARRETT: No, it had nothing to do with that. I consider all that, anyway, as part of other people's contrived legend. The norm is that a pianist will go onstage and say, "I hate this piano," but not know what it needs. So what people usually hear from concert artists, instead of "We have to voice this octave before I play," is undertone complaints like . . . [*growls*].

STRICKLAND: My brother once took me to one of your concerts for my birthday, and I thought the audience was really atrocious—shifting around, squeaking chairs, coughing unnecessarily, all through the first half of the concert. And I was thinking, "Oh God, he's going to give us a lecture." But after the intermission I thought you were incredibly gracious and respectful towards the audience in suggesting, "Look, we're all in this together."

JARRETT: People don't think far enough to realize I go through the exact same feelings. "Oh God, I hope I don't *have* to" . . . give them a lecture or whatever.

STRICKLAND: Actually, I felt ambivalent at the time. I was also thinking, "Go get 'em!"

JARRETT: So imagine yourself *playing* and going through that ambivalence. After a while, it's such a distraction to even conceive of the need for concentrating on anything other than the music that at a certain point you *have* to stop the music. I always feel sorry for the people that *are* listening. I've *always* felt sorry for them, because I know they're going through the same thing, crossing their fingers—"Maybe this will go away" or "Maybe I *do* want him to say something, so then *I* won't have to." But that's an era that I was able to get rid of by various means. One of them by not playing any more concerts [*laughs*].

STRICKLAND: Before we get into your abandoning the solo concerts, may I ask you this? You know, it's very hard for those of us who are not public performers to imagine what it's like for *anybody* to get up in front of three thousand people and perform the Emperor Concerto. But it was almost mind-boggling to imagine what you were trying to do in that context: improvise, compose on the spot while surrounded. What did it feel like?

JARRETT [*after long pause*]: It didn't manage to get to this place all the time, but what it really was was a communion with the whole audience—I saw it a few times. When I saw it once I knew it was important to expose that possibility. But it was always like risking everything. A lot of people thought it became easier as it went along. No. Harder.

STRICKLAND: The last solo concert you gave was in January '84. And you began?

JARRETT: I did a solo concert in Heidelberg in about '72 in a jazz festival context, but I was playing songs, tunes. It gradually got extended.

STRICKLAND: You gave up the solo concerts almost three years ago, and since then you've done many classical concertos, standards with your jazz group, and now *Spirits*. Do you think the mid-'80s have been a period of retrenchment? You were trained as a classical pianist, starting when you were, what, three?

JARRETT: Yeah.

STRICKLAND: And you'd performed in the Academy of Music and Madison Square Garden by your teens.

JARRETT: I think I was seven or eight, something like that. But that was just the Lions Club. I was so impressed that I was playing on Victor Borge's piano . . .

STRICKLAND: How many years did you study classical piano?

JARRETT: Twelve, at least, of continuous study. It ended mainly because we couldn't afford to continue lessons. The teachers had to keep getting better, and it started getting more expensive, and we had to go farther away for them.

STRICKLAND: You're from Allentown, Pennsylvania.

JARRETT: Yes, so I was studying in Philadelphia. I had to get out of school early. Someone had to drive me and wait for me. I didn't always have enough time to prepare. At any rate, at that point it was going to change, because I started hearing, without knowing it—I think I was hearing what I was trying to get at much, much, much later. But I heard it then as a series of negative decisions: "No, I won't study this" or "Yes, this is important, but only for this amount of time." It's as though—not "as though"—to me it is *precisely* that there's a direct line from then to the present. I was responding to as good a sense of intuition as I could have had at that age.

I was looking forward for years to studying composition with Nadia Boulanger and finally had a chance through people who took a lot of time with the usual politics. And then when the scholarship finally came through, I said no, quite spontaneously, without having any idea why I was saying it. That was when I was about sixteen.

STRICKLAND: And then you went to study at the Berklee School of Music.

JARRETT: That was for just a year. But the most important thing at that time was my experience of all types of music I would never have chosen. Cocktail lounges, dinner hour, Dixieland bands, dance bands at the Statler Hilton with two pianos and a vocalist and a violinist. At that time things were beginning to bubble, it was all on the stove, and if I hadn't experienced music in all those different realities I couldn't be so firmly committed now. It's as though I've seen the whole spectrum of music. At the Fillmore I talked to Jimi Hendrix and Janis Joplin. I was going to write some ragtime pieces for Janis and collaborate with Jimi. Then they both died. But the point is that those years I could have spent honing my classical skills, as most people would say, I was honing another kind, and I think it's all led up to *Spirits:* the de-honing, the erasure of anything but perception.

STRICKLAND: Did it seem to you that you were making a radical break?

JARRETT: It was just like going into a restaurant and looking at the menu and saying, "There's nothing here I want." I'd have to go to another restaurant. Or cook it myself.

STRICKLAND: Yet after phasing out the solo concerts you spent a year and a half performing classical works. What led you back to the straight and narrow path? Did you suddenly see something on the menu you wanted?

JARRETT: It's as though I'm using all kinds of fuel for one trip in a certain vehicle. I needed that fuel then. Those concerts came before *Spirits* and produced *Spirits*. There was a moment in May 1985 when I said, "No more of these." I'd seen a lot of the world of so-called classical musicians and had seen almost nothing but frustration in those people, the higher the echelon the more sophisticated the frustration. I was sitting on the front porch looking at *nothing*—not even the trees, just sitting there— and within a split second I had resolved not to do any more of those for the time being. The same split second I decided I *must* get up and come in here and get a flute and try to remember a certain state that I thought was lost. And that was the beginning of *Spirits*.

STRICKLAND: It's odd. The return to classical performance was almost a negative preparation.

JARRETT: *Everything* was a negative preparation. I don't see how it could be any other way. For example, if I want to do a solo improvised concert— and there are four scheduled for 1987 called "Serious Drinking and Inner Vigilance"—I wanted to de–"solo concert" the whole idea—the way for me to do it is to get away from pianos. That's where the core of my work lies—the state I need to be in to do that as honestly as possible and with the greatest amount of awareness. When I began *Spirits* I had no idea it was going to be anything. There was no future. It was a nothing, a nonentity. And it only became something out of a decision to stop something.

You know how people have jobs and say, "What else could I do if I stopped this?" Well, you can't start until you stop—that might be somebody's advice. What do you want to do with your life? "Well, I'm doing this and I don't know how I feel about it, but . . . " Okay, *stop* it!

Spirits was born of drowning in a certain place so I could come up to the surface in another—without forgetting the drowning, and without dying. My leaving the classical concerts was in no way a negative comment on that music; it was a statement about my calling. Now that I've done *Spirits* I can tell you that I can do those other things again—there are *plans*—but I don't know what would have become of me if *Spirits* hadn't happened.

STRICKLAND: Why did you begin the classical concerts in the first place? Was it a sense of unfinished business from your youth?

JARRETT: I wanted to pay back certain composers for the gift of their music to me and participate in playing their music. The solo concerts stopped, which gave me some time to spend *with* the piano—a true improviser has to avoid developing habits, has to know the instrument so well he can be away from it for a long time and then meet it in front of an audience. I could morally afford to be with the piano, and I began playing the classical music I normally practice at home—I've done that since I was a kid, it's never stopped.

STRICKLAND: Is there a connection between the classical work and the standards you performed with your jazz group? It seems as if you were getting back to roots in both efforts.

JARRETT: Yes, but I would put it another way. I was after exposing the need *not* to possess the music. Every artist now has to write his own material, no matter how bad a writer he is. You're not going to get a name in jazz or popular music today without writing your own music. It doesn't matter if it's bad or good. What matters is the publicity behind it.

I spoke with my musicians about the nonpossessive nature of the experiment. Why do people have to have me come and do blah-blah-blah? I would like them to know I can come and do—for example, once I did a Bach encore at a solo concert. Someone came up to me afterwards and said, "But Mr. Jarrett, I thought you were going to *improvise*." I said, "Well, isn't that an improvisation in *this* format?" Until people thought they knew what my music was like and *expected* a recurrence of the Köln Concert—they would *like* that to happen—the format was more or less pure. Then I started to realize, now this *is* a format, something these people would like to treasure like they go out whistling whatever. So I thought why not play what I've been playing at home all these years? Bach, Beethoven, Haydn, Handel. At that point I had been working on the harpsichord for years already. I wasn't going to do Baroque music without knowing what ornaments meant. Yet all over the jazz world that's what happens, and then a classical player like Gulda tries to improvise and sounds like he hasn't lived in the jazz world. So I decided if I was going to do it, I'd have to commit myself a hundred percent.

STRICKLAND: Do you think the solo concerts were in a sense the end of the road? Take it in the context of the whole history of jazz—not to be too grandiose about it. In the '20s you have a collective art transformed by soloists—Ory, Dodds, Armstrong most of all. Then in swing you have a balance of arrangements with featured solo improvisations, and in bop the work consists of a string of solos with maybe an arranged opening and close. By the mid-'50s Coltrane is playing five-minute solos, then twenty-minute solos in the early '60s—"Chasin' the Trane"—and later forty-five-minute solos, sometimes with just a drummer. It hit me when you were doing the solo concerts that this was the last chord in this progression. Now there's no one else there, just Jarrett playing the piano for an hour and a half.

JARRETT: I wonder, though, if it's that objective. I think it's more a matter of what pressures and interests are governing our lives on other levels. The individualism that kept protruding more and more from jazz was a parallel to the American pioneer spirit, which suddenly with the computer age has very little place to go. The pioneers might not be the people anymore at all. Even musicians all want communal bands—they all make the same amount of money that way, for one thing. But my most vivid memory of the preciousness of having a leader was with Miles Davis. Without Miles that band wouldn't have had any reason to exist, and many of his bands would be just shadows of something without him. If Miles were stupid he might say, "Yeah, let's have a communal band." But he isn't stupid, he knows his own value, and that's one of the most important things in the arts.

After *Spirits,* if I do a classical recital it won't be called for for the same reasons as before. *Spirits* also represents what I might have been trying to get at in all my solo concerts. Any future solo concert won't have the hypersensitive quality it might have had in the past.

STRICKLAND: I don't see, though, how it could be so similar. You mentioned that in the solo concerts one of the things of primary importance was the sense of communion. Here you're in the boonies in western New Jersey, locked away in this studio, alone . . . so certainly there's not the same communal element as doing a solo improvisation before three thousand people or so, maybe a thousand or a hundred of whom are listening.

JARRETT: Maybe not the same kind of communion. The search for the core of the process was what a solo concert was about. And sometimes we would all know—the three thousand people, if they were all listening, and once in a while that was true—we'd all know something simultaneously.

STRICKLAND: Know what?

JARRETT: Whatever it was we'd know it, feel it, at the same moment in the same way. Sometimes I interviewed people who came backstage. "Can you tell me the feelings you had?" And they'd go through this string of feelings which would exactly correspond to what I was going through while I was playing.

STRICKLAND: How many solo concerts did you give?

JARRETT: I estimate about six hundred.

STRICKLAND: And how many times did you feel they were a success in that sense?

JARRETT: The percentage was low but the sustenance that it gave me would last for years. Maybe—we're talking about moments? After all, how many concerts do you go to of any music where there are more than several minutes?—I would say maybe a dozen. One time there was a three- or four-minute silence at the end of the set, which wasn't the normal silence. It wasn't a guided silence or the silence after some opera, where it's just *over* and you're sitting there not able to do anything. The music returned to a silent place and everybody sat there. I think we could have sat there for fifteen minutes. Not a sound. It was even quieter than when it was being played.

STRICKLAND: When you first did those concerts it was a revolutionary act. Now it's not so unusual. Is that in part why you moved away from them?

JARRETT: The truth is no one else does it, still. They play solo concerts, but their concept of playing alone is playing without a rhythm section. No one even now goes out and plays from nothing. That was the beginning of the end, when it became "Hey, let's all do this!" when they really had no idea what I was doing.

The whole record industry thought Manfred and I were out of our minds to release that first three-record set of solo piano. "I mean, is there *singing*? You don't, uh, *sing* on it? . . ."

STRICKLAND [*laughing*]: But you do!

JARRETT: Yes, but . . . "I mean, what'll you *do*? Uh, what's *this*?" Even other musicians, friends of mine, their advice was "I mean, this is just . . . it's great and everything . . . but . . . who's gonna buy this?"

STRICKLAND [*nodding to gold records on wall*]: Well, there they are, I guess.

JARRETT: You know, one of my students, who sings with the Harmonic Choir, told me he'd never been a fan of the solo things. And musicians can write them off as, "He's been playing since he was three, he can play a lot of notes . . ." But already I've had hints from my student and others that *Spirits* has affected people's attitude about what the solo concerts were really about. The search on the piano could never have provided the clues that *Spirits* provides. *Spirits* is where the solo concerts often wanted to go, but on piano they couldn't. In my head there were these voices, bent notes—the closest thing to *Spirits* is not the solo concerts but the organ set *Hymns/Spheres*.

STRICKLAND: There's an interesting connection here with Glenn Gould—the singing or vocalizing along with the music, and also the oddness of the posture. He said the reason he was singing or humming or whatever you want to call it was that he was hearing the piece played in a way he couldn't play it on piano. He was vocalizing, articulating a line as if it were an oboe or God knows what. And even more than he you get into some extraordinary postures, and you pluck the inside of the piano, slap the soundboard, and so on. Is it that you're trying to create a nonpiano sound?

JARRETT: Yes. And this is what's changed now. If I play piano tomorrow I won't have to get to this actual sound that I hear. I can think of myself as playing the piano. Whereas before *Spirits* I was playing the music I heard minus the music I heard—only what could be translated by the piano. I *hate* parts of my albums because I know I'm hearing something that doesn't translate to piano—in fact I'm being dishonest by playing piano at all. I should stop and say, "Hey, whoa! This isn't what I hear. Let's all *sing*!" [*Laughs.*] And that would be another of my famous routines . . .

STRICKLAND: In *Spirits* you turned primarily to percussion and winds. Was it simply the greater physical intimacy with the instruments?

JARRETT: Yes. I don't think I used anything apart from the occasional piano that's nearly as mechanical as that instrument. There's a link with the forthcoming clavichord release here too. What I'm finally doing is not regressing into primitivism, as some people seem to think. The clavichord lets me be as close to what I'm hearing on keyboard as I can, even though I can't hear as much as I'd like—it's such a soft instrument. So we miked very close, but without any gimmicks. That or a lute or a guitar—if I had to use the words "essential sound," the tabla drum is to me essential sound. It hits you right in the solar plexus. Like "Umph! *Hel*-lo! *This* is where you are." And for me on the piano the *content* of the music determines whether you're hit. And also the virtuosity of the player and the desire of the player to transcend the virtuosity that he's got are what make any piano piece moving in a way that just the *sound* of the tabla is moving. On *Spirits* I'm using instruments that I know intimately but without having been conditioned to play them. For instance, on recorders I can play hardly anything classical recorder players would classify as virtuosic, but they couldn't phrase the way I do without being shown. You're not supposed to phrase too many notes together without tonguing. But when I was a kid I had a recorder, trying to play jazz lines on it, and that loosened up my way of conceiving of that instrument. There are countless threads that started way back. I was playing drums as early as I was playing piano.

STRICKLAND: The cut "Spirit" on *Birth* also involved a kind of primitive—I don't use the term pejoratively—aura. Also "Algeria" in *Ruta + Daitya.* *Survivors Suite, Eyes of the Heart,* both from '76, open with a similar—

JARRETT: I think if I'd had a different band those sections would have lasted a lot longer. But I was dealing with the musicians I wanted, and *they* wanted to, you know, get into the *jazz.*

STRICKLAND: I think they're the best parts of the albums.

JARRETT: What can I say? I wasn't going to go to India and look for other musicians, who'd play *their* conditioning too. What I really would have ideally as a band would be a bunch of kids, guys, ladies, who'd never played instruments before, get them all together and that would be potentially great. I did that a couple of Christmases ago, in fact. What matters is the *intent* of what you're doing—is it really there? If you're holding a flute and don't know what to do with it, and you suddenly feel there has to be a sound here and you want to make it—that's three-quarters of it.

STRICKLAND: But don't you think someone who wasn't a child prodigy, who can't pick up any instrument and play it, might resent this type of comment from a virtuoso? "Oh, there's nothing to it . . . "

JARRETT: But I'm not saying you should collect those people *without* me [*both laugh*].

STRICKLAND: I want to join the band!

JARRETT: You know, I think musicians are not even listeners half the time. The one world where you're not even *supposed* to listen is the world of classical music. You're guest soloist with some orchestra. And you're suddenly aware of how wonderful the English horn is. And then the conductor turns around and says [*wagging finger, mimicking kindergarten teacher*], "You're *list*-en-ing" [*both laugh*]. But I'm more interested in being a participating listener than I am in being a performer. And solo concerts are that. I know how to play the piano well, but if I didn't it might be more obvious that I'm doing a hell of a lot of listening. Sometimes the notes go by so fast that it's "How could I be hearing this?" But if you slowed it down you might hear little spaces where if I weren't concentrating a hundred percent on the listening I couldn't be playing at all. To me that's what improvising is—a very altered, intense listening. You have to detach the part that's listening and allow it to be there and also play. But you aren't playing and then saying, "Hey! I really *like* that!"—because if you do you've just lost two seconds.

STRICKLAND: One thing *Spirits* has in common with other albums you've done is the overall simplicity of line, which ties into the Gurdjieff album, *Sacred Hymns.* A couple of critics seemed to feel about that, "*We* could play this."

JARRETT: It was a request from one of the Gurdjieff groups in Europe that I work with some Turkish musicians. It was almost a fantasy, though, like when Baryshnikov calls: "I vould like to improvice vith you. You could improvice and I could improvice and it vould be *great!*"

Well, it would be an "event." We're talking about drama and media coverage. The Turks were really beautiful players and wonderful guys, but I ended up doing the original keyboard transcriptions alone. I must have been involved in the path for about fifteen years at that point, so it wasn't something I just pulled out of a hat. If other people say, "I could play that" . . . good! They should! [*Both laugh.*]

As for simplicity, just look at the ending of Rilke's "Archaic Torso of Apollo": "You must change your life." By itself it makes no sense as a poetic statement, yet it's fertile in context, even if it only plants a question—which may be all we can ask of art now.

STRICKLAND: *Spirits* also ties in with *Sacred Hymns* insofar as they both, like other titles of yours, tend to be religious in orientation.

JARRETT: When I started to play that flute . . . there is a state that I would call prayer. That summons up to many people churches, but I'm not talking about that. It was the state I felt I had missed for a couple of years. If a clergyman says, "I used to be able to pray and I can't" . . . well, you've seen films about that problem and so on, but this was somehow related to my involvement in classical music and my calling, some mysterious connection between those things. The second that I said I would not do recitals for whatever amount of time and came into this studio, what I was doing when I took the flute off the wall was to try to regain a state of prayer. While I was in that state every day during *Spirits*—this was American Indian land and if there's any element of that kind of sound on the album I think that it was a kind of spirit communion that was happening while I was in that state. As I said in the liner notes, there was no intention of making an album. After all, people don't go on the radio to pray.

STRICKLAND: Some do.

JARRETT [*laughing*]: Not *nice* people. I was in here all alone dancing around with no belief that it would be heard or seen or felt by anyone else.

STRICKLAND: And this just *happened* that day you were talking about, sitting over there? You said, "That's it, time's up, no more of this." What type of day was it? Was it particularly sunny or something?

JARRETT: You want more details?

STRICKLAND: Sure.

JARRETT: The day before I had received in the mail a fairly good review from John Rockwell.

STRICKLAND: A red-letter day.

JARRETT: I know what that means to other people. "Wow! he said a few good words about me!" I was thinking, why don't I feel something about this? It was as if—if *everyone* in the *world* said, "Mr. Jarrett is the *foremost* interpreter of my *favorite* composer"—I would have had the same reaction. I should have been celebrating and I felt nothing. Literally nothing.

STRICKLAND: What was he reviewing?

JARRETT: My first solo recital at Avery Fisher Hall. There was some Shostakovich, Beethoven, Scarlatti, Bach. Actually the review was quite gracious. I'd done the recital first in Stockholm and *that* review was exciting because it was the very first time I'd done it anywhere. It was in Swedish and someone translated it for me at the airport—what amounted to a rave review. But it wasn't the right kind of exciting. The kind of excitement I had here in the studio—no one here, not thinking anyone would ever hear this—that's what's important to me.

STRICKLAND: When you came in here you didn't know what you were going to do?

JARRETT: Not at all. Even with the recording controls it was totally guesswork. When I was doing an overdub with the headphones on, if it sounded out of balance, I'd just move. You can hear the floor creaking, going *click* because it's glued down. I had no idea.

STRICKLAND: I'm really curious about where the first piece you did that day ended up on the albums. Is the ordering chronological?

JARRETT: Largely. But that piece isn't included.

STRICKLAND: So it turned out to be a kind of lead-in to the project.

JARRETT: Yes. A few days went by during which the state that I was in and the music tried to find each other's level. What exactly was I doing? Was I coming in here and playing a flute or was something else supposed to happen? If I felt the same way when I listened back as when I played a certain piece, that meant maybe I would do something more with it, though maybe not. I don't know what governed it—there were no rules. But at some point the recordings became good enough to actually *use*. Up to that point it was just the state and some stuff for myself. I think I finally started to have an intimation that something big was happening and I'd better get my technology together. All I had was two tape recorders, but instead of fiddling around every day I realized that the music was so intense that there were no second takes—on the whole record there's no Take Two.

Once I was in the studio ready to start a second piece that day—something came into my head, a melody—and I looked at my watch and it was time to go to the dentist. I couldn't write it down because on paper it wouldn't be what it was. It has something to do with inference—if you've ever heard people trying to sing Beatles melodies and missing something in the phrasing, you know what I mean by inference.

So I drove to the dentist's. They have the radio on and the drill's in my mouth and I'm there for forty-five minutes trying desperately to hold on to this melody, which I knew must have changed three or four times. I came straight back, rushed in here and played whatever was left—and that's one of the takes on the first side.

It was like that. I was in the bathroom once and suddenly—luckily I had a piece of music paper—scratched down a Middle Eastern melody for soprano sax now at the end of Side Three. Each piece had its birth in a different way.

STRICKLAND: How, er . . . not to invade your personal life in any way, but . . . how was this [*very gingerly*] affecting your—if you don't want to answer this question, please forget it, but . . . was all this having an effect on your, on the rest of your life?

JARRETT [*quietly, after long pause*]: No. [*Both break up.*] I have two kids who don't live with me, and at that time they weren't staying here. I'm living with a lady that I've been with for over eight years now. She was the only person to hear this music for many months. I'd come back for lunch with a little tape and put it on. Her musical responses are incredibly exposed, accurately and graphically noted. If she had *tried* to like it and didn't I would have noticed everything—I was in a fine state of craziness, my antennae were out. She can't say, "Gee, I don't *think* I like that." She'll *see* whether she likes it or not and whether it's doing something. And that's why the dedication "To Rose Anne" is on the album. She was the only other person. It was her album.

Otherwise, I really didn't know what I was doing. I just knew the state was right and my philosophy was that what came out would have to reflect it. The recording went a lot further than what's on the albums. The state finally turned itself over to the process of recording some "nice stuff," and that was the end of what I would call *Spirits*. It was already a format—I'd created my own format, just like the solo concerts. I started using larger instruments like the drum set . . . more horn . . . then I had to start learning the trumpet, just in case I might need it later on [*both laugh*]. I went to the dentist because my teeth felt loose—I'd just started to play trumpet like a maniac and hadn't ever done it before, so I was worried. He said, "No problem, they'll be all right but . . . you say you've *just* started to learn the trumpet? Do you mind if I ask why? I mean, you play *piano* so well . . . "

Yeah, well . . . thanks!

What I took to Germany was a box of cassettes about ten inches long, and I was hoping the plane wouldn't crash—the one time I was worried about the plane crashing. While the tapes were still in this studio I was trying to figure out—"What if there's a fire in the studio?" [*Laughs.*] And I never felt that way about another album. They were all, in a way, another story in my musical life. This was *the* story of a musical life that I've had and will always have, that could never be told another way.

STRICKLAND: One interesting thing about the set is that even without the stylistic complexity of the solo concerts you still manage to suggest a whole range not only of emotions but of musical styles. Some of the flute sounds Andean. Other parts evoke for me Africa or the Caribbean, where I live, or the Middle East and so on. Was there any effort on your part to aim for this universal music?

JARRETT: None at all. There was if anything a profound *un*awareness [*laughs*] of anything except what was coming out—as is also true of the prototype solo concert, where I shouldn't have heard the piano ever in my life. The better the improvisation the less I'd remember what a piano sounds like, or I'd just be playing "piano music." And I was never *hearing* piano music, even back in the Art Blakey and Charles Lloyd days.

STRICKLAND: What were you hearing?

JARRETT: *Spirits*, I think . . . In the context of jazz, a horn or a voice . . . thus all the singing.

STRICKLAND: There's a lot of incantation on *Spirits*, not the vocalise that to me—no offense—really obtrudes on a couple of the cuts in *Standards*. Earlier you mentioned the Harmonic Choir, who are involved with Tibetan overtone chanting. Since *Spirits* was overdubbed I wasn't sure if you were singing overtones or merely overdubbing them.

JARRETT: I was singing them at the time, not overdubbing that sound.

STRICKLAND: Have you studied that technique?

JARRETT: No. I don't know if you've ever heard Sufi chanting, but when it's real the idea is not whether you're making a pleasant sound but whether you're getting out what has to come out. It might start out being normal enough and by the end you're being attacked by a pack of wild wolves. And yet for them it's purifying. All the voice in *Spirits* is completely related to the music, so when you hear overtones it's just that they started . . . putting in requests, and I did what I could to oblige. Music is intent, and I'm almost certain that every single composer that I might be in love with wasn't writing what he heard—he heard more than what he was writing. *Spirits* might suggest to the listener that that's true—that this person is hearing more than what's on the record, even though it's not in the notes.

That's true of the rhythms too. If I had a click-track I'd end up with *nothing* as an album. Our hearts don't beat the way click-tracks do. I've gotten nauseous being at a discotheque, far enough away from the music to just hear that steady pulse.

STRICKLAND: The pulse in *Spirits* is very fluid at times.

JARRETT: Yes. Even though the melody is saying, "Here you should expect the drum to go *boom*," the drums had to put up with what the flutes were doing, had to listen to their phrasing. In jazz, bass players always want to work with a certain drummer, because of the way he keeps time. In this case I was completely free because I was alone. A melodic phrase could be longer than it was—not just as long as it was. As Lou Harrison said when I did the Mozart K.488 concerto with Dennis Davies and the Cabrillo Festival Orchestra, "The orchestra played better than they could."

If you'd try to turn the melody into a piece, a stable piece, you'd end up with nothing. In fact I tried to do that with one of the melodies. I made it a song. And whatever it had on the original track it lost. No matter what I did—I could've had the Norman Luboff Choir here backing everything up and it wouldn't have made it any worse.

STRICKLAND: Speaking of songs, a couple of the cuts are balladic but not in the pop sense. They evoke Medieval/Renaissance ballads. Does it have something to do with pentatonicism or modalism in those pieces?

JARRETT: It might be the out-of-tune recorder player. It reminds me of when Miles always wanted me to talk to his horn player. He wanted the note bent a certain way and he knew I heard it, but for his pianist to talk to his horn player about this is very wrong politically.

STRICKLAND: It can't be done on your own instrument.

JARRETT: I'd say to him, "*Please* don't make me do this." But with my flutes in unison melodies I'm sometimes staying purposely just under or over the other voice and then maybe just pulling up. But now that I put it in those terms, it's not it, it's not how I felt. That's what's so screwy about talking about an unquantifiable.

STRICKLAND: You mentioned the dentist experience earlier—having a melody but having to hold it until you returned to the studio. Did you always have a melodic phrase in mind to start with?

JARRETT: Sometimes I'd come in just going cha-*kung* cha-*kung-kung* and would have to choose a tabla real fast before I lost what feeling I really intended. Once I played some piano harmonies, then thought, "Maybe that should have some flutes. No, soprano." Listening to the tape I jotted down some scales, fragments—not even chords because I didn't want to think about vertical things. Then I took my horn out, and that's the first thing on the fourth side, the long soprano improvisation. I had no idea what function this piano would have. But listening back, I immediately knew what should happen next.

STRICKLAND: You know, that's an example of the kind of preternatural reliance you've placed on spontaneity in your art for as long as I can remember. In that and in other areas as well—inspiration, isolation, transcendentalism—you seem to have a High Romantic concept of your vocation. In the notes to *Spirits* you don't talk about writing these pieces, you talk about "allowing them to emerge." Elsewhere you use the term "channel" rather than "creator" for the artist, yet obviously you have a high regard for the work you do—if that's the phrase for it. It reminds me of Blake, who described one of his visionary epics as "the grandest poem in the English language," then said, "I may praise it for I claim to be no other than the Secretary. The Authors are in Eternity." Do you identify with that?

JARRETT: I identify even more with the Persian poet Rumi, who was associated with the dervishes and wrote the *Mathnawi*. He said he hated the work, that he was wasting precious time writing. I consider that if I have a purpose it's not to produce records or concerts, it's in the process of perceiving more. Since my specialty is music, that perceiving takes the form of sound. I think Blake's view is the only correct one if you're doing something creative—Bach didn't write his music so we'd all have it on our stereos now. But even Rumi at times must have been pleased that his work was in some sense an image of a state of perception that could be shared later.

STRICKLAND: So you're interested in *Spirits* as a record—not to pun—of the experience.

JARRETT: Yes, as a documentary, the only documentary I think I'll ever have in my life as a musician that gets so close to the silence, the lack of music. Art today has become a substitute in people's lives. Records play the part of a crutch—not that I don't think it's necessary. I'd rather they used that crutch than go bananas. But in my own relationship to music I wouldn't so much wonder *what* to listen to as *when* to listen. Sometimes nothing is what to listen to, and that nothing has all qualities—they're just not activated yet.

STRICKLAND: If the set is a record of a state, how would you describe that state? In twenty-five words or less . . .

JARRETT [*laughing*]: Robert Musil takes three volumes in *A Man Without Qualities* without ever being able to explain it. It either takes a zillion words or Aagghh! I can say briefly all about the state is contained in the moment of making a sound. It doesn't matter what notes you play, or how long you've done your scales and fingering—doesn't matter if you've done that for a zillion years. The only thing that matters is that at the point when you make a sound you're living and breathing that sound—and the only way is by living and breathing the silence previous to it. Otherwise it's an invasion of the silence, it's not an addition. The silence is us sitting around without any clothes on—it's not just about hearing. Often you might ask, "I wonder what so-and-so is like when he's alone? He seems happy—or depressed—with his friends, but I wonder what he's like when he goes back to his apartment?" The society is becoming monotone right now, so I think if someone has a connection to something he should *say* it—not just when he's alone.

But that silence is almost like a private affair to people. "Oh don't talk about that *now!* It's New Year's Eve! We wanna blow our horns!"

To me, New Year's Eve is *when* to talk about it. "Okay, I'll *blow* my horn, but not *this* horn, that's not the horn I *hear* right now. I'm blowing the horn you just heard me blow when you said, 'No, we have to just blow our horns.'" *Spirits* is the New Year's Eve experience without society.

STRICKLAND: Without the forcing . . .

JARRETT: Without the forcing, without the pressure of having to be anything except itself. The only limitations were in the instruments, in my tape recorders, in whether I could play, whether I had the flu or the strength. Most people in their normal lives don't even get a chance to think about those limitations. It's "Did we get the bills paid?" or "Whose version of the Brahms Fourth do we want to hear?" I don't care how many versions of the Brahms Fourth I could hear. If I needed a certain connection to something Brahms would not give it to me. *I* could only give it to me—without Brahms.

I know some African music that's made me cry. It's nineteen eighty-whatever-it-is today, the modern world. It's the same year there. Meanwhile, music made by Central African pygmies makes you cry and other music is able to be played over your CD players in incredibly sparkling tones, but you almost have to *make* yourself cry, or choose the piece you've cried with before.

I once invaded the Classical Cruise—you know, with the English Chamber Orchestra? Everyone else was completely classical, and in fact I was considered a troublemaker. No kidding. We went to an island and from the boat Rose Anne and I could hear onshore this great music being played, drums and so on—it was so vibrant! Meanwhile all the passengers had accompanied the musicians to their Liszt or Rachmaninov concert, straight from the boat down the streets of this poor city to the hall. They listened to their favorite Mozart and Rachmaninov, then back to the boat. In a lecture I gave afterwards, I said, "One thing that's different about an improviser is that he can go anywhere and play with any other country's musicians." Ornette Coleman can go and play in Morocco with musicians with different traditions there and people say, "Well, they're black and he's black." I can do the same thing and I'm Hungarian [*laughs*].

STRICKLAND: You're not crazy about contemporary music in general. Apart from the composers whose work you've performed, are there others you admire?

JARRETT: The Sorabji *Opus Clavicembalisticum* is very rich. I also admire Elliott Carter—for his stance. Not that it's adopted self-consciously.

STRICKLAND: What do you listen to when you're not doing your own music?

JARRETT: Mostly older classical. With the Romantic era it all seems divided into factions—like in religion and politics, various factions claiming they still represent the same thing. Music seems to me to have done that after improvising was no longer part of the player's responsibility.

You've probably surmised that when I do play piano at home it's almost always classical music. I never improvise here, don't come over to play solo concerts [*laughs*]. Now *there's* an idea! Someone could come out with a board game. "Hey gang, let's go play 'Solo Concerts'!" [*Both break up.*] Or "Trivial Solo Concerts"—the other five hundred and ninety of them. [*In quiz-show host's voice*] "At which concert did Mr. Jarrett play *this* phrase? *Twice.*"

STRICKLAND: Take out a patent. When you're not working on a piece, do you often listen to other keyboard recordings?

JARRETT: Yes. But if a recording has in any way a warp towards something it's hard for me to listen really well to what everybody's doing. Most classical artists, I've found out, take very little part in the mixing. They don't even listen to the playbacks. I always work closely with those processes myself. Once I flew to Germany to change two D–Bs in the bass of one of the *Sun Bear Concerts.* I said to Manfred, "I'm not hearing what I did the way I did it." He said, "Well, you'll just have to come over then." To hear it on his speakers, not mine.

I very often listen to Bach, Handel, Purcell . . . at different times, not all at once like some restaurants we know. Mozart has some of the most expressive, almost nonexistent piano writing—everybody who's played it knows this. To me it's potent stuff. With Handel, I find there's a quality in his work that—it just helps me a lot to hear that sound. Even his keyboard music, which is hardly ever played, has a great deal of interest for me because of how much room there is for ornamentation.

STRICKLAND: Have you heard Kenneth Gilbert's version of the keyboard suites?

JARRETT: Yeah, I think it's great. You know, I'm glad you asked me what I listened to when I wasn't working on a piece, because when I start working on one I can find something wrong with everyone else's version [*laughs*]. "Whoops! that's not the right tempo. No no no, that wasn't the right ornament . . ."

STRICKLAND: Do you feel that way when you listen to your earlier records?

JARRETT: I have a great deal of trouble listening to my early piano records—not even early, down to the very last one—because radical changes have been made since then in my touch, and my relationship to what I'm actually doing at the keyboard is much more subtle. I hear things now and say, "Gee, that's awfully gross. Who would have thought anyone would like that?"

STRICKLAND: How do you feel about what was billed and broadcast on PBS as your last solo concert, in Tokyo on January 25th of '84? When you finished the second half of the improvisation and played as an encore

"Over the Rainbow" so longingly, in context it almost seemed as if you couldn't wait to fly there.

JARRETT: No, I'd been playing that as an encore for some time. There wasn't any special reason except that I like the song. I'm not reluctant to be honest about particular concerts not working, especially if I've done six hundred of them. [*Mimics belligerent drunk*] "Oh yeah? Well, there're another fivehunnerdnineynine that're GREAT!"

All in all, I consider that last concert probably one of the best I've ever played. In a way I'm sorry it's not on record. But in a way I'm glad too, because then what would people do? If they liked it as much as the Köln Concert . . . you know, people come and say, "Hey yeah, it's really great! I've bought five of 'em so far, I wear 'em out, 'cause when I go around doing the housecleaning I like to . . ." Okay, go listen to George Winston, I think you'll be in good hands.

STRICKLAND: Speaking of George Winston—not to make a martyr of him— you've often been considered sort of the godfather of New Age music. People like Winston, David Lanz, Michael Jones have taken the pastoral, lyrical, Impressionistic side of your solos and worked on that to the exclusion of the rest, stylized it and made a few dollars.

JARRETT: Somebody I know, speaking of much of Minimalism, said the motto ought to be "Less is less." With New Age it should be "Less is less than less." The whole thing is just opportunistic. If there were a single real artist among them, he'd already be out of that category by now, after a period of several years. I mean, how long is it going to be a New Age?

STRICKLAND: There *is* no New Age.

JARRETT: But now there's a marketing category. I remember once bringing photos for an album to Columbia, which they said didn't look dirty enough. "Nah . . . those aren't *jazzy* enough." Anyway, at ECM Manfred and I have solved those problems.

STRICKLAND: How?

JARRETT: No one else decides anything! [*Both laugh.*] Even misspellings are decided by Manfred and me.

STRICKLAND: You're recording Book One of *The Well-Tempered Clavier* for ECM. How was that decided?

JARRETT: One day the music gave me messages like, "Hey, it's about time you finished this and really did it." I owed a concert to a hall in Troy where I canceled last year. And Lafayette College in Easton, near here, has a nice small hall. So in both places, I thought, I could play at the dynamic level appropriate to the music. Then Manfred got very interested in recording it. And finally I realized it was the optimum way for me to unprepare for improvising—three and a half weeks after the recording and those two concerts is the first "Serious Drinking" concert. My fingers and head will be so busy with *The Well-Tempered Clavier* that afterwards, "Hm, wonder what'd happen if I tried to improvise?" But it does play havoc on my physical system—like having circuitry you're not supposed to have.

STRICKLAND: You're not afraid of having lost it after three years away from improvised concerts?

JARRETT: I was *always* afraid. Even after one day away. Rose Anne can tell you I never knew if I was going to have any music to play before the concert.

STRICKLAND: What's that state like before a concert, facing that void? Could you just sit there, eat, drink, talk to people?

JARRETT: Not before Bach but before improvising, which doesn't have the nervous quality at all of a pre-recital. Everything starts feeling warm. Not secure warm, just a trust in the process. I trust that if I sit at the piano I'll hear something to play. Yet I'm never sure it's going to be again, tomorrow, that way.

STRICKLAND: In physical terms, though, having adapted yourself to Bach tactilely, it doesn't seem threatening—I'm not trying to scare you!—to go back to pure improvisation?

JARRETT: After *Spirits* I did the *Book of Ways* album of clavichord improvisations you haven't heard yet. It's much more linear, less dramatic, more contrapuntal. Then comes Bach. Then the improvised concerts, and I'm not looking for the dramatic anymore, I'm not making the search that way. It might be a much more intimate, small thing that happens. If I have a new commitment in music it might be to remind people that less doesn't have to be less, even to the point of showing what isn't needed in what I used to do. *The Well-Tempered Clavier* has a dramatic smallness but a musical vastness. That's how it relates to *Spirits* and the "Serious Drinking" concerts, which this time will be separate pieces.

STRICKLAND: Without the expansiveness of the two-part format?

JARRETT: Well, I'm allowing for that, but I'm not *counting* on it. [*Note: After the "Serious Drinking" concerts Jarrett returned to the two-part format.*] Maybe an alternative, anyway, to the big electronic bands playing the baseball stadiums. I'm always concerned about what's *missing* in a given society—it seems all of a sudden people just *forget* something.

STRICKLAND: What have we forgotten?

JARRETT: I think surfaces are progressing at an amazing speed, and what's underneath is being forgotten because of that speed. As surfaces become vaster they cover up whatever it was that was to be noticed. In Easton this summer—a small town, no great metropolis—I suddenly noticed I was *living* on concrete and asphalt. I've lived in cities, of course, been on tour, been in Tokyo for what seemed like forever sometimes. Now I didn't say, "I want to save the town of Easton and blow up their streets so they can live with plants and animals and trees." Maybe it would be a good thing to do, but for me it was just the shock—we can adapt ourselves so well to being blind. Even though I'm always checking myself out, to the point of craziness at times.

"Why talk about this? Things aren't going to change." I know that, but I can continue to feel what's under the asphalt.

STRICKLAND: So that's what you tried to communicate in *Spirits*?

JARRETT: A whole pygmy village came from Africa to dance in playgrounds across America, sponsored partially by the government. A very good friend of mine works for the Belgian National Museum. He was hired to do recordings of their music, which had never been done to that point. He went down with his wife, came back a couple of times with tapes, sent me some tapes, went down again, and eventually never came back. He lives in the village now and got a grant to bring his village, all of whom sing and dance—it's not like they've got the singers and the housewives.

And they wove baskets in Howard Johnson's lobby and sat in a circle. And on the floor the pygmy men were assigned, every door to every room was open. I interviewed that man—he's a Frenchman—who as you can tell came to love those people. "So tell me, what did they think?" They'd never been out of their village, completely remote jungle, hadn't even been to the capital of Zaire, and here they are now in New York, *seeing* everything.

And they were as unimpressed as—it was the reverse side of apathy— like young people now, nothing impresses them and we all understand why they must feel weird in this world—these people had a vital connection to life which temporarily they weren't given. "When are we going back? We'd like some good food. You know, those jungle bark things . . ."

STRICKLAND: You wrote once, "I believe in Music to the extent that it was here before we were." Is this a new version of the music of the spheres?

JARRETT: Maybe you could ask Blake where poetry comes from. He'd have one of two answers, either "It comes from me, and I have all these thoughts" or "Everything really did exist already."

STRICKLAND: If there had been no mankind would there still be music?

JARRETT: Yes. There were molluscs, one of the earliest creatures that developed under the ocean, that had incredible colors—not to mention their spirals and other pleasing shapes—before there were eyes.

[*After long pause*] Now even if that isn't true, it's a nice *thought*, isn't it? [*Laughs*.] You know Italo Calvino?

STRICKLAND: I just finished *If on a winter's night a traveler*.

JARRETT: He's got a story—it's great—about love between molluscs. They felt this thing and it was so intense that it just came out in colors, but there were no eyes to see them. But that was okay.

That's almost how I feel about my position in music. If I can radiate that thing, that's what's important. If people hear it or not is the second thing. I don't know, I hope they do. But I wouldn't want someone to say "Hey, far out!" if he didn't really see it or hear it. I would prefer a blind mollusc being in love with it [*laughs*].

© 1989 Martha Swope Assocs./Linda Alaniz, courtesy Elektra Nonesuch.

Born in New York City in 1936, Steve Reich studied piano as a child. In his early teens he switched his attention to drumming, which he studied with Roland Kohloff, principal tympanist with the New York Philharmonic. Reich received a B.A. in Philosophy with honors from Cornell in 1957 and subsequently studied composition with Hall Overton, with William Bergsma and Vincent Persichetti at Juilliard, and with Luciano Berio and Darius Milhaud at Mills College, which granted him the M.A. in 1963.

In 1964 Reich helped organize the premiere of *In C* by Terry Riley and began to find his own voice as a composer with the tape-phasing experiments that led to *It's Gonna Rain* (1965) and *Come Out* (1966). He adapted phasing to instruments for the rest of the decade in such works as *Piano Phase, Violin Phase,* and *Four Organs,* which caused an uproar at its 1970 debut. As legend would have it, after ten minutes, one member of the audience cried, "All right—I'll confess!" and an elderly woman banged her fist on the stage behind conductor Michael Tilson Thomas, demanding that the perpetrators cease and desist.

The same year Reich went to the University of Ghana in Accra, not to escape the lady in question but to study with Alfred Ladzepko, a master drummer of the Ewe tribe. This experience is reflected in *Drumming,* which may also be viewed as the culmination of Reich's phasing (and two decades of small-*d* drumming). The work has been recorded three times, in 1971 at Town Hall by Multiples, in 1973 by Deutsche Grammophon, and in 1987 by Nonesuch—each performance being significantly shorter than the previous one, a reflection of the progressive honing of the Reichian structural aesthetic even as the composer experiments in ever more expansive forms.

The next stage of his career began concurrently with his interest in Balinese gamelan music, which he studied formally on the West Coast. The gamelan influence is normally perceived in the more complex counterpoint and timbral variety of works beginning with *Music for Mallet Instruments, Voices and Organ* in 1973 and continuing with the breakthrough *Music for 18 Musicians* (composed 1974–76), *Music for a Large Ensemble* (1978), and *Octet* (1979). In 1976–77 Reich studied traditional Hebrew cantillation of the Scriptures; and in *Tehillim* (1981), he set psalm fragments. The relationship between these studies and compositions, Reich stresses below, is neither so direct nor so simple as this brief outline suggests and critics generally believe.

In late 1982 and 1983 Reich worked on *The Desert Music,* a piece scored for eighty-nine instruments and twenty-seven vocalists, which premiered in Cologne in March 1984 and has been performed since in both original and reduced settings (thirty instruments and ten vocalists with synthesizer). He has also rescored earlier works, with *Six Pianos* reincarnated as *Six Marimbas* and an earlier chamber piece reappearing in his first orchestral work, *Variations for Winds, Strings and Keyboards* (1979), commissioned by the San Francisco Symphony. He authorized the chamber-orchestral rearrangement of *Octet* as *Eight Lines* by flutist/conductor Ransom Wilson.

Live/tape pieces have been commissioned and performed by Wilson *(Vermont Counterpoint),* clarinetist Richard Stoltzman *(New York Counterpoint),* guitarist Pat Metheny *(Electric Counterpoint),* and the Kronos Quartet *(Different Trains).* In February 1990 the last piece was awarded the Grammy for Best Contemporary Composition. It is an extraordinary montage of live and taped quartets, train sounds transformed through a digital sampling keyboard, and taped voices of witnesses from the very "different trains" experienced by Reich journeying between divorced parents in New York and California and his fellow Jews in Hitler's Europe. The sophistication and imagination of Reich's technique here make his earlier use of tape seem rudimentary by comparison. The common trait of all his work, however, is its precision, which has resulted not in clinicism but in some of the most irresistibly dancelike music ever written.

A piece which exemplifies this is *Sextet,* composed after the large-scale *Desert Music.* It was commissioned by Laura Dean for her dance piece *Impact* and scored for the flexible ensemble the composer began organizing in 1966, Steve Reich and Musicians. Dean and Reich were awarded a Bessie for their collaboration. Reich then returned to orchestral work with *Three Movements,* premiered by the St. Louis Symphony in 1986, and *The Four Sections,* a concerto for orchestra premiered by the San Francisco Symphony the next year.

Reich has been working for some time on a "documentary music theater work" called *The Cave,* which is alluded to in embryo at the end of our conversation. With a text from the Bible and the Koran, the work requires five large projection screens, twenty-four musicians, and six to eight singers. The premiere is scheduled for the Stuttgart Opera in fall 1992, with subsequent performances at the Paris Festival d'Automne, London's Barbican Centre, Boston's Institute for Contemporary Art, and the Brooklyn Academy of Music.

Two decades ago Reich was a leading figure in the arts scene in downtown Manhattan, playing largely in galleries and lofts. Moving in the opposite direction from his career, I took a long walk from uptown to his home near City Hall on a bright afternoon in January 1987, and we spoke in his studio among the instruments and equipment.

STRICKLAND: When you were fourteen you had a musical conversion experience—

REICH: That's right, I did.

STRICKLAND: —which involved composers as diverse as Bach, Stravinsky, and Charlie Parker. I wonder if you could elaborate a bit on their influence as you felt it at the time. Let's start with Bach.

REICH: I had not heard any Baroque music of any sort, so I was hearing an unfamiliar style. I had heard Beethoven's Fifth, the Schubert Unfinished, the *Meistersinger* Overture, the middle-class favorites. Bach led to investigating not only the Baroque but earlier music. He was a signal to go backwards, historically speaking.

I went to Cornell at sixteen as a philosophy major, but I also studied music. The professor who most influenced me by far there was William Austin. Our first course was Music History, which he taught in a very unusual and provocative way. He started with Gregorian chant—now I suppose it's Hebraic chant—proceeded to Bach, then jumped to Debussy and Stravinsky, when contrapuntal music was taken up again, went on through jazz, then stopped. The second part of the course began with Haydn and ended with Wagner. To put it simply [*laughs*], I much preferred the first semester.

Of course, everyone loves Bach, what else is new? But there are a number of things of special interest to me. Baroque music in general and Bach in particular is a rhythmic music in that it has a fixed beat and there are basically no ritards and accelerandos. Your job is to stay with the tempo. Very creative players like Leonhardt can do things with the Goldbergs, of course, and that's wonderful. It's the art of making something flexible out of something that is fixed. Also the terraced dynamics interested me. In addition, during that period you have musicians who are able to improvise within a set of given harmonies, so there's always been a community of interest between jazz players of the bebop period, say, when chord changes were the *modus operandi* for improvisation, and players working with the figured bass of the Baroque.

So you have the fixed beat, relatively straightforward dynamic situations, and working over a ground bass or series of harmonies. I never met a jazz musician who didn't love Bach. And indeed if I were asked who's the greatest composer who ever lived in the West I would say without hesitation J. S. Bach.

STRICKLAND: You too have the motoric pulse and generally a restrained dynamic range. In addition, of the group of composers with whom you're associated—I'm trying not to use the magic word—you're certainly the most contrapuntally oriented.

REICH: The technique always associated with me is phasing, a kind of technocrat word I'm guilty of coining. In *Piano Phase,* Player A plays a repeating pattern and Player B duplicates it exactly. They start off in unison, and Player B begins to try to accelerate his tempo *ever* so slightly so that he goes just a little bit ahead of Player A. They're going to achieve a unison canon—or, if you like, a canonette, since the subject is very short in that case—with the rhythmic distance between voices, which is customarily fixed in Western music, here variable. Even when I stopped doing the phasing, this was still all over the music. A lot of what I do resembles stretto, and you're often squarely back dealing with the kinds of techniques that resemble isorhythmic motets of anywhere from the thirteenth to the fifteenth centuries.

I found recently in the "Agnus Dei" of Josquin's *Missa L'Homme armé,* the upper voices going in very tight canon about an eighth note away from each other, and the lower voices singing the tune forwards and backwards in half and whole notes. And it really analyzes exactly the same as *Octet,* the strings being the tenor and bass and the pianos and flutes being the women's voices. Josquin doesn't sound a damn thing like what I do, but it's the same musical technique—and people say, "Well, Reich, he's from Bali!"

STRICKLAND: We've gone back from Bach to Josquin. In an interview with Donal Henahan about fifteen years ago—I don't want to hold you to the sins of your youth, but—you said that while you admired Bach enormously, you found Magister Perotinus the high priest of Western music.

REICH: What was on my mind in 1971, the year after I wrote *Four Organs,* was augmentation. The most extreme form of that technique in Western musical history is Pérotin's and Léonin's organa, where the notes of the Gregorian chant are elongated over these massive stretches so that one loses one's sense of melodic movement from one tenor note to the next. And over them go what now become really decorative melodies over what appears to be a drone. But it's not a drone, the note changes . . . two or three pages later.

STRICKLAND: I was wondering if the sustained tenor with the melismas above it influenced your own use of figuration above a drone or semi-drone.

REICH: Most of these connections occurred to me after I did what I did in a very intuitive, nonintellectualized way, which is something I try to adhere to to this day. I'd heard Pérotin before *Four Organs,* of course, but if there was an influence it was unconscious. And I encountered the Josquin, for example, *way* after *Octet.* In general, you ought to revisit the literature and then throw it all out the window and write your piece. Forget about it, unless you're doing what Stravinsky did with Pergolesi. After *Four Organs,* a very radical piece, I investigated Pérotin because I asked myself, "Wait, am I all alone here in the ocean, or am I really in someone else's swimming pool?"

STRICKLAND: What about Stravinsky? How did he hit you at fourteen?

REICH: Like a ton of bricks. I hadn't heard anything at all of the twentieth century. Maybe *La Mer.* I heard *The Rite of Spring* at a friend's house, and it was as if somebody had opened a door, saying, "You've been living here all your life, but you haven't seen this room." I just couldn't *believe* that such a thing could exist. It completely changed my idea of what music was about.

STRICKLAND: I don't see this connection as clearly. Was it in part, as with Bach, a question of rhythm?

REICH: No, it was everything, the whole organism. What you suggest is true insofar as I can't trace his influence in my own work as clearly as I can even that of Bartók's. I got the arch form from Bartók. I got the idea of working with canons from Bartók's *Mikrokosmos.* I got clarification of the modes from Bartók. And later, in the late '70s, by looking at the beginning of the second movement of his Second Piano Concerto, I found the resuscitation of parallel intervals, which Bartók may have gotten from Debussy's "Sunken Cathedral," particularly fourths and fifths, as if the Middle Ages were translated into the twentieth century.

I discovered that my own musical heritage is really the French tradition in classical music. This to me is characteristically American. French Impressionism for example, has worked its way deeply into our music: Hollywood, Gershwin, Copland, Charlie Parker, Coltrane. Ives was probably closer to the German tradition.

STRICKLAND: I was surprised when I read of your being influenced by Charlie Parker. Again you have a strong sense of rhythm and pulse, but there's a lot of irregularity of phrasing in Parker, of course, that I don't associate with your music.

REICH: Parker's the most famous of the bop musicians, but the one I really ended up emulating, as a drummer, was Kenny Clarke—as opposed to Max Roach, who had more technique and more notes per minute than Clarke. But Kenny Clarke had a sense of time that propelled the entire band, a buoyant, permanent uplift I found riveting and wanted to imitate and in many ways still do. The rhythm section of Horace Silver, Kenny Clarke, and Percy Heath on the Miles Davis album *Walkin'* was magic—that sense of time which is flexible as to the downbeat—as is African music—and only slightly accented, not the big bombs of Max Roach, and moving steadily, ictus by ictus, pulse by pulse.

STRICKLAND: You took up drumming at this point.

REICH [*laughing*]: *Just* at this point! That was my first reaction!

STRICKLAND: Did you play jazz drums professionally?

REICH: My spending money in high school and at Cornell came from playing fraternities, the Black Elks, this, that, and the other thing—until I got to Juilliard, where it wasn't the nice thing to do. Composers don't play trap drums, so let's sweep this under the rug. The jazz influence that's all over my work is not so specific, but without the rhythmic and melodic gesture of jazz, its flexibility and nuance, my work is *unthinkable*. My music may not recall *Walkin'*, but it lives in a space made possible by those pieces.

STRICKLAND: Later on you heard Coltrane live, you've said, at least fifty times.

REICH: Probably more. Here at the Five Spot, the Blue Note, the Half Note, then Jazz Workshop in San Francisco. I'd go five or six or seven times during each of his stints, and he was playing a lot then. When I was at Mills College from 1961 to '63, most of the graduate students were writing pieces which they didn't play, which one could doubt whether they *heard* in their heads, and which were so enormously complex that they made the page virtually black, but you wondered if they'd ever be performed.

And at night I went to hear John Coltrane, who picks up his saxophone and *plays* and the music comes *out*. It was almost a moral dilemma. It would've been almost immoral not to follow in Coltrane's direction because of the musical honesty and authenticity involved. I became really wrapped up in Coltrane during his period of modal jazz.

STRICKLAND: You're talking about from *Kind of Blue,* with Miles Davis in '59, to just past *A Love Supreme,* heading into '65.

REICH: Exactly so. Particularly *My Favorite Things* and *Africa/Brass.* A lot of music is made over one or two harmonies. *Africa/Brass* has a whole side in F. "What's the change, man?" "F." "I mean, what's the change?" *"F!!"* [*Both laugh.*] That gets tied down and what's played over it is enormously free—which led of course to his later style, when he was playing like Ornette Coleman. In *Africa/Brass* Eric Dolphy has these horn glissandos that sound like charging elephants. Noise begins to enter in. What Coltrane was saying was that over a held harmony finally any note is possible, including noise.

But this was very different from John Cage, and certainly from Boulez, Stockhausen, and Berio, all of whom I felt terribly uncomfortable about: (a) they're the most important people today, and (b) I don't know what to do about it. When I was writing twelve-tone music, interestingly, the only way I could deal with it was not to transpose the row or invert the row or retrograde the row but to *repeat* the row over and over again, so I could *sneak* some harmony in there. At Mills, Berio would say to me, "If you want to write tonal music, go write tonal music." The experience of writing twelve-tone music was an important and valuable one for me in that it showed me what I had to do—which was to stop writing it.

I would say my greatest composition teachers by far were Hall Overton, who was a jazz musician, and Vincent Persichetti, who was also his teacher. What they shared was an ability to see what musical world *you*, the student, were inhabiting without superimposing *their* musical world, while giving specific advice in terms of *this* note or *that*. I don't think that's a gift of strong composers, who are more self-absorbed and have less equanimity of spirit.

I later taught a little composition myself at a community school and found it exhausting, because it requires you to prepare for each student in such individual detail that it exhausts your own creative resources.

STRICKLAND: After Mills you drove a cab for a while.

REICH: I had to do something with my life on an economic level. I either had to apply to X and Y universities to teach harmony and theory or . . . or dot dot dot—we don't know what those three dots are. It turned out to be the Yellow Cab Company. Anyway, I probably made more money there than teaching.

STRICKLAND: So you were driving the cab *and* composing?

REICH: I was bugging the taxi! [*Both laugh.*] Recording this and that, which I turned into a three-minute tape piece played in San Francisco in the early '60s. To get to the authenticity of American speech, which had impressed me so much in the work of William Carlos Williams, I thought, why not use tape? That doesn't lie. So I began to fool around with recorded speech. Not oscillators, not weird sounds. Speech. To me the most important pieces of that period of electronic tape music, which is largely over now, were *Gesang der Jünglinge* by Stockhausen, Alvin Lucier's *I*

Am Sitting in a Room, and, if you like them, my tape pieces, because they all have the richness of sound, an acoustical fact, and meaning, a psychological fact, that are imbedded in human speech.

Come Out is a civil rights piece. Its world premiere [*laughs*], which nobody cared about because it was a benefit for the retrial of the Harlem Six, at Town Hall in 1966, was literally used as pass-the-hat music. I believe they got a pretty good collection. There was a retrial.

STRICKLAND: How did you move from the tape loops into the live pieces?

REICH: At first I didn't see how phasing fit into the rest of Western musical history or any musical history. Clearly human beings can't do this. I felt I was trapped. Someone had locked me in the laboratory and I couldn't get out.

STRICKLAND: First you were locked in by the Serialists and now by yourself.

REICH: By myself. I felt I had discovered something which was addicting me. On the other hand, I felt "If I can't do this for instruments it's a cheap gimmick." For four or five months I just didn't know what to do. Somewhere in late '66 I sat down at the piano, made a tape, and said, "Okay, enough of this. *I'm* the second tape recorder." I closed my eyes, which is significant, started playing with the tape in unison—the first pattern in *Piano Phase*—and found to my surprise, "Wow! I can do it. I'm not as perfect as the tape recorder, but I can do it, and what's more, doing it, performing it is very interesting."

Now what about getting rid of the tape altogether? I had a good friend, Arthur Murphy, who'd gone to Juilliard with me and was a good friend of the jazz pianist Bill Evans. Neither one of us had two pianos, and we were both out of Juilliard without passes to the new, fancy building at Lincoln Center, so it had to wait until January 1967. A sculptor friend invited us to do our first concert anywhere at Fairleigh Dickinson. The night before we went over and did it live, and it was "Look, Ma, no *tape*!" Almost everything up to *Drumming* came out of that experience.

STRICKLAND: Why did you decide to go all the way to Ghana in 1970 to study drumming?

REICH: First of all, William Austin would play recordings of African and Balinese music in his courses—which not everyone would do. More immediately, Gunther Schuller had recommended a book on the subject, *Studies in African Music* by A. M. Jones. His transcriptions made an enormous impression on me at the time—along with Coltrane and Terry Riley—particularly the superimposition without coinciding downbeats of regular repeating patterns of varied lengths in what he notated as $12/8$. I'd heard African music, but how it was put together I'd had no idea. So it was a very potent piece of information, especially for someone fooling around with tape loops, which I began to envision as little mechanized Africans [*laughs*]. Jones had worked with the Ewe tribe in Africa, and at Columbia University I met a master drummer of that tribe, Alfred Ladzepko.

STRICKLAND: You've mentioned Terry Riley. Were you still in California when he was composing *In C*?

REICH: He was still composing it when I met him. I helped him put together the group that did it, which brings up the history of this kind of music.

It does not begin with Terry Riley, it doesn't begin with me, and it *certainly* doesn't begin with Glass. It begins with La Monte Young, who was at the University of California in Berkeley with Terry in the late '50s. Pauline Oliveros and David Del Tredici were in the same composition class with Seymour Shifrin, so it must have been quite a class. La Monte was dragging gongs along the floor, doing neo-Cage things, and was otherwise getting interested in long tones—and we're talking *real* long tones [*laughs*]. He wrote the *Trio for Strings,* a pivotal piece, based mostly on perfect intervals sustained for long periods of time on three strings. This had a profound effect on Riley, who as I understand it was still writing serial-type stuff, and who has tremendous musical facility—he's a very, very fine musician. Terry left the Bay Area to break away for a while, I think. He came back from Europe in '64 and we met through a number of common friends and hit it off and I offered the services of an improvisation group with which I was working. I suggested we could get a drummer to hold *In C* together, and eventually that became the Pulse at the top of the piano. I played, I think, a Wurlitzer electric piano at the world premiere in November '64. *In C* took these various strands—tape loops, African music, John Coltrane—and tied them all together. Undoubtedly this was the trigger for *It's Gonna Rain,* which was done in January '65. I started it earlier, while we were rehearsing *In C,* when a filmmaker friend said, "Come on, you've got to come down to Union Square and hear this preacher!"

Continuing this historical thread, I came back to New York in the fall of '65. At that time I felt very much out of place. Downtown it was basically works by or in imitation of John Cage, Morton Feldman, Christian Wolff, and Earle Brown. Uptown it was pieces in imitation of Stockhausen, Boulez, and Berio. I felt equidistant from both. I didn't know where to go. I felt at home with my painter friends, mostly listening to jazz, and through them I was offered the chance to do a concert of my music at the Park Place Gallery, *the* gallery of minimal art. It was three nights in March of '67, and we did a four-electric-piano version of *Piano Phase.*

After the second night my old friend from Juilliard, Phil Glass, came up and said he was back from studying with Nadia Boulanger and working with Ravi Shankar and had a string quartet he wanted me to see, which was certainly not anything like what he's doing now but which was getting away from dissonant intervals. From then until the beginning of '68, he and I played some things that I would basically give him criticism on and my reactions to. He knew Arthur Murphy from Juilliard. I said, "Listen, whatever you write, we'll get together and play it

with Arthur." I introduced him to Jon Gibson and James Tenney, who
became his group. All of this is in programs and can be verified
historically.

In early 1968 he wrote *One Plus One,* which was for rapping on a
table top in groups of twos and threes. That indeed was his original
insight, and he was very much off on his own from then on. The next
piece he wrote was called *Two Pages for Steve Reich* . . . which subsequently became known as *Two Pages* [*laughs*]. So there's your historical
sketch.

STRICKLAND: In '73 you studied Balinese gamelan music, but not abroad.

REICH: While I was in my teacher's village in Ghana I wore sandals like a
damn fool and got about fifty mosquito bites on each foot and got
malaria. It turned out to be a mild case—that's when you *feel* like you're
dying but you're not [*both laugh*]. So I got myself out of Ghana in a great
big hurry. *Anyway,* the experience made me feel I wasn't going to galli-
vant off to Bali. Probably I made a mistake because Bali's like heaven and
West Africa can be like hell. When I heard Bob Brown had established
the American Society for Eastern Arts, I went out—first to Seattle, next
summer to a church he'd gotten in Berkeley—in a dual capacity, as a
teacher of my own music and a student of Balinese music. They were
two very well-spent summers.

STRICKLAND: It seems to have opened up instrumental possibilities in your
music.

REICH: Well, everybody says that, but the fact is I wrote *Music for Mallet
Instruments, Voices and Organ,* which is most often pointed to in this
context, *before* I went west that first summer. I'd heard recordings, sure.
Drumming is another example. I didn't write it because I went to Ghana;
I wrote it because I'd been drumming since I was fourteen. Everything
African in that piece—$12/8$, repeating patterns—I'd done in *Piano Phase*
and *Violin Phase* back in 1967. Going to Africa was a pat on the back:
yes, repeating patterns are fine; yes, acoustical instruments are richer
than electronic sound; and yes, percussion can be the dominant voice in
an instrumental group. With that green light I allowed myself to write
Drumming.

It became clear to me after Ghana I was going to use my own instruments, not theirs. The same for Balinese music. If someone gave me an
entire gamelan I'd say, "Gee, thanks a lot, but give it to the Smithso-
nian." If it isn't on 48th Street, the hell with it! That's my attitude.

The same with tuning, though composers like Glenn Branca, Terry
Riley, chiefly La Monte Young, are experimenting with it. To me our
piano scale is something one picks up from the cradle. It's imbedded on
an unconscious level, and I don't want to mess with it! What one learns
from African or Balinese music is how it's put together, how to organize
sound—and the knowledge of structure and musical form naturally
comes later in one's education.

I believe this attitude explains why I survived the experience of foreign cultures better than others here, who in a sense got swallowed up and lost in the belly of the whale of Indian music. Because you are, finally, one puny individual, confronting the music of an entire subcontinent. Others end up doing a music which is neither Indian nor Western and finally doesn't add anything to either tradition. They try to adapt the *sounds* rather than the structures of an alien culture, which is really the most superficial aspect of its music—the sitar-in-the-rock-band phenomenon—though the composers I'm thinking of are anything but superficial themselves. I find alien instruments, timbres, tuning, scales, modes, fascinating—but they're precisely the elements I don't want to touch with a ten-foot pole!

STRICKLAND: Hebrew chant was seemingly another of your exotic explorations in music, yet in another sense it's very close to you, since you're a Jew. How did you decide to undertake formal study in cantillation?

REICH: I'm not African, not Balinese, though I respected those traditions. And there's a sadness to the fact that the traditions are going and will never come back. African music becomes variations on James Brown. Anyway, I began to ask myself, "Do *I* have anything like that?" Now I was raised as a Reform Jew, which means I might as well have been a Unitarian. I had not heard Hebrew chant, I did not know the Hebrew language, I did not know the Torah was read in an annual cycle, I didn't know *anything*. When I was Bar Mitzvah-ed I did a lip-sync. I had been given transliterated English and told how to point in synchronization with that. This experience can make you less than enthusiastic about your own background.

So it wasn't until the age of thirty-seven, with the feeling that what I was looking for religiously—which had been sort of associated with this musical enterprise—might be found in my own backyard, that I had to find out indeed what my own backyard was. I studied at the Lincoln Square Synagogue here in Manhattan—it's Modern Orthodox. I studied Hebrew and Torah. As you know, the language is mostly consonants. Then there were vowels, and then a third marking. I asked my teacher, "What's that?" and he said, "That's the musical notation." So I said, "Well, I've got to find out more about that." I got a book and a teacher, as usual. The book was *Jewish Music* by Abraham Idelsohn, a contemporary of Bartók and similar as a musicologist. He'd gone to Yemen, Kurdistan, and Iraq; recorded particularly their singing of the psalms; and established among other things the tremendous similarity between Yemenite psalm singing and Gregorian psalm tone. I studied with Johanna Spector at the Jewish Theological Seminary and then a cantor in New Jersey named Ed Berman and learned to do a bit of it, starting with the opening of the Torah [*chants*]. I thought I'd go to Israel and seek out older men who'd been raised in those places I mentioned, who maintain the closest thing to a survival of the original biblical chant.

So after a 1977 tour of *Music for 18 Musicians* my wife, Beryl, and I flew to Israel from London and spent two weeks working with a man from the national archive of recorded sound in Jerusalem. I told him I wanted to record the first five verses of Genesis with Jews from Kurdistan, Iraq, and India. We went for dinner one night at the home of a Yemenite Jew about sixty or sixty-five who had a couple of younger sons who'd just come out of the Israeli army. After drinking many cups of tea, he finally consented to be recorded. And though I can't sing like he did it was approximately [*chants nasally*]. He then said, "Oh, you must record my son, he's so much better." So we recorded his son and it was [*chants pectorally*]. The voice had clearly moved to the chest—and in one generation a whole musical tradition was over because they'd left Yemen.

And in the West the tradition of singing psalms, as opposed to the chanting of the Torah and prophets, has been lost. If you go to a synagogue in New York, Cologne, Paris, or London you will hear very bad borrowed hymn tunes that would make J. S. Bach roll over in his grave.

On a musical level cantillation involves a single line made up of varying smaller components strung together to make a much longer line. In *Octet* you will find *precisely* the influence of this study, whereas you will find *none* of it in *Tehillim,* which has nothing to do with cantillation whatsoever. *Emotionally,* yes, it's true, a reinterest in being a Jew produced *Tehillim.*

While in the Church you have a tradition even today that welcomes and encourages new Masses, new settings of the Ordinary—which Arvo Pärt is working on right now in the Russian Orthodox church with *great* success; the rest of his life may be spent doing that—in contrast the Synagogue wants to maintain one man, one text, no choir, no organ, just recreating an oral tradition taught by father to son, father to son. I completely support that tradition. I also support the Church's tradition, but I was born into the Synagogue and the Synagogue doesn't need me—it didn't need George Gershwin or Arnold Schoenberg—or Phil Glass or any other Jewish composer to do anything for it. Like Stravinsky's *Symphony of Psalms, Tehillim* is a concert piece and if it's done in a synagogue that's a nice piece of sociological news, but that's all.

STRICKLAND: You just mentioned Arvo Pärt, and this leads me to the question I know you've been waiting for, having heard it roughly ten million times by now. But . . . here it is, anyway. I want to ask if you see your group of American composers now influencing Europeans like Pärt and Górecki. But the first question is, what *is* the group? Everyone calls you, Young, Glass, Riley, Adams et al. Minimalists. What's minimal now about Minimalism? It's not minimal in length—*Drumming,* written fifteen years ago, can last ninety minutes. The Glass operas or Young's *Well-Tuned Piano* can go on for four or five hours. It's not minimal in forces—you have 116 gainfully employed in *The Desert Music.* Even *In*

C can have fifty-three voices, which beats Thomas Tallis by a baker's dozen.

REICH: Debussy resented "Impressionism." Schoenberg preferred "pantonal" to "atonal" or "twelve-tone" or "Expressionist." Too bad for them. "Minimalism" might have been termed by Michael Nyman, an old musician/writer friend of mine from England, undoubtedly thinking about Frank Stella, Don Judd, people like that, a lot of whom exhibited at the Park Place Gallery. Sol LeWitt, whose work you see over there, bought some scores of mine, which enabled me to buy a glockenspiel for *Drumming.* I didn't have enough money, and in those days Sol was enormously helpful. Given some others applied to the music, maybe the term's not so bad.

STRICKLAND: Robert Palmer used "trance music."

REICH: I think that's the worst of them all. He gets the booby prize.

STRICKLAND: I thought Richard Kostelanetz was perhaps more to the point with "modular music."

REICH: Not me. I'd go with the French *musique répétitive,* but basically I wouldn't go with any of them. The attitude which finds names for things is a basic human activity, and I participate in it in areas with which I'm not directly concerned, but in an activity with which I'm concerned in a creative way it would be silly, it would be foolish for me to get involved in it. The most serious answer comes out in the words of the Spanish comedian: "Ees not my job." It's *your* job, the job of people writing for papers, maybe the job of music historians. I don't want to get our functions mixed up. So people say, "What do you call it?" I reply, not facetiously, "I call it music. I call it *Four Organs.* I call it *Work in Progress for the San Francisco Symphony.*" In the early days the term had a little bit of justification when applied to *Four Organs* or *Violin Phase,* where there are no changes of notes or timbre, eliminating normal orchestration and even harmony by using a very restricted contrapuntal technique in its place.

If you'd heard *The Desert Music* before the earlier works you would *never* have said "minimal." The point is that I'm "a Minimalist"—it doesn't matter *what* I do. If I did something that was a dead ringer for Mahler, they'd say "Ah! the Minimalist is doing this, and this is a *new* kind of Minimalism!" [*Laughs loudly.*]

STRICKLAND [*laughing*]: Mahlerian Minimalism.

REICH [*still laughing*]: "It *sounds* like Del Tredici, but *really* it's . . . " According to Donal Henahan, Del Tredici's a Minimalist too. David and I are still trying to figure out *how.*

STRICKLAND: Let's get back to the possible influence on Europeans like Pärt and Górecki. Have you heard the Górecki Third?

REICH: I heard it and I think it's terrible.

STRICKLAND [*surprised*]: Do you?

REICH: I only heard some of it. It was so bad I just turned it off. Maybe I ought to go back and listen to it again. A composer friend of mine sent it to me from Holland, and I wrote him back, "Comparing Górecki to Pärt is like comparing Penderecki to Ligeti, that is, comparing a cheap facility with a real originality." A cheap facility is how I would describe Penderecki. Pärt and Ligeti are major composers. Pärt I've met, and he did tell me he'd heard my music in the Soviet Union. I was very pleased to hear that. But there is no *question* in my mind but that Arvo Pärt is his own voice as opposed to many Minimalists in Holland, England, and Belgium you haven't mentioned and I won't either, who sound to me like the American Serialists—i.e., they're aping some other culture's product.

STRICKLAND: Such as?

REICH: I don't want to make enemies. Schoenberg gives a very honest musical portrayal of his times. I salute him—but I don't want to write like him. Stockhausen, Berio, and Boulez were portraying in very honest terms what it was like to pick up the pieces of a bombed-out continent after World War II. But for some American in 1948 or 1958 or 1968— in the *real* context of tail fins, Chuck Berry, and millions of burgers sold—to *pretend* that instead we're *really* going to have the dark-brown *Angst* of Vienna is a *lie,* a musical *lie,* and I think these people are musical liars and their work isn't worth [*snaps fingers*] *that!*

Minimalism grows out of sources that are non-Western but played in America in abundance by live musicians. An undercurrent goes to jazz, particularly to John Coltrane and maybe Eric Dolphy. It has to do with pop tunes that come out of Motown, like Junior Walker's "Shotgun," which has one repeating bass line for the entire length of the tune [*interviewer hums it*]. All these things were bubbling up naturally, and some Americans responded to it in a natural way. In Europe, Pärt is his own man, doing something quite different. It has to do—while it may be influenced by some of the things I've done, for which I'm very, very proud—really with the Russian Orthodox church. I think that Pärt is the only one of these Europeans I'm aware of of whom I would say this is a man who has his own voice and who's doing something very, very important which is his own.

STRICKLAND: What other composers do you admire?

REICH: Along with Pärt—they've performed his *Johannes-Passion,* and I'm sure ECM will be releasing more of his music—recently I've just taken a good listen to Glenn Branca's music. I heard him up at Alice Tully last year and was struck by the fact that this man's for real. It's sometimes loud to the point of painful, and I'm not about to sacrifice my basilar membrane on the altar of his music, but I salute him. John Adams, it goes without saying, I respect greatly. What I've heard of *Nixon in China* is unfortunate, but I look forward to being at the premiere. These are people saying what's on their minds, conscious and unconscious. With any composer, if his stuff doesn't bubble up of itself, whether you like it or not . . . Buster, you're not welcome in my house! [*Laughs loudly.*]

STRICKLAND: Speaking of welcome in your house, what music do you find yourself listening to at home? Do you listen primarily to contemporary music?

REICH: Not necessarily. Recently the Yo-Yo Ma Bach Cello Suites—the pianists in my group, Ed Niemann and Nurit Tilles, recently made me a present of the three cassettes—I think he plays quite beautifully. Also the Takács Quartet's Bartók, though I'm not sure I don't prefer my old monophonic Juilliard version. It depends on what I'm working on. When I was doing *Tehillim* the model was Bach's *Christ lag in Todesbanden*. My third movement resembles his duet. I don't have absolute pitch, but they're roughly [*sings a line of each*]. The idea of the women's voices in dialogue. Also in Bach the old idea of doubling voices with instruments. Josquin's *Missa L'Homme armé* I could see becoming the basis for a piece or two [*both sing tune*]. Who was *l'homme armé*—some armed man roaming the land? The whole concept of the *cantus firmus* Mass intrigues me.

STRICKLAND: It seems as if your interests, like Professor Austin's course, go up to Bach, then jump into this century.

REICH: Believe it or not, I have no real interest in music from Haydn to Wagner. Of course I love the *Dankgesang* in the Beethoven Opus 132 Quartet, a modal, nonvibrato slow movement very much like what you find in Bartók. In fact, recently in the mornings I've been listening to the *Eroica*—particularly those six repeated dominants in the first movement. Ha! They're fantastic!

STRICKLAND: Those explosions might lead us into *The Desert Music*. It's generally considered your finest work to date, and I think it's fair to say it's been as highly acclaimed as any composition this decade.

REICH: Nice to hear.

STRICKLAND: What musical influences are in it?

REICH: Before I did *The Desert Music* I listened to *Israel in Egypt, Messiah, Dido and Aeneas*—which I'd probably give the highest marks to. Purcell is a genius! I listened to the *Dies Irae* of Penderecki, which is a piece of trash, and *Coro* by Berio. I listened and put it all away, and the piece ended up closer to Bach than any of the works I've mentioned.

STRICKLAND: How did it come about?

REICH: Well, in one sense, as a suggestion from Wolfgang Becker in Köln that there be an evening-length choral piece. He commissioned *Coro* by Berio and wanted to do another piece roughly that length and with roughly those forces. It happened while we were premiering *Tehillim* over there. While I was performing in that, during the many rests I had, I remember thinking, "Why don't I set Wittgenstein? He's German, I did my Cornell thesis on him . . . no, that's not going to work." And at other times I had thoughts about using tapes from World War II, Hitler's voice, Truman's voice after the dropping of the A-bomb, or going back to the tape pieces and making music theater out of that. All these things were sort of spinning around when I picked up Williams and found in his poem "The Orchestra" the material that would take care of the interest in that sort of subject matter in a context that seemed so much more in tune with what I wanted to do. *The Desert Music* was the title of the volume. I went to the typewriter and began copying out parts of poems—bear in mind that in *Tehillim* too I don't set any complete psalms—the criterion in both cases for selecting the fragments was "Can I say this wholeheartedly? Whenever I feel myself drifting off, I'm just going to drop it."

So I typed out the Williams fragments on pieces of paper and physically rearranged them on top of the marimba before I wrote a note, until finally, *voilà!* these pieces of paper were finally in the right shape as a whole, with in the very center "It is a principle of music/ to repeat the theme. Repeat/ and repeat again." Then I went to the keyboard to look for basic harmonic cycles to characterize these texts, so there's one for the first and last movements, another for the second and fourth, and still another for the third.

STRICKLAND: I have a couple of stylistic questions about the piece, the first a very small one. Towards the end of the third movement you have the violas sounding like a siren. You've mentioned that that occurred to you because you heard a fire siren in Vermont while composing. I was wondering if there was also an allusion to the air raid in the Shostakovich Eighth Quartet.

REICH: Are sirens there, really? I don't know his quartets. We both had experience of sirens in World War II—I heard them in movies, he heard them in reality. I've been attracted to sirens off and on, maybe because I grew up with World War II movies . . . but the fact of the matter is I was working at the piano and this thing went off and I said, "That's it! That's what I need."

STRICKLAND: It does have a kind of apocalyptic aura to it . . . which leads to the other question I have. One doubt that I have about the work is whether there is a coherence in the texts chosen between the "principle of music" and the Doomsday warning fragment.

REICH: The piece is all new things following one another till you get to the middle, "It is a principle of music/ to repeat the theme. Repeat/ and repeat again,/ as the pace mounts. The/ theme is difficult/ but no more difficult/ than the facts to be/ resolved." Then the arch form begins to open up. I go back to the string counterpoint that preceded the fragment, only this time . . . those questions didn't go away, they persist. My music, my life will not make them go away. So the music comes back, but why you get those air-raid sirens in the repeat is that it's like turning the screw, because now there are that many more missiles. Those things have not gone away.

STRICKLAND: So there's a duality of focus. You're talking about an existential situation, the possibility of nuclear holocaust, and in "Repeat/ and repeat again" you're using the fragment reflexively in a sense.

REICH: Yes. The very center of the piece is canons on the word "difficult" [*sings*]. It's the most difficult part of the piece, and we always punned about the difficult canon. When the *Grove Dictionary* asked me for a score page, I unhesitatingly gave them a page from that canon and told Beryl jokingly that if I die in the middle of this piece put that on my gravestone. So for me that's the very important center of the work. There's something self-referential about the repeating—it refers to the music itself, but it also refers to the persistence of the whole set of the piece as well as its problems. That's the fulcrum, after which you have the same texts coming back, but coming back differently than when they were first presented.

Compare the fourth to the second movement. It's half as long, but a very successful part of that piece. The second movement asks, *"Well, shall we/ think or listen?"* In the fourth it's *"Well, shall we/ think or listen?"* Now we've introduced this real issue, but we're still listening to music, that's what's really going on. We're sitting in a hall listening to music. *Well,* what are we doing here? You're not about to go on a peace march or write a letter to your congressman or try to sabotage a nuclear plant.

The piece suggests that world, but it also *is* the world of an orchestra and a chorus and a concert and so on and so forth. And that's the tension that's in Williams's poem. The lines "Say to them:/ Man has survived hitherto . . . " are written as if they were a prose insert that he pasted in. It's as if he's at his table writing and he looks up and looks you right in the eye and says this to you. The poem is about the orchestra, but suddenly there's this real question. One of the many things this calls to mind is that music has the same ambiguity of being about nothing and a great deal of things, even when it uses no words.

STRICKLAND: The title *The Desert Music* with its reference to, among other things, atomic testing, is a very dark omen in itself. And your tonal palette is darker than it had been . . . greater chromaticism, dissonance, those violas . . . yet it's very hard for me not to feel more buoyant than threatened. It's like in Byron, where you have the most world-weary comments often couched in jaunty metrics. In *The Desert Music,* as dark as it is in many ways, still there's that Reichian buoyancy of rhythm, and I wonder if there's not a tension between that and the vision that's being presented.

REICH: Well, the last text is taken from "Asphodel," a love poem: "Inseparable from the fire/ its light/ takes precedence over it." To remove the light from the fire is a very delicate operation. "Who most shall advance the light—/ call it what you may!" and then finally you go back into the Pulse. The first movement cadences on a D–Dorian minor. At the end of *The Desert Music* the bass is removed. I find it very difficult to resolve chords using the bass, particularly from V to I, but I find I can do that if I remove the bass and go high enough in registration—this happens at the end of *Sextet* too—and make a more ambiguous resolution where I'm returning to the home chord. It could be interpreted that way, but because I don't have a bass, it could be a possible major ending in F or the D-minor Dorian or that we're still in the dominant.

STRICKLAND: Is this tonal ambiguity a reflection of the ambiguity of the vision of the piece?

REICH: Absolutely! I mean, *Tehillim* ends with a hallelujah! in D major, and that's the way it should end if you're setting Psalm 150. But in *The Desert Music* to have a conclusion that could be nailed down would be childish, foolish. It would be wrong, musically wrong and humanly wrong. So with this very large harmonic structure working itself out—I wanted to confront the basic axes of Western music: if there's going to be a conclusion it tends to go to either the major or the minor—in my case a modal minor—or it rests on the end of the dominant—*Four Organs* is one long dominant chord, which gives the sense of pushing yourself forward without reaching your conclusion yet. And at the end of *The Desert Music* one is left with a situation where those three harmonic candidates are all equally up there. To say which one it is—well, it is musically accurate to say they are equally represented. And that's precisely the situation I wanted to get to. Because really what's going to happen is that the conglomerate energy of the human race is going to determine what happens. And I would like to, I would *like* to feel at least that it's an open situation. It would be naive to say I could plunk down on major. Reading between the lines, you may find in fact that I have other feelings about it which are more positive.

STRICKLAND: Do you anticipate doing a work of that scope again?

REICH: I may be doing something radically different, a theater piece—don't ask me. I may work with just my ensemble. I may collaborate with other artists. I could spend as much as two years working on it. It would not be an opera. It could use audio tape. It could use video tape. It could use choreography. But it would not use 116 musicians, it would use probably under twenty. But it could be a very, very long piece, a very big piece, and as I hope you've seen from *Sextet,* a lot of things can be done with a small number of instruments.

© 1990 Marian Zazeela.

La Monte Young's music is like no other, making no concession to conventional concepts of intonation, structure, dynamics, or duration. His marathon performances, described by one critic as "unutterably boring," are to others transcendentally beautiful, at once uncanny and on some subconscious level intimately familiar.

Like his work, the composer is an American original, born in a log cabin (as was Roy Harris) in Bern, Idaho, in 1935. As a student in the '50s he played in black blues bands and led on alto saxophone a jazz group including Billy Higgins, Dennis Budimir, and Don Cherry. As a graduate student at the University of California in Berkeley, Young composed the long-tone works now generally recognized as inaugurating musical Minimalism, most notably the Webern- and *gagaku*-influenced *Trio for Strings* (1958), in which minutes pass slightly more quickly than notes.

In 1959 he studied with Stockhausen in Darmstadt and in turn influenced the overtone chanting of that composer's *Stimmung*. In New York in 1960 Young directed the first loft concert series at Yoko Ono's studio and affected the course of post-Cageian concept art and the Fluxus movement with *Compositions 1960* (#10: "Draw a straight line and follow it"; #15: "This piece is little whirlpools out in the middle of the ocean"). In 1963 he edited the avant-garde compendium *An Anthology* and continued his experiments with drone simulation on the sopranino saxophone.

The following year marked the beginning of Young's still-evolving *magna opera, The Well-Tuned Piano* and *The Tortoise, His Dreams and Journeys*. The *Well-Tuned Piano,* released on five discs by Gramavision in 1987, was recorded in live performance in 1981 on a custom-designed and completely retuned Bösendorfer. The piano has an additional bass octave and is tuned in just intonation rather than in equal temperament, each of the keys corresponding to a harmonic of an E-flat ten octaves below the lowest on the keyboard. That E-flat is, of course, never heard, but it pervades—perhaps "haunts" is a better word—the piece and its listeners as a drone encountered on some subliminal level. In addition, acoustical properties peculiar to this harmonics-based tuning at times create the unsettling illusion of timbres of instruments other than the piano, so that one momentarily "hears" a horn or a gong. Texturally, the piece varies from very spare, ruminative passages on six chords and myriad thematic permutations to extremely dense "cloud" sections, in which Young seeks, with the same dexterity he demonstrated over three decades ago as a jazz saxophonist, to lose the identity of individual notes in the mass. The nomenclature of the sections is also unheard of: "The Magic Harmonic Rainforest Chord," "The Homage to Brahms Variation of The Theme of the Dawn of Eternal Time in The Deep Pool," "Young's Böse Brontosaurus Boogie," "The 189/98 Lost Ancestral Lake Region." The last reflects the mathematical precision of Young's pioneering research in just intonation, and his work has attracted the interest of MIT mathematicians and Columbia University psychoacousticians.

His explorations in drones and dynamics have been seen as the forerunner of both dreamy ambient music—Brian Eno has called Young "the daddy of us all"—and punk rock—founders of the protopunk Velvet Underground performed in Young's own Theatre of Eternal Music. Founded in 1962, this flexible group has realized performances of sections of *The Tortoise, His Dreams and Journeys* in which musicians and singers (including Young and his wife, Marian Zazeela) improvise within strict guidelines over electronic drones. This inspired the Dream House projects, semi-permanent sound and light environments the couple has realized internationally since the '60s, most notably in the six-story Dream House at 6 Harrison Street, in New York. After six years of perfectionist effort in continuously renovating the old New York Mercantile Exchange (purchased for them by Heiner and Philippa de Menil Friedrich) while maintaining a constant sound-light environment, Young and Zazeela were forced by the decline in oil prices (their patrons derive their wealth from Schlumberger) to leave 6 Harrison in the spring of 1985.

In 1987 the Dia Foundation presented a retrospective of Young's work, including seven performances of *The Well-Tuned Piano* on successive Sundays. Young will perform *The Well-Tuned Piano* only in the setting of Zazeela's *Magenta Lights*, a breathtaking composition which manages by precise manipulation of lighting tones and angles to abolish the distinction between solids and space, image and reflection, all in a hauntingly crepuscular ambience that unites audience and spotlight-free pianist.

The couple continues to perform and exhibit internationally. In February 1989 Dia opened a year-long sound-light environment composed of Zazeela's *Time Light Symmetry* and Young's *The Romantic Symmetry (over a 60 cycle base)* from Young's new long-term project, *The Symmetries in Prime Time from 112 to 144 with 119*. In March 1990 the exhibit closed with four performances by the Theatre of Eternal Music Big Band, the Theatre's first incarnation since 1975 and its largest ever, consisting of twenty-three musicians improvising over the seventeen-frequency drone of a Rayna synthesizer.

Young continues his studies, now of two decades duration, with North Indian singer Pandit Pran Nath, master of the Kirana style of perfect-pitch singing. Young and Zazeela have produced frequent concerts by Pran Nath in New York, as well as his album, *Ragas of Morning and Night*.

Young and Zazeela pioneered downtown loft-living in the 1960s in the TriBeCa loft where we spoke from seven to two one May night in 1987.

STRICKLAND: How did you come to composing? Or vice versa.

YOUNG: We can go back to the very beginning in the log cabin, with the wind blowing between the crisscrossed logs. I was born in Bern, Idaho, in Bear Lake County, maybe ten miles from the lake. It's very cold there. My dad told me they once had a blizzard on the Fourth of July. My grandfather said, "That's nothing. One year it snowed every month." He later moved to Utah, he said, because he got tired of watching his overalls standing in the corner after he waded home through the snow [*both laugh*].

STRICKLAND: From what age does the memory of the wind date?

YOUNG: I've thought a lot about that. There's no way I can pinpoint whether it was my first or second year, but I was born on October 14th, so we were already into winter. I definitely remember lying in bed and being fed a bottle. We left the cabin when I was about three and a half and moved to Montpelier. I suspect it was probably the second and third winters that I remember so vividly. They say when blizzards came you couldn't see your hand in front of your face, and when the wind came off that lake it was something really fierce. And it was just a little two-room log cabin. Once the stove and the cabin caught on fire and they ran out with me into the cold while the neighbors helped put the fire out.

STRICKLAND: This was a Mormon community.

YOUNG: Yes, a little Swiss dairy community. There were 149 people when I was born, and the way they tell it they were all Mormons but one, and he was a very good soul. But the population has since exploded—it's about 172 right now [*both laugh*].

STRICKLAND: Was it a very clannish community?

YOUNG: Oh, yes, the Mormons are very in-group. You can't go with girls not in the church and so on. The church has you programmed seven days a week all day long. You pay ten percent of your earnings, so if you mow a lawn for five dollars you give fifty cents to the church. The symbol of the Mormons is the beehive—they're very hard-working, try to be self-sufficient . . .

STRICKLAND: Apart from the Mormon Tabernacle Choir, it's not a religion that I, as an outsider, would associate with music.

YOUNG: They start you at a very early age speaking in front of the congregation. If you can play an instrument you do solos in church. Or you sing in the local ward choir. You start bearing testimony as soon as you can talk. In certain meetings they have people with musical talent play numbers.

STRICKLAND: Spirituals?

YOUNG: Not necessarily. On Tuesday nights they had Mutual Improvement Association—MIA. Now they call it something else, that's gone.

STRICKLAND: Missing in action?

YOUNG: It was the youth group for high-school kids. One week we'd go miniature-golfing as a group, next week a play that we'd all participate in; other weeks a dance and my group or someone else's in the church would be the band. Another night they'd have a more normal service, including a couple of musical solos, and I would maybe play one and maybe my dad would sing "When the Swallows Fly from Capistrano"—you know that one? It's a beautiful song.

STRICKLAND [*crooning*]: "When the swallows come back to Capistra-a-no . . . "

YOUNG: That's it. Or maybe he'd sing "Red River Valley" or a more spiritual song like "In the Garden of Gethsemane" or maybe the ward choir would sing. In church services on Sunday nights the more spiritual side of musical performance would be presented. I played a number of classical saxophone solos then. The whole audience sang hymns, as in the normal Protestant service.

STRICKLAND: When did you first pick up an instrument?

YOUNG: My mother and Aunt Norma started me singing cowboy songs, and then my Aunt Norma started me playing the guitar to accompany them when I was about three or four. I was trying to learn "A-ridin' old Paint and a-leadin' old Dan." Very frustrating. I just couldn't get the whole thing together. By the time I was four and a half they had me tap dancing and singing at the Rich Theater in Montpelier. When I was seven my father bought me a saxophone and started to teach me. This was a greyish silver Holton. It was probably my birthday and Christmas present combined. It wasn't until high school that I bought my first Selmer alto, working in a machine shop after school. I was earning forty cents an hour, and it cost three hundred with the case on the installment plan. I went to the store with my teacher, William Green, who told them I was good for the money.

STRICKLAND: When did you move to L.A.?

YOUNG: Dad first hitchhiked down when I was about four and a half—this was the end of the depression and there was no work. He was a sheepherder—you can poeticize it or depoeticize it as much as you want, but that's what he was doing. My parents were hillbillies. We lived in L.A. through my fifth grade. Then Dad's Uncle Thornton, who had taught my father to play saxophone and had a swing band in L.A., brought Dad up to manage his celery farm in Utah. We Youngs—like Brigham—have a very strong organizational streak. We stayed through the ninth grade on the shore of Utah Lake, and there Uncle Thornton coached me on saxophone, introduced me to more popular music, and gave me his old dance band arrangements. I composed the first thing I remember, a waltz on the saxophone, now lost. At that age you're not thinking about preserving anything. But I was still living in the world of two- or three-chord cowboy music—I used to listen to cowboy music on the radio every day.

STRICKLAND: Before your uncle introduced you to swing, what were you playing?

YOUNG: Standard stuff that comes out of the lesson books, and from the second grade on I played in the grade school orchestra. I played in bands and orchestras the entire time I was in school. When I got back to L.A. I was listening to polkas and Spike Jones, and when I went to John Marshall High School, somehow I got introduced to Dixieland. Once I hit Marshall it was all over. Music of all types was brought immediately into my presence.

STRICKLAND: Your own sax playing was more bop than swing.

YOUNG: That happened at Marshall. I hadn't been hearing swing from bands—I was learning it through Uncle Thornton's books and his coaching. I had no records—we were very *poor*. I had a radio but it didn't work most of the time. One of the big experiences of my life was when I got some classical music on the radio and I was *just* sitting by it and listening to it—I don't even know what it was I heard now, because I was very naive. Except for what I'd learned in school and from my family, I was very uneducated musically. My dad was a very strict teacher. He'd absolutely beat me if I made a wrong note. By the time I got to high school I could play better than he could.

STRICKLAND: What type of musical training did you have at Marshall?

YOUNG: There were some very fine teachers. My harmony teacher was Clyde Sorenson, who had studied with Schoenberg at UCLA. I took every possible semester of harmony I could. There I did my second composition, also lost, something I'd written in the whole-tone scale, to which he'd introduced me.

STRICKLAND: You were being trained classically but were involved with jazz.

YOUNG: Very much. I met all of these students there who were introducing me to jazz left and right. Charlie Parker, Stan Getz, Lee Konitz. Jazz was something we did at noontime, before school, and after school. In the school orchestra we were playing typical music—I remember playing Glinka's "Russian Sailor's Dance" [*sings tune*]. Very nice piece. Then of course we played some semi-jazz pieces like Leroy Anderson's.

STRICKLAND: Was the school integrated racially?

YOUNG: All kinds of us went there, but we were all from the wrong side of the tracks. It was just wild! A lot of Mexican kids. One of the most fantastic musicians there was Gordo, David Sanchez, a sensational trombonist. By tenth grade he had already been on tour with Perez Prado, and he could play just anything you'd put in front of him. His tone was so beautiful! It just . . . oh, what a sound, what musicianship! How he could just sit there and rattle things off! He came to band practice, first period every day, drinking a quart of beer. The teacher would go *crazy* and Gordo would raise hell. He was too good and he didn't give a damn about [*laughing*] the teacher, the school, the class—he was just there because he had to go. It was the law, you know?

It was a very tough school. The big rage then was Big Jay NcNeely's "Cornbread." You know that one? [*Sings*] *Da*dadat *da*dat *dah*, *da*dadat *da*dat *dah*, *da*dadat *da*da—with about, you know, three or four tenor saxophones and he would roll around on his back and at noontime the kids were doing these dances called the Choke and so forth, just very beautiful popular dances.

STRICKLAND: After Marshall you went to L.A. City College.

YOUNG: Their dance band was world famous. At Marshall all I heard about was the alto saxophonists that had been there before me, and the only goal they set up for me was to make the dance band at L.A. City College my first semester. That was the meaning of life.

STRICKLAND: You found it. Is it true you beat out Eric Dolphy for a spot?

YOUNG: I sat there while Eric auditioned and I thought he sounded *fierce*—I thought he sounded just like Charlie Parker. I was playing saxophone like Lee Konitz. We were competing on saxophone for the second alto chair, and somehow I got it instead of Eric. In the orchestra Eric was a better clarinet player than I was. He played first and I played second. We'd both studied during high school and L.A. City College with William Green, a saxophonist's saxophonist who also taught clarinet at the Los Angeles Conservatory. He was a black musician and really got my saxophone playing in shape. I also began studying clarinet with him because I knew you had to double in the L.A. City College dance band, as I soon did in the Marshall orchestra.

STRICKLAND: Before finishing your B.A. at UCLA you attended L.A. State College for a year.

YOUNG: I had to make up some credits that weren't given at City. But the music department was hopeless. I moved on to UCLA because I wanted to study composition, I stopped playing jazz because I felt I couldn't expand. In high school Clyde Sorenson took us to hear the L.A. Philharmonic play the Bartók *Concerto for Orchestra*. I just loved it. I also remember Mr. Sorenson playing the Schoenberg Opus 6, which must have been the inspiration for the Webern *Bagatelles*. But I had certainly not heard much modern classical music. Then in college Leonard Stein and others began to introduce me to it seriously—Debussy, Schoenberg, Webern, Stravinsky.

STRICKLAND: You were playing jazz and learning about Serialism. An interesting combination.

YOUNG: By the time I wrote the *Five Small Pieces for String Quartet* in '56 I was heavily into Serialism. It seemed that the expanding horizons of modern contemporary music, such as Webern's incredible imagination, just made me feel that—you know, with jazz, you're in clubs and people are talking and spilling their drinks—I felt that classical music offered much broader horizons. In jazz there was constantly the pressure to conform. Maybe if I'd been playing jazz in New York there would have been greater freedom, just as there was much greater freedom here in composition. But I took up saxophone again in '61 in New York—sopranino.

STRICKLAND: At Berkeley as a graduate student you majored in composition, still composing serially. An interesting thing is that the group—might as well use the word, the Minimalists—

YOUNG: No problem there.

STRICKLAND: You, Terry Riley, Steve Reich, and Philip Glass all were raised in the twelve-tone tradition.

YOUNG: Did Reich and Glass study that too? Riley definitely was writing like early Schoenberg when I met him. One of the things I liked about Webern, in addition to all the internal detail and complexity, which was very interesting to me, was the very static sections of his works.

We can divide my influences into environmental and musical. The environmental we can divide into the natural and the electrical or mechanical. In nature the wind, crickets, cicadas, outdoor natural resonances like canyons or the owls in the woods near Utah Lake. Under electrical we have the sounds of the power plant next to the Conoco station my grandfather ran in Montpelier. I can remember just standing next to the plant a lot of times and listening to it. I just found the transformer sound completely interesting.

STRICKLAND: What was it that fascinated you about the hum?

YOUNG: I later thought it was the harmonics. Also there was a favorite telephone pole I used to like to stand by in Bern. I went back with Dad and Mom and tried to find it, but you can't tell anymore. Things have changed, poles have been moved, wires have been run. Transformers that used to hum don't hum anymore. But the power plant is still there. I stood next to it and listened to it again.

Motors in the machine shop at school—I used to sing and whistle along with them. I don't know if I was aware of drones yet. I probably encountered them at L.A. City College or UCLA hearing Indian classical music.

STRICKLAND: You've also mentioned train-switching signals.

YOUNG: Because in L.A. the second time I lived next door to the L.A. River and across the river was a train yard. All day and night trains would be pulling in . . . *oo-oo, oo* . . . and there were train whistles in Montpelier too.

STRICKLAND: You just had some instinctive attraction to drones.

YOUNG: It seems like it. Musical influences I can divide into American, European, East European if you want to place Bartók in a separate category, and Eastern—not just Indian but *gagaku* and gamelan too. The American line begins with the slow harmonic movement of cowboy songs, then in high school American Indian music, which is very static as opposed to the dynamic, directional, climactic form of classical Indian music. I played drums for an Apache friend in high school who danced at great big church gatherings at amphitheaters and so on. I left out African pygmy music, by the way, the static music where each performer has only one tone and they come in in hocket [*sings*]. I grew interested in pygmy music at L.A. City College and later transcribed an African wedding song. And of course jazz is a strong Afro-American influence.

Then we get to classical music and Debussy. I worked my way back from Debussy to chant, Pérotin and Léonin, the Notre Dame school. I see that line going to Debussy. His music to me—"The Sunken Cathedral," "Sirens" in the *Nocturnes*—all of that to my ear comes out of the organum tradition.

But the static element in my music I see very much as coming out of the land of America. Gertrude Stein said, "The music comes out of the land," and Cage and I often discussed this. In Ruggles, Cowell, Cage, even some of Copland, the static American style features sounds in and for themselves, suspended in time.

Then the Viennese line—Webern and Schoenberg. In Webern's *Bag-*

atelles there were little static sections, like a chime, or a music box, or time ticking off. Then later in the slow movement of the Opus 21 Symphony, there's a very beautiful section many people talk about, where each time A comes or B-flat or B or C or E-flat there's a certain octave placement maintained throughout that movement. It's a very beautiful technique, and he did this in a great deal of his later work.

STRICKLAND: Is this the point of transition between your serial work and the beginning of Minimalism?

YOUNG: I think this is one of the transitions, absolutely.

STRICKLAND: The work that's always cited here is the *Trio for Strings.*

YOUNG: It's dated September '58 and I was copying the score on onion skin when I got to Berkeley, my first semester. No doubt I'd written the piece over the summer. Maybe I'd started it during the spring semester.

STRICKLAND: How did they react to it at Berkeley?

YOUNG: Oh, well, the only people who understood the *Trio for Strings* at the time of its composition were Terry Jennings, Dennis Johnson, and Terry Riley. I would say that probably nobody else understood it at that time, but there were other close friends who participated in it. [*Turns over cassette, speaks into mike*] "Well here we are, it's nine forty-nine and about eighteen seconds p.m. on the same studio clock. We're at Church Street with Edward Strickland." Terry Jennings was an incredible jazz alto saxophonist who followed me at Marshall. You could play any chord on piano and he would just run the notes up and down. Play another chord and he'd run them up and down.

STRICKLAND: It's interesting that he'd be attracted to the *Trio for Strings,* in which virtuosity is negated.

YOUNG: But not his very fine sense of intervals and harmony. He was a child prodigy. When he was two he was selecting his own records from the collection. When he was four he was playing Beethoven four-hands with his mother. When he was twelve he was working on the Cage *Sonatas and Interludes.* When he was thirteen they say he'd written an opera, although I've never seen it. At thirteen he went down to the L.A. Conservatory of Music, where the teachers were rehearsing the Schoenberg Opus 29 suite, and sight-read the E-flat clarinet part on a B-flat clarinet.

I used to play jobs for money occasionally with the Willie Powell Big Blues Band when I was at L.A. City College. They would play dances, mainly for black crowds. And there was Terry sitting next to me. People had been bringing me his cassettes—he knew Lee Konitz's solos inside and out. I might have met him once before at a session I did with Gordo in Toonerville, the Mexican section of the Silver Lake district. At any rate, Terry Jennings was the first composer to follow me in the style that I originated, long sustained tones. He died in 1981. You can read my entry on him in the American *Grove.* He wrote very beautiful music and was very talented.

STRICKLAND: Terry Riley also caught on to this.

YOUNG: Terry and I had become very close friends.

STRICKLAND: His *In C* was the first Minimalist piece to make a public splash.

YOUNG: I think so. And later Glass, and then Reich.

STRICKLAND: It was recorded by Columbia.

YOUNG: Yes. Columbia offered me a contract at the same time they did *In C*. They even gave me an advance and recorded me, but we couldn't come to terms.

STRICKLAND: Why did you turn down Columbia—as you also did Lincoln Center when they wanted you to lower the volume? It must have been attractive.

YOUNG [*standing up and walking around*]: I won't put out a record with *anybody* unless I have complete artistic control, from A to Z. Never. Under any circumstances. For any amount of money. That's it. Period. I won't do it.

STRICKLAND: That explains it.

YOUNG: I didn't go into music to earn money. I went into music because it was my life's work and I'm driven, consumed by the creative passion. It's true that I insist on earning money with my music, but I am only interested in producing great works of art. Life is too short. That's why I stopped playing in dance bands. I could have earned a living in dance bands, sure. I could have also become a doctor or a lawyer or an Indian chief, anything. I went into music because I was drawn like iron filings to a magnet. The reason I'm here on Earth is to make music. I'm not here to make deals with Columbia Records.

STRICKLAND: What had they recorded?

YOUNG: This was in '68, and at that time I was very interested in singing outdoors with natural resonances. John McClure, who was the head of Masterworks, had a house on the beach in Westhampton, which he gave us for a week so that I could practice with the ocean before he sent out the sound truck. And it just so happened that the day the truck came was a very, very choppy, windy day, so the ocean was not pacific [*laughs*]. I guess it couldn't be since it was Atlantic.

The ocean didn't sound good, and the wind was blowing my pitches all over the place. Sound frequencies exist in the medium of air, so, for example, when I'm tuning the piano or tambura I don't allow anybody to move or speak in the room. Because if somebody does it moves the air molecules around and you can't tell whether it's in tune.

I would listen to the waves break and hear which frequencies were set into resonation and then determine the fundamental frequency of the area. Marian would sing the drone pitch from "Map of 49's Dream The Two Systems of Eleven Sets of Galactic Intervals Ornamental Lightyears Tracery" from *The Tortoise, His Dreams and Journeys,* and I would sing the intervallic relationships improvised within a set of given rules over her drone tuned to the resonance of the area.

It was a bad day, so I asked John to keep the sound truck out for another day. John said, "We've already spent thousands of dollars on this project. We can't keep the sound truck out." You know Columbia's just out to make money, they're not out to do anything, and as a side effect they produce a little bit of serious music to satisfy people like you and me who think that, you know, we're getting a little bit of classical music now and then.

We talked about this for months and John said, "The singing's great but the ocean's . . . I want to send David Behrman back out and record the ocean and . . . " I said, "Never. You're *never* going to take ocean and paste it in over my singing. Ever. No way. I'm singing in *real time* with the ocean—this is me and the ocean *together.* I'm listening to what's going on and it's got to be that way. You send *me* and *Marian* and the sound truck and David out again or else we're not going to do it." We talked about releasing other things of mine—the sopranino saxophone, the original version of *The Well-Tuned Piano*—but it wasn't in stereo and he didn't want to spend more money. Their loss.

STRICKLAND: Let's jump back to the sopranino saxophone and the early '60s.

YOUNG: I came to New York in '60 on the Alfred Hertz Memorial Traveling Fellowship. John Cage had already introduced my *Poem for Chairs, Tables, Benches, etc.* in New York, Cologne, Venice when he and David Tudor, Earle Brown, and Christian Wolff were on tour. John and David Tudor really introduced me to New York and European audiences.

STRICKLAND: Was Cage the main influence on the concept art?

YOUNG: Without doubt, John and also David Tudor. But I'd gone to Darmstadt in '59 too, where I heard David play live—a great experience, especially since I couldn't afford records. I used to get the salesman in Berkeley to let me take them into the booth by pretending I was thinking about buying them, but in those days I was so poor I lived on bread and mustard. Once a week I'd treat myself to a garlic sausage sandwich. First semester I was on a Woodrow Wilson, which I got at the insistence of the brilliant musicologist Robert Stevenson. Second semester I had a teaching assistantship.

In Darmstadt I was in Stockhausen's composition seminar, and I considered him at that time the greatest living composer. The concept art grew directly out of *Vision,* which I wrote immediately after Darmstadt—it was eleven really wild sounds to be played on classical instruments but in logarithmic relationship to one another with the performers placed around the room and the lights turned out. It was only thirteen minutes long, but the audience at Berkeley really went wild. They were very childish and giggled and tore up their programs and commented during the performance.

STRICKLAND: They were more disdainful than riotous?

YOUNG: At that performance I would say they were silly. And the music department was very upset.

STRICKLAND: Is this about the same time as *2 sounds?*

YOUNG: That was a shade later. I wanted to apply the idea of sustained tones with independent exits and entrances over a long period of time to other sound sources to which I'd been introduced by John Cage. Through John I learned that perhaps an infinity of sounds could be considered music. With *Poem for Chairs, Tables, Benches, etc.* there was one performance that was about a quarter second long. I just moved a bench. I did other performances in which I had large groups of people moving chairs and tables over cement floors, and the whole building would sort of rock and resonate.

ZAZEELA: You have to see it in performance. You know, it's possible to get some really lovely cello-like sounds if you very carefully drag a chair or a bench and impinge it against either a wood or a cement floor. And you can really control it if you avoid the rhythmic element—if you don't let it bump. And you can change the pressure. It's incredible!

STRICKLAND: Sustained tones again. Wasn't there some sort of riot at a performance of *2 sounds*?

YOUNG: Oh, yeah. You have to understand that when I hit New York I became the darling of the avant-garde. That's how Yoko Ono met me.

STRICKLAND: I was wondering if your conceptual art influenced *Grapefruit*.

YOUNG: She would have never written it without my work. She may say she was headed in that direction and maybe she was. I love her dearly and she may . . . you know, I don't want to take credit for inventing the world! [*Interviewer breaks up.*] Honestly, really, to my knowledge she certainly was not publicly presenting any work like that. *An Anthology*, which I edited in '60–'61, included what I considered the most avant-garde work of the time and most of the people I had presented in the Yoko Ono loft concert series at 112 Chambers Street. That concert series, which began in December 1960, was to my knowledge the first ever to take place in a loft. I called my 1960 pieces the Theater of the Singular Event when they hit the scene, and Henry Flynt later coined the term "concept art." I strongly admit that I didn't come out of a vacuum. I deeply appreciate people like Cage.

I was doing very far-out performances in New York. The one story everybody knows is when I burned the violin during a performance of Richard Maxfield's *Dromenon*, I think it was. It was my conceptual composition—"Build a fire in front of the audience"—*within* his piece. I'd bought a cheap violin and a couple of cans of lighter fluid that afternoon. I think it was with the last ten bucks I had. The audience went wild, but we continued with *Dromenon*. Richard always trusted me implicitly and let me do whatever I wanted, which was the precondition of my performing.

STRICKLAND: Jimi Hendrix picked up on the idea with his guitar six or seven years later.

YOUNG: Did he do that? Nam June Paik started dropping pianos out of airplanes and so on. A number of people took up the idea. I thought it was kind of destructive, and besides, I was always into moving on to other things.

STRICKLAND: How many times could you perform a conceptual piece of that period—for example, "Bring a bale of hay and a bucket of water onto the stage for the piano to eat and drink"?

YOUNG: It has maximum effect the first time somebody becomes aware of it, yet every time I see that cartoon in Bob Palmer's article in *The Atlantic* I get a kick out of it. But I didn't do those pieces from the point of view of humor but of conceptual art. One or two have humor in them—that one certainly did.

STRICKLAND: Did the piano ever eat the hay?

YOUNG [*laughing*]: Not as far as I know. Anyway, you can perform the pieces different ways. I collect cartoons, did you know that? One I like is of a group of cavemen hanging around a fire, and one guy is leaning against the wall with his legs crossed and his head in the air looking very arrogant. Two other guys are by the fire, one whispering to the other, "Okay, so he invented it. But what's he done since?" [*Both laugh.*]

STRICKLAND: Now . . . before we forget . . . our old friend Sopranino Saxophone . . .

YOUNG: Jennings introduced me to Coltrane. "Hey, there's this new guy!" He'd bring me the newest Miles Davis records while I was moving into classical music. No! Billy Higgins first played me *Tenor Madness* with Sonny Rollins and John Coltrane.

STRICKLAND: That's fairly conservative Coltrane, around '56, four years before he brought back the soprano with "My Favorite Things."

YOUNG: You can hear the influence of "Favorite Things" on my sopranino work.

STRICKLAND: Everyone and his brother suddenly picked up soprano saxophones. Why did you jump to sopranino?

YOUNG: It was in E-flat, and I was an alto player basically and knew my tunes best in that key. By then the performers I thought were the best were T. R. Mahalingam, the South Indian flutist, who was probably my major influence on sopranino; Bismillah Khan, the North Indian shenai player; and John Coltrane.

STRICKLAND: Whose sound has often been compared to the shenai.

YOUNG: I found I could approximate the shenai better on sopranino than on soprano. You might hear "Early Tuesday Morning Blues" or "Dorian Blues" on our next Gramavision record, *The Blues According to Pandit Pran Nath, Terry Riley and La Monte Young*. This is a style of blues I invented, where I'd stay on each chord, the I, then the IV back to I, then V–IV–I for as many minutes as I wanted, according to feeling.

STRICKLAND: Sounds like an odd combination of blues and modal jazz.

YOUNG: Of course the blues is a very strong mode of its own.

STRICKLAND: Yes, but I was speaking structurally about the relative infrequency of changes in modal jazz.

YOUNG: Within those changes my idea was to play combinations and permutations of sets of specific tones so fast it would create the impression of a set of sustained tones. I then translated this approach into the clouds of *The Well-Tuned Piano.*

I think that work deep down somewhere has another jazz influence, Bud Powell. You could never imagine from his records what he played like live. Oh, it was just [*gasps*] thrilling! Oh, the depth, the beauty, the space, the serenity, the solemnity of his ballads!

But just as jazz influences classical music, I like to point out that apart from blues much of the rest of jazz derives from Western classical music. There would be no bebop like Sonny Stitt plays without Mozart. There'd be no big extended chords in jazz—ninths, elevenths, thirteenths—without Debussy and Ravel.

STRICKLAND: What influenced the Theatre of Eternal Music?

YOUNG: One of the strongest Mormon influences was their doctrine of Eternal Life, life after death. They have the whole mythology outlined, so that you know what it's like after death, and they have rituals so that you'll be married after death. They baptize the dead so they can be in the highest kingdom in the afterlife. They baptize their ancestors posthumously. There's a connection here too with the Dream House project, of music eternally playing.

STRICKLAND: How would you imagine eternity as a child?

YOUNG: The imagery was provided. You didn't have to imagine anything at first. They came to you with ready-made imagery.

STRICKLAND: So as a child you developed or inherited an obsession with eternity and seemed to have an instinctive attraction to drones. The two seem to tie together in the sense of timelessness in the Dream House concept and *The Well-Tuned Piano,* or even in the early *Trio.*

ZAZEELA: A work like *The Second Dream of the High-Tension Line Stepdown Transformer* in 1962 represents a vast extension of the use of sustained tones in the *Trio for Strings.* It's a piece consisting of four pitches, each assigned to one performer. This, as well as the Dream House concept, is an influence on ambient music as practiced by Brian Eno.

STRICKLAND: The title *The Well-Tuned Piano* is an answer to Bach, and in the work you're turning your back on almost three centuries of the dominance of equal temperament by returning to just intonation. Minimalism has become almost trendy in this decade, yet it's radically retrospective. Glass has a sort of neo-Gregorian chant and hocket in the opening of *Einstein,* Reich goes back to Josquin and organa, and you seem to go all the way back to Pythagoras and a concept of music as both harmonic mathematics and mysticism, though maybe that's not the best word.

YOUNG: It's all right. Nothing wrong with being mystical.

STRICKLAND: I guess my question is whether this was an attempt to get back to roots in an almost cosmological sense. How did you develop this idea? Did you wake up one day and say, "I'm not going to use equal temperament anymore"?

YOUNG: Not only do we have Pythagoras but Indian roots. Take the tambura and the vina, the two oldest Indian instruments along with the ektar, a one-stringed instrument which may be a bit like the tromba marina. And then you have the Chinese system. Harry Partch says that in Chinese music the understanding of harmonic relationships goes back to 2800 B.C. And then we have Helmholtz's writing, Harry Partch, Lou Harrison, Ben Johnston, and so forth. Terry Jennings had told me about the Indian flute players he'd heard at UCLA listening to harmonics. When Tony Conrad was playing in the Theatre of Eternal Music—he was a mathematician and one day pointed out to me how with the integers you could basically understand and manipulate the overtone series. Then I just took off. I just sailed into just intonation and in 1964 I retuned the piano for the first tape version of *The Well-Tuned Piano*.

Then I introduced the group to the aquarium motor I'd been running when we used to keep turtles. I put a contact mike on it, amplified it, and had Tony and John Cale tune the strings to it. Then eventually I was able to buy a sine-wave generator. I tuned that to an interval above the motor drone. Gradually over the years I got more sine-wave generators. Then when I got some funding I started buying better oscillators and tuning up ratios and . . .

STRICKLAND: What effect did you find this had, living here in just intonation?

YOUNG: Oh, it was very harmonious, so beautiful, so right, so natural, so consciousness-expanding, so much a key to the understanding of the old idea, the harmony of the universe.

STRICKLAND: We're back to Pythagoras. Is your effort in a sense a musical search for that primordial music?

YOUNG: In part yes. I have to say that the way I create is to follow some very strong inspirational drive. And I try my very best to never let my mind, my preconceptions, interfere with that. With *Trio for Strings* I didn't exactly just sit back and say, "Well, I'm going to write some long tones here." They were coming, starting to flow out of me. Let the creativity flow and analyze it after the fact. In teaching me singing in the ancient oral tradition, Pandit Pran Nath would say, "Listen. And learn to repeat what I'm doing. If you *think* it, you can get in the way of hearing and learning what it is."

When I sit down to play *The Well-Tuned Piano* I basically pray that I can become the servant of this source of information that comes through me, that I will be able to realize it in the most pure and direct way, and that I will be able to have the energy and strength to perform what comes to me. I follow the dictates of this stream, source of information that comes through me, and I don't get in the way of it. It's true I practice, it's true I've composed this piece, it's true I've set it all up in advance, but when I sit down to play I just let it happen. And the way the first tone comes, the first sequence evolves . . . every note evolves out of every note that came before it.

The tuning determines how I play the piece. If Michael Harrison tunes a certain chord extremely well, you can be sure I will linger on that chord and do new things with that chord.

STRICKLAND: The recording we have is just over five hours. I realize this piece has evolved over more than two decades, but how long was it originally?

YOUNG: In '64 I recorded the forty-five-minute tape, stopping the tape recorder between sections. I was young, it was all I could do to get a taped piece on the program, let alone ask for a piano, retune it . . .

STRICKLAND: And leave it there for a couple of weeks.

YOUNG: All this stuff! I couldn't do that, so I was mainly playing the tape . . . Museum of Modern Art, Metropolitan Museum, later in Germany and France. As I explained in the liner notes, it wasn't until '74 that we could afford to mount a live performance. I became the most expensive composer, even more than Stockhausen. But as Pran Nath said, I took the instrument of Europe and literally, before their eyes, transformed it.

STRICKLAND: It's a far cry from forty-five minutes to five hours on disc.

YOUNG: Yeah, well, you know the last concert I played at Dia on Mother's Day lasted six hours and twenty-four minutes. Week before that I played five hours and forty-one minutes and forty-two seconds. Every concert in the Mercer Street series was longer than five hours.

STRICKLAND: May I ask a simple question? How does it feel to sit at the piano for six hours and twenty-four minutes?

YOUNG: Wonderful. Absolutely fantastic. It's one of the most elating experiences . . .

ZAZEELA: You look like you can't quite believe it, Edward [*laughs*].

STRICKLAND: I can't imagine sitting at the piano for . . .

YOUNG: I give myself up to the piece—you have to understand this! The piece carries me to the highest state of meditation.

STRICKLAND: You've studied with Pandit Pran Nath for how long?

YOUNG: Formally since 1970, after listening to his tapes for three years.

STRICKLAND: I know you keep your composing and your Indian music separate. Yet couldn't we consider *The Well-Tuned Piano* a La Monte Young raga?

YOUNG: Well, yes, very definitely.

STRICKLAND: Is there always—as in raga or jazz—so much room for improvisation? You could play *The Well-Tuned Piano* in three or six hours?

YOUNG: Let's go back. By the time of the world premiere in '74 the Theatre of Eternal Music had already evolved into the Dream House. When I went on tour with Dream House I would take two tons of electronic equipment, six to eight musicians, two projectionists, a technician, and maybe a road manager. Fabio Sargentini had just held a Dream House—

ZAZEELA: At the Contemporanea Festival in Rome in '73. Under the Villa Borghese gardens they had built an underground garage and wanted to publicize it so Italians wouldn't keep on parking on the nearest sidewalk. So they held an arts festival there.

YOUNG: The next year Fabio produced the East-West Festival at his Galleria L'Attico. He had Pandit Pran Nath, T. R. Mahalingam, Terry Riley on organ. When he invited me I intended to do another Dream House, but he said, "No, you just did Dream House. And I can't afford another one." So we had the idea of doing a tape concert of my saxophone playing, *The Well-Tuned Piano,* and so forth. "I can get you a Bösendorfer," he told me. He made some sort of deal—you know how Italians love to make deals—with a music store.

By then I'd *forgotten* the idea of playing the piece live—this was *ten years* after the initial tape. The performance lasted about two and a half hours, and the next night fifteen or twenty minutes longer. They were such an enormous success that Fabio bought the piano and had me sign it and made it available exclusively to me for the rest of my life for performances of *The Well-Tuned Piano,* commissioning two more performances two or three weeks later.

STRICKLAND: Why did it take so long to release a recording of the work?

YOUNG: I have very high standards. Now I take a month in the performance space to practice, because each space has its own acoustical properties. Which cloud is going to resonate in that particular space, and which cloud is not going to be as lively? The piano needs time to adjust to the temperature and humidity of the location. The tuning technician needs time. Okay, he could tune it in a day—but then it shifts and the strings adjust. He *fine*-tunes it over the process of weeks. Another extremely important factor is that I won't perform the piece outside of Marian's light environment, and that itself takes several days to set up. Also I won't play unless the performance is recorded, so that brings up the costs even further. So now it's a very expensive piece. Now we're also video-taping the performances. I'd very much like to release a video tape of *The Well-Tuned Piano.*

STRICKLAND: But the performance on disc was recorded in October '81. I know this is just another temporal question, but why did we have to wait five and a half years?

YOUNG: First of all, there were a number of companies fighting over it. Once we decided on Gramavision, a lot of time was spent in determining side-breaks. It wasn't meant to be chopped up into half-hour—or hour on the CDs—fragments. A lot of time was spent editing extraneous noise, steam pipes, and so on. And meanwhile there was an absolutely enormous amount of work to do with 6 Harrison Street, which we built from the ground up. We thought it was a permanent center for our work; it was even written in the contract. Otherwise I would never have done all that work—run carpets through the hallways, run wires through the entire building from top to bottom. I may be a fanatic, but I'm not crazy [*laughs*].

ZAZEELA: We saw it as a place of pilgrimage, where people would come for ongoing periods of performance, including Pandit Pran Nath, a research and listening center. Records and books would emanate from it.

YOUNG: In order to have *The Well-Tuned Piano* come out the way it is, I really had to negotiate contracts. And it took time to make sure that everybody understood I absolutely would *never* put it out unless they let us do it with full artistic control on every level.

ZAZEELA: We also rejected a lot of test pressings. We were told that without direct-to-disc it wouldn't have been possible to transfer so much material to LPs. Also, the climate might not have been right in '81 or '82. Now a lot of musicians are working in just intonation—Terry Riley's *Harp of New Albion* has been well received. Also the booklet and box took a lot of time. And various record companies were interested in it, but the others finally fell by the wayside. Believe it or not, we never signed the contract with Gramavision until a week ago, a month after *The Well-Tuned Piano* was released.

STRICKLAND: Now you've got so much material it can't be played in its entirety. Are you going to keep on playing it?

YOUNG: Absolutely, just as I fully intended to keep *The Tortoise, His Dreams and Journeys* going, though it's in a lull for the moment. But even at six hours and twenty-four minutes I had to leave out a lot of themes and just touch on others that I used to play for long periods of time.

STRICKLAND: Given the open-ended, improvisational nature of the piece, it could theoretically go on forever.

YOUNG: Michael Harrison likes to point out that in the early days [*chuckles*] when I had fewer themes, a cloud might go on for forty-five minutes. These days that would be a real rarity.

ZAZEELA: The material La Monte is creating in *The Well-Tuned Piano* he will utilize in other aspects of his work. Already in the sound environments he's using chords from *The Well-Tuned Piano* tuned in sine waves. He's starting to work again with a group using sections of *The Well-Tuned Piano*.

STRICKLAND: Is there such a thing as a definitive performance of the work outside eternity?

YOUNG: There are very definitive performances.

STRICKLAND: How do you rate the performance on disc?

YOUNG: The best I'd ever played to that day. That's why I released it.

STRICKLAND: Okay. How do you feel about the term "Minimalism" applied to this?

YOUNG: Well, I think it has its place and defines a subset of the music I've generated. It's valid, but all terms have their limitations. It's difficult to find small units of linguistic expression to convey big ideas. You can see haiku as Minimalism, the Webern *Bagatelles,* certainly the Rothko and Newman works that were probably the early inspirations for the word "Minimalism." I think it should always be pointed out that whereas I spawned the Minimalist movement, my work covers not only Minimalism but a much larger universe of creativity. It's all right to be a Minimalist. I *am* a Minimalist, but that's only one of the things I am.

STRICKLAND: It's taken you a long time to release a commercial recording in your own country, after the 2,800-copy limited *Edition X* in Germany in '69 and the '74 French Shandar disc. Your emulators, followers, whatever you want to call them, have preceded you. How do you feel about that?

YOUNG: Well, I was a little concerned when it first started happening that I wasn't being recognized. When I first hit New York there were articles on me in *Esquire,* later *Vogue, Newsweek,* all the big magazines . . . but Terry first, then Phil in a bigger way, then Steve in a very big way, though not as big as Phil's way, all had bigger successes. I was concerned, but there was nothing I could do about it. I had to keep doing my work. I never felt any of this would change my work.

STRICKLAND: It's really to your credit that when the hoopla began you didn't say, "Okay, let's grind out *The Well-Tuned Piano!* Full speed ahead!" At any rate, you're now finally generally recognized as the "inventor" of musical Minimalism. Do you ever feel like Dr. Frankenstein?

YOUNG: No. I'm very proud of what everybody is doing. Do I like it all? Well, you know [*laughs*], I don't have to take full responsibility for everything these guys do.

ZAZEELA: Jill Johnston, who wrote an important article on La Monte in the *Village Voice* in '64, went to John Cage in recent years and told him La Monte had said he was convinced he'd influenced Riley, Reich, and Glass. Cage said, *"Well, if he wants to be responsible . . . "*

STRICKLAND: Are there compositions of those gentlemen—or John Adams or others—that you particularly like?

YOUNG: I very much like Terry Riley's *In C* and *Poppy Nogood's Phantom Band.* That modal, two-tape-recorder stuff was very beautiful and really the forerunner of Steve Reich's phase work. I thought Steve's *Desert Music* was very well orchestrated, his best work; and I also liked *Music for 18 Musicians,* though I think Steve's work till *The Desert Music* comes out of Terry and Africa.

There was one and only one concert, as far as I know, where works by the four of us were played in the same concert. It was put on by a group working out of New Haven called Pulsa. It was a tape concert. I brought a tape of *The Tortoise, His Dreams and Journeys*—you know, very evolved stuff. Terry brought *Dorian Reeds* or something like that. Steve brought a phase piece. Phil brought a piece that was just a single line.

ZAZEELA: A single meandering violin line, sort of unfocused.

YOUNG: Clearly before he had worked with Steve Reich. But I did like some things he played at a concert in around '69. I don't know the operas, maybe they're very good. I very much like the music of Terry Jennings and Dennis Johnson, who hasn't made his work public, and Jon Hassell.

I like what David Hykes and the Harmonic Choir do with harmonics. John Adams, who owes a great debt to both Terry Riley and Stravinsky, gets much better in his later work, but one piece . . . *Grand Pianola Music* was it? . . . very derivative, becomes bombastic. I think Henry Flynt, Christer Hennix, Michael Harrison, and Alex Dea will all be composing fine things.

STRICKLAND: We've covered a lot of ground, but apart from all the background and analysis I want to tell you that the last time I played *The Well-Tuned Piano*, when it was over . . . what was odd was that I just didn't know *what* to do. I just walked around for about fifteen minutes still feeling that unheard drone which seemed to draw everything into itself, including me.

YOUNG: That's wonderful.

Anthony Davis

Photo by Paula Court, courtesy International Production Associates, Inc.

One of the most inventive and versatile composers of his generation, Anthony Davis was a Pulitzer Prize nominee for the piano concerto *Wayang* (pronounced *why-ang*) *No. 5*, which he premiered with the San Francisco Symphony in December 1984. Characteristically, the concerto used themes from an earlier Davis work, *Wayang No. 4,* and was his first attempt "to explore my rhythmic concepts with an orchestra." The piece is written in four continuous movements—the last, "Keçak," referring to Balinese ritual monkey chant, just as the *wayang* pieces take their name from the Indonesian shadow-puppet theater.

Wayang No. 6, for two pianos, was commissioned by the Laura Dean Dance and Music Foundation, and *Hemispheres*, for ensemble, by the choreographer Molissa Fenley. Other commissions include *Middle Passage*, a programmatic work on the slave ships for pianist Ursula Oppens, which Davis performed himself on his album of the same name; *song was sweeter even so,* for the MIT Experimental Music Studio; and *Still Waters,* for the Brooklyn Philharmonic, recorded as a trio with James Newton and Abdul Wadud (with whom Davis has recently released the album *Trio2*) on *I've Known Rivers*, and again as a septet on his album *Undine.*

Among the most accomplished of Davis's works is the Violin Concerto commissioned by Shem Guibbory with assistance from the Kansas City Symphony and premiered in 1988. The concerto is titled *Maps*, after the obsession of the composer's son Timothy with real and imaginary cartography, and its movements are named after the drawings "Timothy Island," "The Ghost Factory," and "Planet J."

Davis is perhaps best known for his opera *X: The Life and Times of Malcolm X,* with scenario by his brother Christopher and libretto by his cousin Thulani Davis. It was first produced in October 1985 by the American Music Theater Festival in Philadelphia and had its world premiere at New York City Opera eleven months later. The work not only integrates various jazz styles with classical form but also incorporates earlier Davis works, such as *Middle Passage* and *A Walk Through the Shadows*, into the operatic context. Even more important is the composer's refusal to trivialize American history and emotionally castrate music theater in deference to mainstream politics.

In June 1989 the Opera Theater of St. Louis premiered Davis's second opera, *Under the Double Moon* (*Undine* was the working title at the time of this interview), a space-fantasy opera, based on a novel by his wife, Deborah Atherton, who wrote the libretto. Davis's third opera, tentatively entitled *Tania*, with libretto by Richard Nelson, is based on the story of Patty Hearst and the Symbionese Liberation Army. Production by the American Music Theater Festival is planned for 1991.

Davis has also been completing a voice and piano work on commission from Dora Ohrenstein; a violin sonata; and an *a cappella* choral work co-commissioned by Chanticleer, the Dale Warland Singers, and Musica Sacra and funded in part by Meet the Composer/Reader's Digest Commissioning Program.

Davis was born in Paterson, New Jersey, in 1951. From the fifth grade he was trained as a classical pianist, while interesting himself concurrently in jazz. His father, a professor of English, became the first Black Studies chairman at Yale, where Davis did his B.A. in music. As a student he explored Indian, African, and Indonesian music, and after graduation he performed in avant-garde jazz groups led by Leroy Jenkins, Leo Smith, and Anthony Braxton. Davis's own music may prove to be a landmark in the ongoing dissolution of the catergorical boundaries between the ever more tenuously segregated styles of music.

Davis returned to Yale in 1981-82 to teach piano and Afro-American Studies. He was Senior Fellow in the Society of Humanities at Cornell in fall 1987 and Composer in Residence at Columbia in spring 1988.

Specifically, Davis has attempted in virtually all his compositions to provide room for improvisation within the context of formal composition. This is true of his solo piano albums *Lady of the Mirrors* and *Middle Passage,* ensemble works, and even his operas. It is especially striking in his work with his flexible instrumental ensemble Episteme (the Greek word for understanding or knowledge), with whom he recorded three albums for Gramavision—with greatest success in *Undine*—and more recently Group/Davis, which includes a vocalist for arias from the Davis operas. Both groups have toured the United States and England. Since June 1987, with augmented forces, they have performed *X-cerpts,* the concert version of *X*.

I met Davis at his midtown Manhattan apartment building on a hot afternoon early in August 1987. We spoke over a long lunch at a nearby restaurant.

STRICKLAND: You've worked in a lot of forms for someone so young. Let's talk about the operas first. How did you get interested in that genre?

DAVIS: I've had an interest in opera for some time. I studied it in college, particularly Wagner and Strauss, and I'd been developing the skills to write opera—using large-scale forms, working in drama and dance as well as poetry. Finally I felt really ready to write an opera, and when my brother came to me with the idea of doing a musical theater work on Malcolm X, I thought the best way to do it would be as an opera.

STRICKLAND: Why start out your operatic career with a work on Malcolm X?

DAVIS: It seemed like a natural. I was shocked that no one had done it, because I thought that Malcolm X was in a way a hero for my generation. Also I felt that his life had so many different facets to it. It was a real odyssey, a classic story of a man changing and becoming something— the whole idea of the three conversions in his life. I felt it was just a natural for opera. The type of story that Wagner drew from Norse mythology I felt was here, in a sense, as our real mythology, our American mythology.

STRICKLAND: You ran into some real difficulty in financing the opera.

DAVIS: Oh, yes, because of the political aspect. But it turned out to be successful. We managed to sell out the City Opera for every performance. I suspect that if we hadn't run into any problems, then we wouldn't have been doing our job, since Malcolm X was always controversial, and I think that's what drew me to him too. I felt it was important to do something about a figure in American history that people have different feelings about. It made it more interesting to me and made the opera more confrontational too. I felt very comfortable there, but I realized it would be hard to do, hard to put on, and would be a chore since there would be extra hurdles put in our path doing it, but I thought it was worth doing for sure.

STRICKLAND: Other recent operas, like the Glass and Wilson works, have focused on specific historical or contemporary figures. Did it occur to you that you might have obviated some of the financing difficulties by choosing as a subject a black leader who would be more accepted by the mainstream? You could've written an opera named *King,* for example.

DAVIS: That to me wouldn't be interesting. The confrontation interested me, and I felt that I didn't want to stage a pageant, I wanted to write an opera. I think there's a fundamental difference there.

STRICKLAND: And you don't think that King would have—

DAVIS: No, because I was interested in dramatic tension. Where's the dramatic tension? I was interested in all aspects of Malcolm—his prison life and so on—because I felt there was a real story to be told, in a sense not that different from Julius Caesar's or other classical stories. It was a story about the search for self-discovery. I don't think an opera on King would have been as interesting. And I was kind of sick of the idea of safe art, which I think a lot of my contemporaries are doing—art about subjects that won't cause tension.

It's part of the postmodernist esthetic, to produce art that's marketable so you don't alienate the Phillip Morris Corporation and other foundations, etc., who have their own political interests, which are essentially conservative. What we're seeing is this art that basically has very little content in terms of politics or in terms of ideas. You see an art that everyone is free to interpret, that's infinitely marketable in the sense that it doesn't bring along with it the beliefs and the ideology of the creator.

So in those terms I felt somewhat at war with the postmodernist idea of presenting a commercial, marketable art, not really an art that challenges an audience, that confronts an audience with ideas. I didn't want to do an opera just about icons. I wanted to do an opera about someone who is a hero to our society, let's say black Americans—and a lot of white Americans too—but who has provoked a lot of discussion, etc. I think art can be confrontational.

STRICKLAND: Malcolm X was of course a very confrontational figure, but I was wondering—you were only becoming a teenager when he was assassinated. Did he mean as much to you at that time as he came to mean?

DAVIS: No, I don't think so. I really became aware of him when I read his book when I was in college. I think that was true of a lot of people, though a lot of people my age who grew up in New York or other cities knew more, grew up more in touch with that. I grew up in university towns, such as in rural Pennsylvania, which was very distant.

STRICKLAND: Your father was an English professor, first at Penn State?

DAVIS: First at Princeton, then Penn State, the University of Iowa, and Yale.

STRICKLAND: Before we get into your own academic background I'd like to ask you something else on the matter of the operas. In *X* you collaborated with your brother Christopher, who did the scenario, and your cousin Thulani, who wrote what is often a very poetic libretto. Now you're collaborating with your wife, Deborah Atherton, on the new opera, which was originally called *Xola*. Why the change to *Undine*?

DAVIS: The title became *Undine* because there are two twins in it, Xola and Targ, and the opera doesn't really focus on one character above the other. The novel was really about Xola—but this is based on only a few chapters. I think the story we're telling in this opera—it all takes place on the planet Undine, and it really focuses as much on the dilemma of the mother as it does on the children.

STRICKLAND: You've crossed a lot of frontiers in your music, jazz/classical and so forth. You've made another big jump here, from black revolution to outer space. Is there any connection or continuity between the two?

DAVIS: Well, I think there'll be continuity. In the opera there'll be a multiracial cast. The twins are different races. But it's not really about the issue of race, though I think it will be interesting to present a future world in which black music will be part of the landscape.

In terms of politics, in *Undine* I have, for example, an inspector who comes to take away the twins. Anyone who has telepathic powers goes to this special school for reprogramming and training by an inspector who comes from another planet that's part of the empire. This time I felt an interesting idea would be to have the Fascists be the hipsters.

STRICKLAND: Sometimes true today.

DAVIS: Right, exactly. So for me it was really fun to do something different, more about fantasy, and it was a challenge to see if I could write a completely different opera rather than another historical work. Rather than the Wagner model I used in *X*, which I think is very evident, this is more in a Mozartian mode, with an eight-member cast, more intimate scenes.

STRICKLAND: We've already got on the last Gramavision album a selection from the music for *Undine,* which is also the title of the album. How exactly does it fit into the opera?

DAVIS: It doesn't at all. The music has nothing to do with the opera at all! [*Both laugh.*]

STRICKLAND: So much for that one.

DAVIS: I used the title, and because I used it I might try to take something from it somewhere, but the music that I'll be writing will be an extension of my wayang music, based on the Balinese shadow-puppet theater. Originally the piece "Undine" that comprises the second side of the album was written for a dance work I was going to do based on Debbie's stories. But the new opera is a completely different set of challenges— there won't be the chorus, the same kind of dynamic that I had in *X*—it really has to be about character, about intimate scenes, people making choices in their lives—which is also true about *X* but in a different way.

STRICKLAND: I was assuming that the relationship between the piece "Undine" on the album and the opera *Undine* was similar to that between what you've called *X-cerpts* and the opera *X*. That's not the case though.

DAVIS: No.

STRICKLAND: You've recycled, transformed material from a number of your works over the past decade. What was involved with *X-cerpts*, for example?

DAVIS: The idea was to make a concert presentation of parts of the opera, with an ensemble and four singers. And we also use a narration that Thulani's done that ties together the various scenes. In a way it's to broaden the audience for the work. We thought we could get to places we couldn't get with the opera. And it's been very successful.

STRICKLAND: Speaking of broadening your audience, I know you were offered by one foundation the possibility of presenting a small-scale version of *X* in inner-city playgrounds.

DAVIS: Well, it wasn't an official offer. We were discussing it. I thought it was ridiculous, basically because I took as racist the whole idea that somehow black art belongs in the playgrounds. So my response was just that.

STRICKLAND: But there have been jazz performers, for example, who've brought their groups to inner-city playgrounds with—

DAVIS: There's nothing wrong with that. I'm not saying that.

STRICKLAND: —with the idea that a lot of the kids or adults who live in these areas don't have the money to go to a concert or a club or whatever, so they're losing out on their artists. You didn't think that was viable, however, for *X*.

DAVIS: No. Because it's really made for an opera house. *X-cerpts* perhaps . . . *X-cerpts* you could go and do in performance there. But the whole idea was basically a kind of apartheid approach that we have in America, the idea that we look at our art by our white artists as being something that can be presented in a concert hall or an opera house—the whole high art/low art distinction that we make. Somehow what black artists produce is something that can be shown in a playground. Because in a sense they look at what they do for black culture as public service, not as something for art, and that was my only point.

STRICKLAND: When I mentioned to Robert Farris Thompson, a friend of yours from Yale, the Central African pygmies performing in playgrounds across America—however well intentioned the idea was—he objected immediately. He *jumped* on the comment and snapped something like, "They should invite them to Carnegie Hall!"

DAVIS: Right, of course. I think there's this idea about what the role of Third World art is—the kind of cultural segregation that we've tolerated over the years. And *X* did a lot, I think, to break it down, being presented at Lincoln Center at the New York City Opera. I think it was a shock to a lot of people that that could happen. I think that was good.

All these institutions are public—we the people of New York City, New York State, the United States, through our tax dollars support these nonprofit institutions in their presentation of what is known as American culture. And if they don't represent every aspect of that culture, in a real and positive way, then to me they have reneged on their mandate. My point with the man at the foundation was not that I disdain the idea of presenting my work in playgrounds—I've played in playgrounds, I do programs for kids all the time—it was just the idea that that's where *X* belonged, the opera belonged—

STRICKLAND: By definition.

DAVIS: By definition. To me that was a racist remark, that was racially motivated, and had nothing to do with the work and had nothing to do—if he'd bothered to check out what the work was about and what it entailed . . .

STRICKLAND: On the question of stereotyping, I go to a lot of record stores, and I've found that your discs are more often to be found in the jazz section than in the classical—you know, black, Miles Davis, Eddie "Lockjaw" Davis, Anthony Davis. You've managed to cross borders in your music, working in both jazz and classical settings, but I wonder if that's restricted your classical audience in a sense. Do you have the traditional jazz audience or classical audience?

DAVIS: No, I don't think I have either. I think I'm developing my own audience.

STRICKLAND: Tough job.

DAVIS: Sure. I think it's the easy sell to fall into a category—the most commercially successful jazz today is basically a revival of bebop, which, ironically, was a revolutionary new style forty years ago while the so-called Dixieland revival was packing them in. But to me that's not lasting fame. I'm interested in people coming to know my work and looking for *that,* not for "something in the jazz vein" or "the classical vein" or whatever it is—not Minimalist or not . . . I feel very uncomfortable in a sense being seen as part of any cultural group. I always feel at war at all times with any kind of classification.

X was sold out for every performance. It had its own audience and its own momentum. I think people were drawn in by the subject matter as much as the music, but I think they were left with something more. And I would hope that bodes well for the future, because I think that too many record companies and people just blindly accept these categories and blindly—rather than market the individual artist—want to take the easy way out and market you as part of a bunch of artists, part of some group.

Especially with black artists. Look at a *New York Times* article on "black music"—it always seems that in order to be in the article and to justify your existence you have to be part of some kind of social phenomenon. You can't just be an individual artist who has created an individual thing that is unique. That uniqueness, I think, is sometimes a hard thing for the white critics to grasp. Black artists always seem to have to be justified by their tradition. Now I'm very sensitive to and aware of my Afro-American heritage, but I don't feel at all trapped by it.

STRICKLAND: Okay. We think in categories. Magazines and record stores are arranged in categories. Even listeners tend to categorize themselves. For example, someone who might *love* the counterpoint in the Second Brandenburg would never listen—the average guy—to, say, the Hot Seven or—

DAVIS: That's too bad, because the counterpoint in the Hot Seven is pretty good too.

STRICKLAND: They'll listen to Berg but not Cecil Taylor, or Debussy but not Ellington. Or vice versa. Do you think these boundaries are evaporating slowly?

DAVIS: Well, I don't know. I think it's a constant battle. Again, it's how art is sold in America, how you transform something that is a personal expression into an object that can be bought and sold. It almost necessarily works that way, but as an artist I just try to ignore it.

STRICKLAND: I wonder if you do so to your own economic detriment.

DAVIS: I think a lot of my contemporaries are hung up on the idea of our art as being commercial art. It's hard for America to accept black art as art for itself, for its own sake rather than art that is popular or has commercial value. The only way, traditionally, that black art has been tolerated in America is if it sells. But for me, as for my white contemporaries, it's not really whether the ticket sales justify the production or not, because in *no* opera in the United States do the ticket sales pay for the production. The economics don't work that way.

The way I look at it is that my audience is quite large for a classical composer's—and it's a very faithful audience. I mean, I'm not competing with Stevie Wonder! That's not my interest [*both laugh*]. I'm trying to create new work and develop interest in that work, and for a classical composer I think I've gone very far in that direction.

STRICKLAND: You've done this with—like the old Beatles song—a little help from your friends, and also your family. You've collaborated very closely through this decade with your group Episteme as well as your relatives.

DAVIS: Episteme has been very stable for over the last few years. The group presented on the last record has been playing together for about two or three years. We augment the group to fourteen to do *X-cerpts,* with four singers added too. I look to the septet as the core group and add other people for certain compositions. For some time most of the music I've been writing is not for a seven-piece ensemble—more for larger groups, with voice or narration, for orchestras as well . . .

STRICKLAND: I was very impressed by Episteme's most recent album. But I have to tell you that before *Undine* I much preferred your solo piano albums to the trio or ensemble works. It seems to me that in *Undine* you have a much more colorful tonal palette and it seems somehow to congeal more, seems more interesting texturally and structurally. Did you see it as a breakthrough?

DAVIS: I don't know. It's hard for me to say because it's music I've been working on and playing for a number of years, a culmination of my work on those pieces. It represents what my work with the group has been about for the last few years. Remember, the earlier *Hemispheres* record was music commissioned for a dance and required a beat through the whole piece—that was part of the concept. I like that music too, but in *Undine* I'm involved with a very intricate interplay between improvisation and the notated element, which has grown and developed over the years.

STRICKLAND: That's my next question. I know the balance of notation and improvisation has always been a central tenet of your compositional faith. Listening to *Undine*, I was asking myself, "Is there any improvisation here or is it composed throughout? Did he give up on improvisation?"

DAVIS: Oh, no. I'm really interested in the seamless interplay of the two elements. To me this is my most successful record so far if you can't really distinguish between the two. That's always been my goal. I'm very excited about it. I've been trying to do this record for a number of years as we've been exploring these areas. In a way I'm glad it took so long to do it, because we've reached another level of performance, of chamber music. I brought the same idea to *X*, which is ninety-five or ninety-nine percent notated but also incorporates improvisation by particular people in my ensemble. With a smaller group you have, of course, more freedom for improvisation.

STRICKLAND: What about improvisation in your piano solo albums, *Lady of the Mirrors* and *Middle Passage,* which are the albums I've liked most up to now? I think "Beyond Reason" is a wonderful piece, for example.

DAVIS: Oh, there's quite a bit of improvising, though not in "Beyond Reason," which is a passacaglia. Generally, when you start dealing with larger ensembles you need more structure. Otherwise it descends into chaos. I try to apply my ideas as a solo improviser to the group, moving from texture to texture, to integrate the notated element with what the individual improviser might do. It's really imperative that the improviser try to realize the direction and flow that comes from one mind, the composer's. It's interesting you mentioned the solo records, because they've been the model for the ensemble in a sense.

STRICKLAND: Even in the solo records you've recorded twice "Behind the Rock," first on *Song for the Old World,* then on *Middle Passage.* Why did you decide to re-record it?

DAVIS: Sound quality mainly. That piece had a lot to do with overtones, and I couldn't really hear what I was going for on the earlier recording. I also thought the piece worked well within the whole structure of the *Middle Passage* record.

STRICKLAND: The later version runs two minutes longer than the earlier. Were those notated or was the improvisation simply longer?

DAVIS: I added new elements, a rhythmic texture. It's not totally notated, yet it's a realization of elements common to all performances. That's one thing people think is very funny in my music, the idea of realization of a structure that will always be there—as in "Still Waters," for example. Each performance may vary, there may be different choices made in each performance, but the overall structure is the same.

STRICKLAND: The example you mention, "Still Waters," is probably the most shocking and successful transformation of a piece that you've achieved. Some of the earlier works—for example, "Under the Double Moon" was used in different contexts, as was "A Walk Through the Shadows" and various other pieces. In "Still Waters" you took what was originally recorded as a trio and adapted it for the septet, though in fact it sounds like a larger group. How difficult was that to adapt? It doesn't sound like an adaptation, and I think it's considerably more successful than the original trio on *I've Known Rivers*.

DAVIS: The trio was a sketch, a first draft. I actually did an orchestral version that's been performed by the Brooklyn Philharmonic and the New York Philharmonic. The intermediary step was for the ensemble.

STRICKLAND: I want to ask you about this whole matter of transforming existing material. What is the process like for you? Is it entirely different from original composition? Do you find that it's as stimulating intellectually or emotionally?

DAVIS: Oh, definitely. I love the idea of taking something I have and developing it. To me it's about developing a language, building upon the past, my past, my own personal language and means of expression. It's its own world, communicating with yourself and taking things and transforming them like a landscape. I guess maybe I got this from my father, who was a literary critic who would do that with Edwin Arlington Robinson or Walt Whitman revisions.

STRICKLAND: "A Walk Through the Shadows" is a good example of that ongoing process. It was first a piano solo, then an ensemble piece in *Hemispheres,* then you had it in *X*—

DAVIS: Right, "Mecca."

STRICKLAND: Something I wanted to ask you relates to the title, which comes from the Twenty-third Psalm, as does "Still Waters." In the piece "Behind the Rock," which I like very much, you move to the New Testament, referring to Holy Saturday. Is this from a strong religious background?

DAVIS: Definitely not [*laughs*]. With "Still Waters" and "A Walk Through the Shadows" . . . my father's death in 1981 affected me and I wrote them thinking about the Twenty-third Psalm. They really work together, using the same tonal rows.

STRICKLAND: Speaking of tonal rows, "Still Waters" is not strictly tonal music, yet you use a technique of intervallic repetitions which suggest tonality or a facsimile of a tonal center. Where did you develop this technique?

DAVIS: In my piano playing. I think my music is always tonal in that it always suggests the next pitch. Anything that creates the idea of expectation to me is employing the concept of tonality. When you suspend expectation you create tension. When you satisfy the expectation there's resolution. And I think there's that sense in the music. A lot of times I might think of it in a vacuum, like major sevenths piled up. I might put the next note in the bass rather than the register you'd expect—to me that's still a resolution you'd expect from the progression of the intervals. Rather than using a twelve-tone method or working on serial composition, I try to do it more instinctively, intuitively. I also think in terms of counterpoint—in "Still Waters" you have the section with the passacaglia theme in the bassoon and various other interjections and it builds from there. I like the idea of developing both my contrapuntal abilities and the vertical harmony.

STRICKLAND: You mentioned Serialism. You did your B.A. in music at Yale in the early '70s—

DAVIS: And took some courses in world music at Wesleyan.

STRICKLAND: When you studied composition did you still have Serialism drilled into your head as, say, the Minimalist composers did fifteen years earlier?

DAVIS: Not so much. And of course I decided not to continue in the academic environment on the graduate level. As an undergraduate I studied South Indian music, Balinese music, other kinds of music.

STRICKLAND: There wasn't a serial straightjacket by the time you got there.

DAVIS: Not for me. The composition teachers I had at Yale had of course come through the serial thing and really been involved in it and in a sense were trying to liberate themselves. They were more the generation of Steve and Philip Glass and those people. They were exploring chance operations . . . I think the regimen that more upset me was the Cage stuff and the idea of overcoming that. I think every generation has its demons. In a sense I think the Minimalists had the serial period, and we have them! [*Breaks up.*]

STRICKLAND [*laughing*]: They'll be glad to hear that.

DAVIS [*still laughing*]: It's just natural, just nature . . .

STRICKLAND: What influence did studying South Indian and Balinese music at that time have on you?

DAVIS: We had a gamelan at Wesleyan, and I heard it there for the first time. I studied with a South Indian master drummer, a guy named Ragavhan, so I was exposed to a lot of music. A lot of work I did on my own. I had my own group. And I was studying and learning from records about the whole Afro-American tradition. At Yale I was studying Medieval and Renaissance music—motets and so on—and that was an influence later.

The pretonal structure of classical music interested me. Later on I studied Wagner and nineteenth-century music, which influenced me a great deal too. But I kind of avoided serial music for a long time. I wasn't really drawn to that music.

STRICKLAND: In terms of this century, you know what I hear more of in your music? Bartók's work.

DAVIS: Oh, yes. Oh, definitely. I used to play along with Bartók records, especially *Music for Strings, Percussion and Celeste,* treating it the way I would learn a Charlie Parker solo.

STRICKLAND: We're getting more into your eclecticism. Along with training in the Western classical tradition, were you exposed academically to the Afro-American tradition—or jazz, if you don't object to the term, as some do?

DAVIS: I primarily learned it on my own. I took courses in jazz, but I'd heard Art Tatum records when I was seven. My father was a big Art Tatum fan, also Erroll Garner. I didn't hear Parker till a little later, though I'd heard a lot about him. I think my father got a Thelonious Monk record in 1965. Then I started getting my own records—Mingus and . . . I think I first went through Coltrane, a lot of Coltrane stuff.

STRICKLAND: I hear Mingus in the brass in *Hemispheres.* I don't hear Coltrane in your records.

DAVIS: I love Mingus, and Coltrane influenced me a great deal. I went through a whole period in the late '60s and early '70s where he really affected my whole style of playing. When I came to New York in the early '80s people were really trying to get away from that sound—all the piano players had been trying to sound like McCoy Tyner—or Herbie Hancock, one or the other—and all the sax players like Coltrane. I sort of rebelled against that.

But you can hear Coltrane in *X.* When I came to Malcolm's conversion to Islam I naturally thought of Trane. What is American Islamic music? *A Love Supreme* by John Coltrane is the great example. So in the scene where Malcolm finally embraces the Nation of Islam I have the melody [*sings*] "Dark is our history/A flame is our prophecy/Allah's Messenger/Carries His word. . . . "

STRICKLAND: "Psalm" from *A Love Supreme?*

DAVIS: A little bit, yes. Then it goes right into the saxophone solo with [*singing, snapping fingers*] "Allahu-Akbar, Allahu-Akbar. . . ." Boom! Ding! Then it goes right off into swing $^4/_4$, E-flat—even in the key of *Love Supreme.*

STRICKLAND: In some of your notes you've mentioned that you see yourself as part of a tradition of pianist-composers, going back to Scott Joplin, Duke Ellington, Monk, Taylor. Do you think it might be the dawning of the age of—if not our old friend Aquarius, at least the composer-performer?

DAVIS: Oh, I think so. The composer has to get out there. The idea of the composer staying in the academic institution in isolation I don't think can work. I think it's been proven over the years, from people like Ellington to people like Philip Glass. The idea of taking the music on the road, taking it to people, I think is always to the composer's benefit. We've played in places from Stillwater, Oklahoma, to Kansas City to California to England. It's very important to be really involved with the audiences.

STRICKLAND: Yet you've also been involved with academic institutions. You were the first Lustman Fellow at Yale in '81–'82. This semester you'll be at Cornell as a Senior Fellow in the Society for the Humanities. You seem to like to go on the road, unlike a lot of people who just hate it. But how do you find being in residence academically?

DAVIS: I hope it'll be fruitful. I'll be there and in New York on weekends. But actually I shouldn't say I'm a person who likes to be on the road. Maybe two weeks at a time. There are people I call the Road Warriors, who are out there four months a year—I couldn't do that. At Cornell I have big works I have to finish—two symphonic works along with the new opera. Cornell will give me the opportunity to get to work, have some peace with an office and a lot of support while I teach one course. Basically the idea of the Society is to enable me to do my work.

STRICKLAND: Let's jump back to Bali for a moment. You've named a number of your works after the Indonesian shadow-puppet theater *Wayang* Nos. 1 to 6. I think the influence is probably most evident in *Wayang No. 2 (Shadowdance),* which also sounds at times a bit like Reich—you don't want to hear this?

DAVIS: No, that's okay.

STRICKLAND: Along with studying gamelan itself, were you also aware of how that influence had been absorbed by people like Reich?

DAVIS: Sure. I guess I was influenced by *Music for 18 Musicians.* Friends of mine, Shem Guibbory and Elizabeth Arnold, were members of his ensemble. I was attracted to the music, but I felt we could bring something else to it in terms of improvising and our approach to rhythm. I think *Wayang No. 2* is very different from Steve's things. The similarity is the use of vibraphone and marimba, the mallet instruments in sustained rhythm, which I love. In my pieces the rhythmic structure is entirely different—not the displacement of rhythms, as in Steve's work, but the juxtaposition of repeating rhythms, sevens against fives and so on. I'm more interested in the clash of rhythms with contrasting tonalities that clash harmonically much as the rhythms clash. I was interested in expanding the notion of antiphony that you hear in Minimalism, taking it to the next step. Maybe the antiphony could be violent. In the opera I took that to more of an extreme.

STRICKLAND: Confrontational rhythms are a dominant characteristic in your work. Apart from Bali, you seem in general to be fascinated by repetitive patterns. Even the passacaglia form we've mentioned twice is an example.

DAVIS: The first piece I ever wrote, when I was sixteen, had that in it. I find repetition is emotional, and I like the idea of expanding from that core.

STRICKLAND: Another influence we haven't talked about is Ellington. You've said that the bop tradition and later the free jazz approach were in a way retrogressive in their movement away from arrangement in favor of pure improvisation.

DAVIS: Ellington is more a model to me, but a later bebop model might be [Thelonious] Monk or John Lewis. I would never denigrate, I *love* Charlie Parker for the way he expanded the vocabulary, as Louis Armstrong did in the '20s and early '30s. Ellington is a composer who consolidated the gains of the improviser and synthesized those elements into a very sophisticated, nuanced form of personal expression, as opposed to the improviser-innovator—like Parker, Armstrong, or Ornette Coleman, to talk about three *major* figures—who invents a whole new language and tension. And I think there's always been a really healthy tension in the tradition between the people who are trying to forge ahead as improvisers and those who take those ideas and try to synthesize them. Ellington represents the master synthesis of New Orleans music and the whole dance-band thing of the East Coast. It's unfortunate to me that there haven't been enough critical studies of his music to show the kind of dynamic that was going on, instead of anecdotal works.

STRICKLAND: You're trying to consolidate a *very* wide range of influences— Bali, Africa, India, jazz, Minimalism to some extent, Mozart, Wagner, Bartók. Do you see your synthesis moving in a certain direction?

DAVIS: I'm going to continue on the same path. I'm very interested in opera, and I'm going to write more operas over the next few years.

STRICKLAND: Do you have another idea for an opera after *Undine?*

DAVIS: Four or five! I'd like to do something about the Middle Passage story, the mutiny on the slave ship with Cinquez in it. I have sort of a secret plan to do something about Patricia Hearst [*laughs*].

STRICKLAND [*laughing*]: You're not shying away from the controversial.

DAVIS: Oh, no. No no no. I'd like to vegetate ten years and do *The Invisible Man,* a three-part . . . [*laughs*].

STRICKLAND [*laughing*]: You're talking about Ralph Ellison, not H.G. Wells.

DAVIS [*still laughing*]: Ralph Ellison, Ralph Ellison. It could be either, right!

STRICKLAND: Which contemporary composers do you listen to?

DAVIS: I don't listen to music! [*Breaks up.*] I've been in my own world the past few years . . .

STRICKLAND: Are there any contemporaries you particularly admire?

DAVIS: Earl Howard I think is very good. I've worked with him a lot.

STRICKLAND: You recorded his "Particle W" a few years back, and since then you've worked in electronic composition yourself a bit, as in *song was sweeter even so.*

DAVIS: I think he encouraged me along those lines. Then this commission from MIT came along to do a piece for the computer. Of course it used different kinds of technology from what Earl uses.

STRICKLAND: Are there plans to record it?

DAVIS: Not at the moment, but I'd like to do a song-cycle record. Another composer I like is Henze. I've been listening mainly to opera lately, and I wish I could hear more of his work in that area.

STRICKLAND: Which operas have you been listening to?

DAVIS: A lot of Janáček, Berg, Schoenberg—*Moses und Aron*—Birtwistle, Peter Maxwell Davies, Benjamin Britten of course . . . I used to *hate* English composers, had this absurd hatred of English composers. I'm growing out of that [*laughs*].

STRICKLAND: We're mellowing with age. In your notes to *Lady of the Mirrors* you mention that you're primarily interested in music as form.

DAVIS [*laughing/moaning*]: They take something I said back in 1979 and . . .

STRICKLAND: The spectre of the past returns to haunt you.

DAVIS: Well, I'm basically a classicist and look for a kind of perfection in form. People always say to me, "Why don't you loosen up?" No. Can't do it. That's why I like the idea of developing small nuclei of music, everything growing out of one idea. But I think opera has helped me rediscover the more lyrical aspects of music, and that's been a great thing for me. Melody was always the thing that came easiest to me as a composer, even at seventeen. I had to develop my rhythmic and harmonic abilities before rediscovering melody through setting texts.

STRICKLAND: When setting the street language in *X* did you find it tough to reconcile the rhetorical or even grandiloquent tendency of opera with the jive talk and so on?

DAVIS: No, that's just another kind of heightened expression. So's Fats Waller, who was my musical model for the Street scene with the rap and the stride piano. There was no contradiction at all. When I was handed the libretto I knew that section had to be blues-based. In Mozart's operas, if you analyze them, he would think of which dance form he would use for a given aria or section of the opera, and that choice had significance to his audience. My drawing upon blues form was the same concept.

STRICKLAND: Getting back to the libretto by your cousin Thulani, how much did you have to say about its revision?

DAVIS: I felt like an editor. She would write more than I would need, and I would cut it down. We had a very good *modus operandi*. Occasionally if I changed things too much she would say, "Hey, wait a second!"

STRICKLAND [*laughing*]: Do you find working with your relatives—brother, cousin, wife—conducive to familial peace?

DAVIS: No, definitely not. But that's all right. It's brought me back to my own aspirations to be a writer when I was at Yale—I wrote poetry and tried to write a novel. For me to go back into the written word with them was really an exciting thing. I found that the words inspired musical ideas—that's what I love about opera! Sometimes you find it's hard to write *without* words afterwards, without that springboard. "What am I going to do now?"

STRICKLAND: *X* has been called both a "jazz opera" and a "third-stream opera."

DAVIS: I don't like "jazz opera" at all. It doesn't really come from the "third stream" either, since I wasn't trying consciously to synthesize classical music with jazz. I'm just writing music that I think is integrated in a way third-stream music couldn't be. That was kind of an artificial thing in that formally it didn't really confront each music. I think John Lewis was in a way far more successful than the others.

STRICKLAND: What about Miles in *Sketches of Spain,* which could be seen as influenced by Schuller's third-stream concept?

DAVIS: I always thought that was totally corny [*roars with laughter*]. A lot of people, I know, love it. I listen to it and say, "Oh, God." He's a great player, but to me *Filles de Kilimanjaro,* that period, would be more formally interesting. I think third stream was a noble effort, and one of the nice things about it was the recognition it brought to Ornette when he came up, or John Lewis. But I find that most of the time the interaction between the notated music and the improvisation wasn't refined enough, the integration didn't have the same refined esthetic as composition. It was a natural step in the evolution of music, trying to bring together warring, divergent traditions.

I think now we're in a much better position to create a new American music that's not an artificial synthesis but a product of people who have grown up with the improvisational as well as the compositional tradition, not seeing them as separate things. I think that's a new phenomenon—with James Newton, George Lewis, maybe me, other people . . . who when they think of twentieth-century music regard Ellington and Stravinsky, or Charlie Parker and Toru Takemitsu, with equal respect. That's the idea, a new and pure American classical music that couldn't really have existed before in the kind of cultural apartheid system we have.

Meredith Monk

Photo by Bob Shamis.

Meredith Monk is one of the most versatile, innovative, and accomplished artists in the U.S. or any country. For over a quarter century she has pursued her goal of creating "an art that breaks down boundaries between the disciplines [and] seeks to re-establish the unity that exists in music, theater and dance." Joseph Papp has called her "today's Renaissance virtuoso . . . probably our most original composer and her own most moving interpreter."

Monk has danced and sung as well as choreographed and composed. She has scripted and scored as well as directed films both as independent works and as part of her multimedia productions. She has been awarded two Guggenheim fellowships; a Brandeis Creative Arts Award; Obies for the 1971 *Vessel: An Opera Epic,* for the 1976 *Quarry: An Opera,* and for Sustained Achievement; a Bessie for Sustained Achievement; Villager Awards for the 1979 *Recent Ruins: An Opera* (Outstanding Production) and the 1983 *Turtle Dreams: Cabaret* (Outstanding Composition); numerous ASCAP Awards for Musical Composition; and the German Critics Best Record Award for *Dolmen Music* in 1981 and *Our Lady of Late: The Vanguard Tapes* in 1986. Her film *Ellis Island* and her video *Paris,* in collaboration with Ping Chong, have each won several awards and have appeared nationwide on PBS. *Book of Days,* her most recent film, has been presented on European television as well as on PBS. Her seventh album includes music from that film and bears the same name.

Other albums include *Key* on Lovely Music, *Songs from the Hill/Tablet* on Wergo, and *Turtle Dreams* and *Do You Be* on ECM. *Dolmen Music* is for me the most powerful of her recordings, but the other ECM albums represent equally imaginative explorations of extended-vocal technique.

It is as futile to attempt to explain Monk's vocalise as to notate it. Along with a transparently beautiful "straight" soprano, Monk has explored a startling variety of whispers, moans, glottal stops, siren-like and Siren-like wails, overtones, sobs, and whoops. Her songs tend to use words elliptically or not at all, for Monk has sought to reveal—with astonishing success—"emotion we have no words for." In her best work, experimentation with extended-vocal techniques is subordinated to that goal—to alternately devastating and hilarious effect.

Monk is a unique presence among the various notable experimenters with extended vocals, from Stockhausen and Berio to Diamanda Galas and Joan LaBarbara to George Crumb and David Hykes. Her groping for articulation of the unutterable recalls Cathy Berberian's *parole* in Berio's *Visage,* her more manic moments Jan DeGaetani in Crumb's Lorca settings. What distinguishes Monk is, first of all, her deeper rootedness in folk and popular music, and, secondly, the ironic counterbalance provided by her unshakable wit and humor. The personalities of both the music and the woman are of an extraordinary and irresistible vulnerability not cloaked in but crowned with indomitable vivacity.

From her offbeat performances (one introduced by her mother with "Hi! I'm Meredith's mother" and an abrupt departure from the stage) to the black-and-white/color shifts of *Ellis Island* to the multimedia "apocalyptic cabaret" of *Turtle Dreams,* Monk has always played with the artistic context in an attempt to wake up the audience. She avoids offering the treacherous complacency of the artistic "event" as an imperfect alternative to a contemporary reality, "where feelings are being systematically eliminated." She refuses to lull the audience into another phenomenological trap. Gregory Sandow has described her vocal works as "scraps of melody that might be folk tunes of a culture she invented herself." More simply, she is the voice(s) of our dreams.

Monk has worked from a downtown Manhattan base since 1964. In the past few years she has composed a music/movement sequence for David Byrne's film *True Stories;* scored Bob Rosen and Andrea Simon's *The Fayum Portraits;* had a video retrospective and a sound installation, *Silver Lake with Dolmen Music,* at the Whitney Museum of American Art; presented *The Travelogue Series* with Ping Chong at the Joyce Theater; put on *Duet Behavior* (with Bobby McFerrin) and *The Ringing Place* at the Next Wave Festival at the Brooklyn Academy of Music; and given a concert of songs and piano duets with Nurit Tilles at Town Hall. As of this writing she is working on a commission for the Minnesota Opera and another for the Houston Grand Opera, Walker Arts Center, and American Music Theater Festival.

On a bright October afternoon in 1987 I limped up several flights of stairs to Monk's TriBeCa loft. It is typical of her graciousness that after we introduced ourselves, she immediately asked if she could bandage the ankle I had twisted en route.

STRICKLAND: Let's take it from the top. Is it true you sang before you spoke and read music before words?

MONK: Yes. I started reading music and taking theory when I was about four. I still have a little workbook from those days that I found when my parents were selling their house. I had a piano teacher who was also teaching me to read, and I was also studying Dalcroze eurhythmics, which is a system of teaching music through very simple movement, so that you actually see the relationship between rhythm, pitch, and space. For example, children working on a scale might start with their arms down and raise them for the higher pitches and finally at the high *do* their arms would be straight up.

STRICKLAND: Were you studying dance at that age?

MONK: Dalcroze eurhythmics involved movement but not so much dance *per se.* It was more simple physical exercises like skipping in time to music or throwing hoops in certain rhythmic combinations.

STRICKLAND: What about voice?

MONK: Well, I always sang. My mother was a singer, my grandfather was a singer, and my grandmother was a concert pianist. I always had music at home. My mother said that I sang back melodies at a very early age.

STRICKLAND: Where were you raised?

MONK: I was raised in Queens, New York, for a while and—[*interviewer raises arms in triumph over head; Monk waves imaginary pennant*] Ya-ay! And later Connecticut.

STRICKLAND: Did you study music and voice formally through high school?

MONK: Before I went to high school I started studying voice with my mother's teacher. My mother did commercials and musical variety shows on radio and early television. She was also studying classically, so I started working with her teacher when I was thirteen or fourteen. I remember at school singing solos and choral concerts at Christmas and other occasions.

Strickland: Where did you go to high school?

Monk: The George School in Bucks County, Pennsylvania, a Quaker high school. In high school I started studying theory again, and composition. There was a wonderful music teacher that I loved, Mr. Richard Averre.

Strickland: You then went to Sarah Lawrence. Did you major in music?

Monk: I had what they called at that time a Combined Performing Arts program. So by the time I was a senior two-thirds of my program was in performing arts—I had one academic course [*laughs*]. I'd figured out a way to do that. The combined program included music and voice. I had two voice lessons a week, and I was coached the other days. I was taking Opera Workshop, so I was singing in operas and learning about staging. And I was taking vocal chamber music with a composer by the name of Meyer Kupferman. That was a wonderful class. I had a great year. He was doing small chamber pieces with voice and maybe one or two instruments— things like the Stravinsky piece for violin, clarinet, and voice. Twentieth-century repertoire basically. And I was taking theory and harmony, dance technique, composition, history, and also some theater classes.

STRICKLAND: All of which stood you in good stead.

MONK: During that time I started getting a feeling, a glimpse of a musical form that combined all those elements: music, movement, visual images, character, costume, light—that kind of thing.

STRICKLAND: You also sang folk music and in a rock group for a while.

MONK: When I was in junior high and high school, I was singing folk music, but I was also singing—especially in junior high school—things like "Be-Bop-a-Lula." I was entertaining in functions like the prom, singing calypso. But a long while later, after college, I was singing in a band called the Inner Ear. That lasted about two months [*laughs*].

STRICKLAND: I know it wasn't a sustained commitment, but I mention it since you've said that you found a lot of the classical music at the time seemed to be written for people whose bodies extended down as far as the chin. I was wondering if the rock and folk influence was complementary.

MONK: I'm sure it had a lot to do with how I started writing my own music. What happened to me in that band was that I had really been doing my own work for a number of years by that time, and it seemed that singing in a band wasn't something you could just do on the side. It wasn't really my main interest. My main interest was making pieces, writing pieces, so that's why I didn't stay longer than two months.

STRICKLAND: What type of music was in the air? It was a good time for pop culture, but in terms of contemporary classical music . . .

MONK: Really the most vital music at the time was rock'n'roll. The Beatles were coming out with *Rubber Soul, Revolver,* and *Sergeant Pepper.* I don't remember thinking very much about contemporary classical music, though I was still singing *lieder* at that time, and I remember singing in a concert of Satie music around 1966. I sang some of his music-hall pieces with a wonderful composer and teacher by the name of Philip Corner. Actually, now that I think about it, there was a very interesting group of people working in classical music—Philip Corner, Malcolm Goldstein, Morton Feldman, James Tenney, that generation. Nam June Paik, Dick Higgins. And in '66 Dick Higgins had a Satie festival at his house in the West Twenties. We did a concert at night that included some of his music-hall pieces, and then we did *Vexations* starting at midnight and going on till about noon. People stayed overnight, brought sleeping bags, and it was really amazing.

STRICKLAND: It's odd you mention Satie now, because I was wondering if you were conscious of a Satie influence in your multimedia works, *Turtle Dreams,* for example. I don't know if you're familiar with his *Relâche,* but did you know that was the first time film—by René Clair—was incorporated into dance?

MONK: I actually performed in *Relâche* in 1965. I played the Woman. We did it very much like a '20s period piece. It's funny that when I started using film in my own work that direct connection didn't occur to me. But when I was about ten years old I had a piano book of various short modern pieces, and I remember playing Satie, and I had never heard of who this person was. And I remember loving that music, *Gymnopédies.*

STRICKLAND: In *Turtle Dreams* you have a very apocalyptic aura in the film of the turtle as the last survivor in Manhattan. Clair had a camel dragging a hearse around the Eiffel Tower.

MONK: I don't remember the film very well. I think I was offstage. I think it comes in the middle with a piece of music that was played by James Tenney and Philip Corner, four-hands. It's a wonderful piece.

STRICKLAND: Very repetitive too. A measure repeated eight times then another repeated eight times and . . . he calls it *Entr'acte.*

MONK: Yes. I remember the music but not the film so well, since I couldn't see it from backstage.

STRICKLAND: How much mixed media was going on at the time?

MONK: A lot. I came to New York at the end of the happenings period. What they would do visually was very strong, though sometimes the time element was not taken into consideration because they came from the visual arts. In the Judson era, just before I came to New York in the mid-'60s, there was a lot of cross-fertilization of ideas. It wasn't exactly taken for granted, but nobody had to fight for it very much anymore.

STRICKLAND: In a way you fused drama and song in your extended vocals. You also experimented with the performance context right in this loft.

MONK: That's right. I was very interested in trying to do concerts that were not eight-thirty-get-tickets-in-lobby-and-walk-into-theater. I liked the idea of performances that were experiential for the audience, so I would do concerts in the morning here, and the audience would get coffee before the performance. The first piece I did in my loft dealt mainly with darkness and silence. The events would come out of the darkness, and the music would cut through the silence. It was a very quiet piece. Or I did performances that took place in different spaces. The audience would either walk to the next space or I would take them by bus, so that they were experiencing environment in a very direct way. A piece called *Vessel: An Opera Epic* in 1971 started out in my old loft in Great Jones Street, and then I had a bus to take the audience to the Performing Garage. And then on the weekend there was a large outdoor piece that took place in a parking lot near there. History is not very accurate, and a lot of people think these works were big free-for-alls, but each piece was very rigorously put together.

STRICKLAND: The impression's been given that you had your audience racing for the subway to catch up with you.

MONK: It was *never* like that. I think that was in John Schaefer's book, and that was very odd, because it's a wonderful book—and he's a wonderful person, one of the great friends of new music. But if you actually read reviews from that period, you'll see it was all carefully planned, because the logistics were very difficult. In the outdoor piece I was working with almost a hundred people, and we had to work with the police department, etc. The environment gave the pieces their resonance, but it all had to be very rigorous.

STRICKLAND: Now you're making me skeptical of these early legends. Is it true you composed a piece for eighty-five singers with eighty-five jew's-harps?

MONK: At the Guggenheim in 1969. I was using the sound of that space, which has almost a half-second delay. The performers were all up on the ramps, so the audience down below had the sensation of being *inside* the piece, getting waves of sound coming from all different directions. Then there was a section where the audience walked around the Guggenheim encountering events at very close range. Then finally the audience was on the ramps and the performers down below. The piece was called *Juice*. In those days I was very involved with how an audience perceived in terms of distance. The architecture of the building contributed very much to the idea of the piece.

STRICKLAND: You have a wonderful voice—an incredible range and a lovely lyric soprano. You could have been singing mainstream classical vocal music for the last twenty-some years instead of doing what you've been doing.

MONK: Thank you. But I knew that I couldn't go into that because of my temperament. I didn't have the kind of temperament that easily did what was expected of me [*laughs*]. Sometimes I wish that I did! I think it would be a lot easier if you knew what to do next as a soprano—you know, you do this step, then the next step, then the next step. Somehow I had the kind of spirit that needed to find new ways. I wanted to make my own work, explore things, discover things.

STRICKLAND: Maybe I'm making a false distinction, but could you say you had more a creative than an interpretive impulse?

MONK: I think that was more my impulse. I was very interested in seeing how different things worked, how to combine forms. But I loved to sing so much—I mean, it's the thing I love most in life!—and I didn't exactly know what to do about it. I just sat down and started vocalizing every day. And one day at the piano, doing straight vocalizing, I realized the voice could have the same kind of flexibility and range that the body has, and that you could find a language for the voice that had the same individuality as a dancer's movement, that you could find a vocabulary that was actually built on your *own* voice. That really excited me, and right from the exercises I started branching out. That was the beginning.

The irony is that the first piece I did for voice was with an Echoplex, a little echo chamber machine that my cousin, an engineer, had. I would sing, and he would do things with the echo. We would record that and later on in the piece it would be played back and I'd sing against that and he'd record *that* and we'd keep on adding layers during a live performance. Now after working all these years with the voice I've realized that the voice can do almost anything that electronics can do. I've stayed very much away from electronics.

STRICKLAND [*laughing*]: When I play your pieces for friends they assume you're programming your voice. Other artists involved in extended-vocal techniques haven't shied away from electronics, for example, Joan LaBarbara.

MONK: She's a wonderful singer, and I'm sure in the right hands it's a fine thing to be working with. It's just that for me there's still so much to find within the voice itself. It takes all my time and energy to work with that. And the exciting thing is that the group and I can perform almost anywhere, even if we don't have microphones or lights or anything.

STRICKLAND: Other people were working around the same time with modifications of the voice. Crumb, Berio, Stockhausen in *Stimmung* . . .

MONK: Do you know that I've never heard *Stimmung*?

STRICKLAND: I don't believe it! You've got to hear it!

MONK [*laughing*]: I keep on saying I've got to hear it. Every time we do *Dolmen Music* people ask, "Have you ever heard *Stimmung*?" I even know one of the singers in the original record.

STRICKLAND: It's amazing, because I thought you were actually quoting *Stimmung* in one technique you use in *Dolmen Music* [*attempts to sing it*].

MONK: You mean where the two women [*sings*]?

STRICKLAND: Yes! So when you started out with this, did you feel you were working in a vacuum?

MONK: I was pretty much working by myself with my own instrument, trying to find out what it could do and reveal. But as for the sound in *Stimmung*, when you've been working with voice for a while you realize there are universal sounds, even archetypal songs. Working with your own instrument you come upon, say, the glottal break. Now in many cultures that glottal break exists: in yodeling, in Balkan music, African music, North Carolina hollarin'. That's comforting and one aspect of it. The other aspect is that each person's voice is unique. There are certain sounds that I can get that other people have a hard time doing, and some people in my ensemble can do sounds I have a hard time getting. That's the excitement of working with the voice—having the *universal* human experience yet working very much with your *own* instrument. It's a little bit like phylogeny and ontogeny.

STRICKLAND: What type of music were you listening to when you began to explore these techniques?

MONK: I always liked all kinds of good music. Classical music, jazz, rock'n'roll, folk, ethnic music . . . in jazz at the time I was conscious of Albert Ayler, as well as the singers Ella Fitzgerald and Mildred Bailey. Also African folk music, which I *loved*.

STRICKLAND: Many have seen a Minimalist influence in your work. Do you identify with the term?

MONK: I really don't. First of all, I don't like the term. It bothers me. People like Steve Reich, in the early days, were working more with pattern and over-pattern. There was a similar kind of movement in painting, so-called pattern painting. It's hard to be labeled. The repetition in Steve's music seems to set up a long enough time base so that when things shift it becomes an event, whereas in my music I use instrumental repetition more as a carpet for the voice to fly off—to fly from and back onto.

STRICKLAND: Your vocals are anything but minimal. They're extraordinary in their range, rhythm, and variety of timbre. But there *is* a similarity insofar as you tend to use accompanying drones, repetitive broken chords, etc., beneath complex figuration, in your case vocal. Talking about other influences now, obviously a strong one in your work is chant. I don't know your religious background but—

MONK: I'm Jewish.

STRICKLAND: I'm Catholic, so your work hits me very immediately, very viscerally—it's not something I had to acquire a taste for, since I was raised with Gregorian chant. Did you have anything similar?

MONK: Jewish liturgical music is mostly single lines. It's a vocal tradition but usually without harmony, usually unaccompanied in the Orthodox tradition. But I grew up as a Reform Jew and didn't really have a strong religious upbringing. In our temple there was vocal music but often with organ behind it.

STRICKLAND: Maybe that carries through in your work. You often use just a simple organ or synthesizer background . . .

MONK: I wouldn't think of that connection consciously. It's always hard to tell how your ethnic background influences your work, but the only thing I would connect here—not that I think about it in a conscious way when I'm working on it, but just as a temperament thing—is that I usually write modally and in minor keys rather than major diatonic. You could say that minor modal feeling is a very Jewish tendency, but I'd hate to generalize about things like that. And actually [*chuckles*], I don't really know where some of this music comes from in me at all.

STRICKLAND: The chant influence is very strong not only in *Dolmen Music*— you've got the antiphonal element in the "Rain" section, for example— but "Scared Song," which lives up to its title. It's not only scared, it's *scary*. That's an odd piece insofar as it conveys an extreme emotional state yet has a very liturgical feel to it. I saw it as a kind of liturgical psychodrama.

MONK: I'm so *curious* about that—it seems so secular to me, but somebody else said that to me. I think it was more like dealing with the *human* tendency in this society to be afraid of being afraid.

STRICKLAND: Yes, but with that organlike synthesizer . . . it sounds to me like someone trying to confess—here we go again, Catholics . . .

MONK: I love it! [*Laughs.*] Not beating their chests but confessing.

STRICKLAND: It's very churchlike to me. Someone confessing his or her soul in an empty church.

MONK: I just hope this music would evoke people's *own* images. That's why in the past few years I've sometimes thought I prefer just doing the music concerts to the big theater pieces. I really love that subjective element.

STRICKLAND: I can get very subjective here—though I almost feel I'm going into analysis! When I first heard "View 1" I just about fell over because the childish, mocking voice in the piece sounded like a voice that I some- times heard as a child trying to sleep and have remembered periodically since then.

MONK: Wow! In my own conception of the piece it was as if I were in a spaceship looking down at the earth, seeing someone in one place going [*sings in childish voice*] and someone in another place going [*sings in lyrical voice*]. It was as if you could see the whole world at once—that's how I was getting the images: some were like children and some were like old people. I was thinking of calling the piece "Aerial View."

STRICKLAND: Another influence is organum, for example in "Astronaut Anthem."

MONK: I've always loved Medieval music. I love music through Bach and then go to the twentieth century. One of my absolute favorites is Perotinus.

STRICKLAND: In *Our Lady of Late* you're adapting organum technique with a kind of *upper*-voice drone in the water glass.

MONK: Yes. It starts in E-flat and goes up to G.

STRICKLAND: What about your use of overtones? Were you familiar with Tibetan and Mongolian overtone chanting?

MONK: In the late '60s someone gave me a jew's-harp, and that's given me a lot of ideas. Now I sometimes sing through the jew's-harp, pulling my breath in at the same time, which creates a partial between the jew's-harp and the voice. I translated the jew's-harp to voice, and that's how I began with overtones. I heard about Mongolian singing in 1976, when someone came backstage after my *Songs from the Hill* concert at Town Hall and said, "You should really get an album"—and so I heard those techniques.

But I'd never heard them live till last week, when the Mongolians came to New York for the first time. The man doing the *hoomi* singing was *unbelievable*—it was so inspiring! Bob Een in my ensemble was also there and told me he went right home and started practicing! I was doing overtones in my mouth and cheek area. Now we're all working on very high fundamentals and overtones that go *way* over, right through the forehead. I don't know why it's taken me so long to get to that—I had to be inspired by this wonderful *hoomi* singer. He's the best I've ever, ever heard.

STRICKLAND: You've mentioned your ensemble. How did that begin?

MONK: I'd been working on *Quarry,* a big opera piece of mine, and I needed a chorus of twenty-seven who could sing and move well. From the twenty-seven I chose three of the women singers who were outstanding: Andrea Goodman, Susan Kampe, and Monica Solem. That's when I started working with extending *Tablet* from a solo version with piano to a piece utilizing four voices in as complex a way as my own voice as a soloist.

STRICKLAND: *Tablet* was on the same album as *Songs from the Hill,* written in New Mexico in '75 and '76. What took you there?

MONK: I was visiting my sister. That's one of my favorite landscapes—in Placitas, New Mexico, between Albuquerque and Santa Fe—in the hills.

STRICKLAND: There's an American Indian influence in a couple of those pieces, especially "Mesa." I felt that carried through in *Tablet,* written the next year. Did you feel a continuity between the pieces?

MONK: I never think of *Tablet* as the same landscape. I always think of *Tablet* as ancient Greece—winds and goddesses, Furies, that kind of mythic quality. Whereas *Songs from the Hill* really came from my sitting out in the hot sun every day, deciding that my discipline for the summer was to work on solo voice pieces, which I hadn't done for a long time. I had mostly worked with voice and keyboard. Basically I was writing a song a day—not the whole song, but the idea.

STRICKLAND: Do you notate all your songs?

MONK: At that time I didn't because some of those songs are hard to notate. I would take a little tape recorder with me.

STRICKLAND: If it weren't for recording technology it would be hard to pre-
serve your work at all. You could look at a score and have *no* idea of
what's really going on.

MONK: It's very difficult.

STRICKLAND: What about your singers? Do they come from a homogeneous
classical background?

MONK: I met Andrea Goodman when I was doing a series of workshops at
Oberlin in 1974. She was not a conservatory student but studying music
in the liberal arts school. She had the room across the hall in the dormi-
tory and knocked on the door and said, "Hello, my name is Andrea."
Somehow we started going through a book of hymns from the Ap-
palachians called *Sacred Harp.* Then an organ player down the hall heard
us singing, and he came in and we started reading through these
hymns—all beautiful modal hymns. It was my first afternoon in Oberlin
and I thought, boy, this is really going to be *fun!*

In late 1975 I was in Morocco and thinking about changing *Tablet* to
a group piece. I'd been working with recorder and called a friend in New
York asking if Andrea, who'd graduated just before Christmas, knew how
to play one. "Well, yes, she *does!*" "Tell her I'll be back in a week and
we're doing this concert for Merce Cunningham and can she be in it?"
That was a primitive version of *Tablet,* working with two other voices.
Andrea had been studying piano and when she got to New York started
studying classical voice—she's always had such a naturally beautiful
voice, but in recent years it's grown, it's gotten more body, a wonderful,
wonderful dark sound and a beautiful light sound. And like everyone in
my ensemble, she's very quick with new ideas.

The person working with me the second longest, Robert Een, came
from a musical family and had studied cello with the Suzuki method and
also voice—an excellent, excellent musician. Then came Naaz Hosseini,
who I started working with in 1980. She had been a violin major at
Wesleyan and told me how in the middle of her senior exam one of the
strings broke and she sang the rest of the exam [*both laugh*]. She also had
classical voice training. Those are the three who've been with me the
longest. They all have a fantastic technical base, but what I love about
their singing is that when you hear them it's not that you go, "Opera
singer!" It's *Andrea's* voice or *Bob's* voice or *Naaz's* voice. I don't want
them to sound like an imitation of my voice.

STRICKLAND: Let's talk about a couple of the other extended extended-vocal—have to do something about this stutter—pieces, the longer works.
What inspired *Dolmen Music?*

MONK: When we were performing in Brittany in 1977 someone said you have
to see the Fairy Rocks, *Les Roches aux Fées.* Monica Solem, Tony Giovan-
netti, and I were driving down little back roads past farms and suddenly
there were these huge rocks in the shape of a table. It was a very *strong*
place. You could feel the energy of those rocks. It had a very mysterious

quality because it was hard to figure out exactly how they had been placed that way—a huge horizontal slab over four uprights, so you're talking about tons of weight. And the uprights were about ten feet high.

Somehow Monica and I started singing. We just felt like singing. When I went back to America I started writing some phrases and realized the connection to these rocks, so I called it *Dolmen Music*. I was thinking about Druids, the ancient people who had constructed this table. I was trying to make music which had a kind of primordial quality but also a futuristic quality at the same time. Because when you were there you felt that it could have been creatures from another planet that had constructed that table. That's what it felt like.

STRICKLAND: A lot of your music presents emotional extremes, and I wonder if that accounts for your reliance on temporal extremes, primordial or imagined future landscapes to . . .

MONK: To get deeper into the present. I think we're living in a society that is not really that interested in emotion [*both laugh*]. So in a way you have to go outside it a bit to have the human memory of feeling. And I think the voice is a wonderful instrument for dealing with emotion that we don't have words for. It can get between the emotions that we can catalog. It has so much nuance and yet a very direct connection to the center of each person.

STRICKLAND: That's true even of a less dramatic piece like "I Don't Know."

MONK [*laughing*]: "Mid-life Crisis," you mean?

STRICKLAND [*laughing*]: Don't look at me when you say that!

MONK: I was thinking about calling that piece "The Ambivalence Waltz."

STRICKLAND: Why do you think emotion is at such a premium in our society?

MONK: Things have sped up so much, sometimes it's hard for people to be open enough to feel any pain. If you're intelligently—not ignorantly or stupidly—open and things hit you, you can move through them. Instead, people are so afraid of feeling and so closed-in that if something does hurt them they hold on to it so hard that it's actually more painful. I don't think these defense mechanisms are very accurate in terms of what reality is. They have to do with fixating—fixating the way you think about yourself and other people.

STRICKLAND: My single favorite of all your pieces is directly related to this— "Biography."

MONK: It's certainly one of my favorites too.

STRICKLAND: In terms of how you perceive our society, it's almost as if that piece functions on the level of primal therapy. I'm not trying to reduce art to therapeutic or cathartic utility, but do you see a connection?

MONK: "Biography" is from the second act of *Education of the Girlchild*. It was one woman's life, from death through old age to youth, kind of a revery piece. I don't think of it as therapy so much as I think that music has the power to be a healing force in offering its energy and expansiveness to people.

STRICKLAND: "Biography" is *so* moving . . . *[laughs]* but the funny thing is that on *Dolmen Music* it comes right after your *craziest* piece ever, "The Tale." When I first heard it I couldn't stop laughing *[starts laughing, tries to stop]* all through the piece—and then "Biography" came on and I felt as if I'd completely lost my balance.

MONK: That was Manfred Eicher's idea. He's very good at ordering pieces. I had never sung it that way in a concert situation before. I sang "Biography" before "The Tale," but now I do it the other way.

STRICKLAND *[laughing again]*: Just thinking about your voice in that piece, the kind of pinched . . .

MONK: It's sort of an old woman doing an inventory, talking to Death and going *[adopts creaky, high-pitched voice]*, "Well, you can't take me away 'cause I still have my this, I have my that . . ."

STRICKLAND: "My money, my telephone . . . my allergies, my philosophy . . ."

MONK: And then Death's going *[shakes head, snaps fingers, drops voice]*, "Too bad!" I've always loved comedy and I think it would be a shame to do a work without it. I would hope every concert we do would have at least one funny piece in it. When audiences come to our concerts, it often takes them a while to figure out that they can have a good time. But then they do. Art doesn't always have to be totally serious.

STRICKLAND: Getting back to "Biography," what do you draw on for a piece like that? I'm not trying to psychoanalyze you—"Have you had a rotten life?" and so on—but it's so pulverizing.

MONK: I think I worked on vocal qualities first. I thought of the opening section as a dirge, then towards the end the young girl's voice comes in *[sings]*. I saw it as a dialogue of her selves. So I don't start with emotion as my base. I really start with voice as my base and if it moves towards an emotion naturally, then that's what it is.

STRICKLAND: How vulnerable do you feel when you're performing? Because you certainly destroy your audience's defenses.

MONK: When I'm singing "Biography" I'm just listening very hard. If you as a performer are going through this catharsis I don't think the audience is. When I'm performing well it's a combination of pinpointed awareness, absolutely focused, like a needle—focused on the moment, being there completely—and complete openness, so that it feels very expansive.

STRICKLAND: You're conveying emotions either without words altogether or using words fragmentarily. One example is the waltz in *Turtle Dreams*, where you have the most prosaic statement in the world transformed into something terrifying.

MONK: "I went to the store." I was starting with a very ordinary reality that goes farther and farther and gets more and more extreme as the song goes on.

STRICKLAND: It reminds me of Peter Handke's saying we must experience a nausea at words similar to Sartre's protagonist's nausea at things. What led you to begin *Turtle Dreams*?

Monk: I started realizing that I was living right here in this time in New York and that I was hearing a lot of dissonance and sounds grating against each other and that I was being bombarded by sensation. It seemed interesting to me to work on a piece that acknowledged that. Even in *Girlchild* you're in an ahistorical world, and *Dolmen Music* is out of time. In *Turtle Dreams* I was looking at this culture and trying to have some reflection of it in the music. That's why it has an edgy quality— very much like New York City.

Strickland: In the "Waltz" section you have a lot happening at once. People moving robotically with excruciating cries, on the screen the turtle moving through New York, and meanwhile a woman in a hoopskirt waltzing with an imaginary gallant. Was she meant to suggest the nineteenth century?

Monk: It was just a collision of worlds, as if you sliced through the world of four city people—I always think of them as contemporary types, definitely urban, that have a lot of surface to them, yet the emotions come from inside. The waltzer is as if another galaxy suddenly cut through that world—I always think of her as coming from the Moon and cutting through this reality. I deal with that a lot in my pieces, different realities presented simultaneously so that you get the feeling of a multidimensional spectrum of things.

Strickland: If we compare your work to a lot of contemporary compositions, it seems much more committed emotionally and at times politically—the Fascism in *Quarry,* the apocalypse in *Turtle Dreams* or *The Games*—than the norm.

Monk: In those last two works I thought it was important to state the problem. After I finished them it seemed more appropriate to continue working but in a sense offer an alternative in behavioral terms—to show in a concert how people could work together creating an environment where tenderness, sensitivity, humor, emotional commitment, a certain kind of bravery and rigor can exist—that's already an alternative. Everybody pretty much knows what the problem is at this point. I still feel responsible.

Strickland: There are all sorts of concerts you or I might go to where the music may be technically or formally interesting or experimental but leaves you feeling "That was good, let's have a beer." Know what I mean?

Monk [*laughing*]: Yes, I do.

Strickland: So one statement of yours that impressed me was "I'm still interested in reaching people's hearts." There aren't a lot of composers today who'd use those words.

Monk: It sounds too romantic or something, right?

Strickland: No, it sounds great!

Monk: But I mean to a lot of people. That's been going on for at least the last fifteen years. That's why reaching feelings is so important—it's the only thing we *can* do now. Everything else is covered by the mass media.

You can sit in front of your TV all day and not have any kind of feeling at all. Live performance seems a very important thing to try to continue doing. A direct connection with the audience on the level of heart is something music can do and a lot of other media can't do so easily.

STRICKLAND: I think the reason a lot of artists might *not* say, "I'm interested in reaching people's hearts" is that the currency in mass culture is pre-packaged emotions. People in the coffee shop . . . most of them are stars in their own sitcom or soap opera. They've learned how to act with one another by watching *Cosby* or whatever. Friendship is emulating the same TV show.

MONK: But do you go along with that or just do something else?

STRICKLAND: I think a third alternative taken by artists today is simply an abnegation of emotional content.

MONK: But that's what I would call going along with it.

STRICKLAND: "We can't feel anything. We're all so corrupted by false images that even if we think we're feeling something we're not."

MONK: I don't believe that's true.

STRICKLAND: I don't either, but I *do* believe we're facing a *massive* proliferation of freeze-dried emotions.

MONK: I totally agree with you. Something like "I Don't Know"—it's a very elusive song. I worked on it and worked on it and worked on it, and it can go in a lot of different directions. In some performances I've sung it with more irony than on *Do You Be*. For some reason that day it just went a little more towards tragedy. It has that funny edge of both self-irony and being in quicksand a little bit. It just eludes me all the time. That's the kind of emotion that's very delicate and complex, and that's something you don't usually have on TV.

STRICKLAND: Just the uncertainty of the title and performance is something I think people are very loath to admit. I remember when I was a student, a friend of mine who'd dropped out of college asked me, "How many times did you ever hear a professor say 'I don't know'?" Now I'm a professor, so I know the answer—*far* too few. Or on a personal level: "Do you love me?" "I don't know." [*Both laugh.*] What happens is "Of *course* I love you." "Me too." So your piece is poignant because it points to something that's fundamental yet constantly evaded. But what about the ambiguity of the title of the album. Is *Do You Be* an ungrammatical question?

MONK: Uh huh. I tried to translate that into Italian on my last tour. They'd translated the song "Do You Be" into *Si!*—exclamation point and all. And that did *not* seem to be it.

STRICKLAND: The song was first recorded on *Key* back in '70.

MONK: I'd like to hear that old recording again.

STRICKLAND: I think it stands out from that album. But the new version has better sound, and your voice is more incisive. It's the only piece I know of that you've recorded twice.

MONK: It just seemed right to put it on this record. Working on *Do You Be* was very complicated. Manfred was more interested in an intimate album this time, and I was more interested in recording *The Games* as a whole. We talked and talked and talked about it and started working with some of the songs from *The Games*. "Memory Song" was the first we recorded. It became clear that the first side would be the piano and solo voice pieces, mainly from *Acts from Under and Above*, and that the second side would be mostly choral work from *The Games,* going from an intimate to an epic quality. It had a nice progression.

I was doing a duet concert with Nurit Tilles with some of the songs from *Acts*. At the end of that set in Munich we performed "Do You Be." Manfred was in the audience, and he said, "That sounds like it would be really nice for this album." I felt it was so many years since I'd recorded it, and it's very different with piano instead of organ. It felt right as the end of the first side of the album, and I did like the idea of recording it as a very young person and an older person. I also liked recording digitally for the first time. The dynamic range is unbelievable! I remember when we were working on *Songs from the Hill*, the engineer was going *crazy*! It would go from a whisper to full voice in one song and he had limiters on it, he had compressors . . . it was just ridiculous.

STRICKLAND: On the question of keyboards, one thing that interested me in *Do You Be* was a new use of organ against acoustic piano, drone against riff, in "Scared Song."

MONK: I'd never tried that combination before. I'm getting to love playing the piano so much now that I've had to get my chops up to play duets with Nurit. I'm becoming so interested in writing for piano again. I used to like organ or synthesizer better because you could have a drone feeling and connect tones. But I love the articulate quality and richness of sound of the piano.

STRICKLAND: The central section of "Scared Song" is very virtuosic. In my notes I've got this jotted down: "How avoid hyperventilation?" Was circular breathing involved?

MONK: Not there. It just doesn't bother me at all. I guess I'm used to it. It's just a matter of getting enough air in.

STRICKLAND: That simple. Let me ask you about the two "Panda Chants" on *Do You Be*? Why a panda?

MONK: "Pahn-da pahn-da" had a really nice sound to it, and the people in Germany said that the sound was actually an animal.

STRICKLAND: You weren't originally thinking of the bear?

MONK: No. Not panda but "pahn-da," just the sound. But it turned out that panda's pronounced "pahn-da" in German. If it had the meaning of a bear, it was fine with me. A lot of people think it's some kind of song for keeping the species alive.

STRICKLAND: "Save the Panda." Well, it's a good idea . . .

MONK: "Save the Panda"—okay! *The Games* was a piece about the end of the world and the survivors living on either another planet or a spaceship remembering Earth's culture. The older people, that is—the younger people don't remember it. They don't remember what a cup of coffee is or a football game or a chair or an aspirin. Every year the society has games to reenact Earth's culture, but everything gets a little askew. In that song I was taking the idea of a chant, the way people would chant at a football game, but putting a word in there that doesn't usually belong. But that's the way the society is in *The Games*. A lot of other things are a little off like that.

STRICKLAND: "Memory Song" from *The Games* is itself one of your most lyrical pieces, with beautiful use of Naaz Hosseini's violin and that bell-like synthesizer. The feeling of nostalgia and absurdity at once.

MONK: *"Foott-ball . . . Foott-ball . . . "*

STRICKLAND: In *Turtle Dreams* the most commonplace phrase becomes terrifying. Here the commonplace becomes vaguely disorienting. Towards the end the tone changes with the overlapping voices from nostalgia to haunting.

MONK: I like the fact that it sounds like more than three voices, as in *Dolmen Music*, when it sounds like a lot more than six voices singing.

STRICKLAND: It sounds like a whole monastery. One other piece we haven't mentioned is "Wheel," which is a beautiful ending to *Do You Be*, especially with the bagpipes.

MONK: Thank you. I've been wanting to work with bagpipes for years and it just happened that a wonderful player named Wayne Hankin—he plays all Medieval and Renaissance reed instruments: rauschpfeife, shawm . . .

STRICKLAND: You should use them! The double reeds and your overtones . . .

MONK: I'm working with him now on a new ensemble piece called *The Ringing Place*, Nurit playing hammer dulcimer and Wayne playing didgeridoo and maybe some of his other double-reed instruments. In *The Games* what inspired me to work with the bagpipes was that I love the idea of juxtaposing something as futuristic and spaceship-y as the synthesizer with the bagpipes, which are so fundamental, universal, and ancient.

STRICKLAND: "Wheel" has the otherworldly quality of Celtic music. "Double Fiesta" is spaced-out too, but in a different way.

MONK [*laughing*]: I always think of "Double Fiesta" as someone going to a party and getting more and more out of it. It starts out very light and gets darker as it goes along.

STRICKLAND: Here's the question I've been asking everyone. Which composers today do you particularly admire?

MONK [*after long pause*]: That's a hard one. Think about that one for fifteen minutes. I don't get a chance that much to hear other people's work, and when I have time off I go to the movies, almost any kind of film—I love old films. I like music across the board—the Mongolian singer I mentioned, the Brazilian percussionist Nana Vasconselos, who's a good friend of mine. I love to hear good jazz singers or players. I have a lot of records, but when I'm working on a piece I have a very hard time listening to music. Sometimes I just like to have silence.

I love a lot of Steve Reich's work. And of course I love La Monte Young's. A performance of *The Tortoise, His Dreams and Journeys* in 1966 I'll never, never forget. I remember going into a three-story building and hearing one note, which you could hear all the way down in the street. You could stay on the floor where La Monte, Marian, and John Cale were playing and singing or you could go to other floors, but you had to sign a paper that said if anything happened to your mind after you left, they weren't responsible for it! Which put kind of an edge on the situation [*both laugh*]. I remember going in there having a very bad headache, staying about three or four hours, and leaving feeling wonderful. I love La Monte's music, and the visual aspects that Marian does are so beautiful. I remember when Charlemagne Palestine was playing—he strummed the Bösendorfer—I also loved his music.

STRICKLAND: What are your plans?

MONK: That's easier than the last question. At the Next Wave Festival from November 20th, my birthday, to the 22nd we're doing *The Ringing Place*, which we'll present as a work in progress if I haven't finished it. I'm also working on music for the score of a film that a friend of mine is doing called *The Fayum Portraits*, pieces for solo voice with Nurit playing the hammer dulcimer and also some really interesting things for voice singing through a double ocarina and getting a three-note chord and a lot of partials. In March I'm going to France to shoot a film of my own that I've been working on for about five years called *Book of Days*. I've written the music for it already and am working on the film aspect of it.

STRICKLAND: What does it treat?

MONK: It deals with the Middle Ages and contemporary life, going back and forth between the two times. It's basically a film about time. It's a little hard to explain, but I'll show you the story boards, drawings of the film from beginning to end, so you can *see* what it's like. I'm also starting to work on an opera for the Houston Grand Opera in 1990. I mean, I love these things planned so far in advance! You just wonder. There was a time years ago when I hated knowing what I was going to do in advance. I was kind of a hot-rodder and I could never plan and always felt very constricted if I had to. Then Merce Cunningham said to me, "Just plan. It's never going to end up being like that anyway" [*laughs*]. Anyway, the working title of the opera is *Three Ghost Stories*.

STRICKLAND: Are they traditional or are you inventing the ghosts?

MONK: I'm inventing them [*laughs*]. Inventing ghosts . . .

Terry Riley

In 1989 the Silver Anniversary of Terry Riley's *In C* was celebrated with performances in, among other places, the People's Republic of China, and one of the Chinese performances was released later that year by Celestial Harmonies. The initial release of the piece by Columbia Masterworks in 1968 marked the beginning of public acceptance of Minimalism a decade after La Monte Young had originated the style with the long-tone experiments of works like his *Trio for Strings*, in which Riley performed as a fellow graduate student at the University of California in Berkeley. Although Riley has always acknowledged Young's influence with great respect and affection, he has left an even greater mark on the subsequent development of the tonal and repetitive style adopted successively by Steve Reich, Philip Glass, and numerous others.

The increasing expansiveness of the compositional explorations of those composers as well as Riley in recent years has rendered the adjective Minimalist ever less adequate if ever more popular. His recent works, such as *The Harp of New Albion* (1984), display a still motive-centered but more relaxed lyricism, while the string quartets on which Riley has worked for the past decade—see the double albums *Cadenza on the Night Plain* and *Salome Dances for Peace*—at times recall Bartók and late Shostakovich. They and the quintet *Crow's Rosary* (1988), commissioned by the Kronos Quartet and Lincoln Center, mark both a development of and a departure from the modular and layered structure of Riley's work with instruments and tape in the '60s and his solo keyboard compositions/improvisations of the '70s. His activities have been remarkably varied: saloon piano player and professor of Indian music, off-Freeway film scorer *(Les Yeux fermés, La Secret de la vie, Les Metamorphoses du regard, Crossroads, No Man's Land)* and part-time farmer.

Riley was born in Colfax, California, in 1935. After graduating from San Francisco State, he moved across the Bay for graduate studies in composition, still writing in the then accepted, if not expected, serial style. Young led him to investigate long tones but, unlike his friend, Riley soon applied them to a tonal context in his 1960 *String Quartet* and 1961 *String Trio*.

In 1961 Riley completed his M.A. and moved to Europe, where he became involved in a strange variety of musical endeavors, the most important of which proved to be experimentation with tape in the ORTF studios of French national radio and television. Through manipulation of tape he created the techno-canons of *Music for the Gift* from Chet Baker's performance of "So What."

Finding himself unemployed in Europe in late 1963, Riley returned to the Bay Area with his wife and daughter (now a Bay Area physician). He continued his tape experiments at the San Francisco Tape Music Center and his jazz piano playing in North Beach. At this time he applied the modular repetition of his tape pieces to live performance in *In C*, while advancing tape-feedback technique further in *Dorian Reeds* (1965).

In 1965 Riley rejoined Young in New York, singing with The Theatre of Eternal Music and later recording *In C* for release in 1968. His second Columbia album (1969) simultaneously culminated his tape experiments with *Poppy Nogood and His Phantom Band* and anticipated his keyboard work of the next decade with *Rainbow in Curved Air*.

After meeting Pandit Pran Nath in 1970, Riley devoted the decade largely to studying Indian music and teaching it at Mills College. His recording in the '70s was restricted to electronic-organ improvisations like *Persian Surgery Dervishes*

(1971). *Descending Moonshine Dervishes* (1976), and *Shri Camel* (1976). Toward the end of the decade at Mills he met the Kronos Quartet, who in a sense inspired him to return to composition, which has been in good part devoted to string quartets ever since. On a 1982 commission by Radio Bremen, however, Riley sang and played synthesizers in *Songs for the Ten Voices of the Two Prophets* (the title a pun on the brand name of the instruments). Shortly thereafter he returned to acoustic piano, now tuned in just intonation and often muted, for *The Harp of New Albion* and *No Man's Land* (the latter with Indian sitarist Krishna Bhatt, with whom Riley has collaborated in composition as well as performance). Riley has continued to write for saxophone from time to time, most recently for the Rova Saxophone Quartet in *The Pipes of Medb* (1987), based on Celtic mythology.

Despite the variety of his compositions, constants in Riley's music are, technically, the often wildly imaginative transmogrification of a motivic (or modular) base and, emotionally, an abiding sense of wonder. The latter is conveyed by the total lack of pretense in the composer himself and his résumé, which still begins by acknowledging, under Music Education, "Piano lessons with Mrs. Halton, 1943. Piano lessons with Mrs. McGorvin 1945 . . ."

We spoke in December 1987, two days after the odd incident described in the Preface, on an afternoon of rain and light snow. We sat on floor mats by a wood-burning stove in the studio the composer had built beside his home in the foothills of the Sierra Nevada. Dubbed by him Shri Moonshine Ranch, it is located near a stream and is reached by an unpaved road. Early in our conversation I joked that the setting indicated no burning ambition to besiege Carnegie Hall, and Riley in turn expressed no burning interest in orchestras in general. Not long afterwards what became *Jade Palace Orchestral Dances* was commissioned by Carnegie Hall for its centennial. Riley has recently completed a fifty-minute work for the St. Louis Symphony.

STRICKLAND: What are you working on at the moment?

RILEY: A new piece for the Kronos Quartet, which is supposed to become a quintet, since the piece involves my playing with them on keyboard. Originally it was planned for piano tuned in just intonation, but because of our schedule it looks like I'll have to do it on an electronic instrument. We have performances every night in a different city, and there's no chance to get the piano tuned, which requires a few days.

STRICKLAND: La Monte requires a few weeks.

RILEY [*smiling*]: He's famous for long-term installations. We'd be happy with two or three days. But the schedule's too tight.

STRICKLAND: What's the piece called?

RILEY: The working title is *Crow's Rosary,* which doesn't mean anything— just a title that came to me in a dream. The essential thing I'm working with in this piece is the harmonic series involving nine, ten, eleven, twelve, thirteen, and fourteen. Those will be the principal notes of the scale. I've been curious for some time to build a scale with that part of the harmonic series. Eleven and thirteen are higher primes than I've used in my other pieces.

STRICKLAND: Speaking of titles, what about *Poppy Nogood and His Phantom Band*? When it came out in the late '60s, many of us took it as some kind of allusion to controlled substances.

RILEY: My daughter, when she was a tiny little girl, called me Poppy instead of Daddy. And Poppy Nogood sometimes when she was mad at me [*both laugh*].

STRICKLAND: There goes that theory.

RILEY: The Phantom Band, of course, was the time-lag tape system I'd developed in order to overdub my playing.

STRICKLAND: The last section of *Cadenza on the Night Plain,* written just after Billy Joel's song "Captain Jack," is "Captain Jack Has the Last Word."

RILEY: Most of *Cadenza* is on Native American themes. I thought it would be nice to be able to rewrite history. Captain Jack was one of the Modoc Indians who held out in northern California and was murdered, I think, after he surrendered. So I thought in the string quartet he should have another chance in a musical reincarnation. Also, that section was written as a little concluding solo for David Harrington, the leader of Kronos.

STRICKLAND: You've been writing string quartets for how long?

RILEY: I wrote a string quartet in 1960 at Berkeley. I'd always loved the sound of Beethoven string quartets and also those of Debussy and Bartók. I'd always thought the string quartet was one of the purest musical forms. For years I wanted to do another, but I'd sort of given up on writing music. When I met David Harrington around '77 or '78 he kept badgering me to do something for the Kronos, who came to Mills College in residence, then in an earlier incarnation with two different members. I hadn't been writing any music but I taught there for over ten years and that was pretty much my life, which revolved around practicing Indian music and teaching privately and at Mills in Oakland while living up here. I was performing a lot during the '70s but not writing as much as I have since I left in the early '80s.

STRICKLAND: In terms of the American discography, you kind of disappeared in the '70s. Then *Shri Camel* came out in '80.

RILEY: It was recorded in '77 but Columbia didn't release it for years.

STRICKLAND: What did it feel like not to be composing for ten years or so?

RILEY: Well, I was always working with improvisation and other musical ideas. It felt natural and still does. I don't like to do anything unless there's some kind of inspiration. I was working very hard in developing my knowledge of Indian classical music. It felt right, because in Indian classical music there's an oral tradition and things are passed on anonymously. It felt good to be part of an oral tradition and still does, but now I'm doing and will probably continue doing from time to time more actual scoring of musical ideas for Kronos and others.

STRICKLAND: During that period we had electronic keyboard improvisations from Europe, and in recent recordings like *No Man's Land* and *The Harp of New Albion* you've gone back to the acoustic piano. Along with the Kronos work you've done ensemble work, most notably in *In C*. Some of the people with whom you're popularly associated have branched out into orchestral work.

RILEY: I'm not terribly interested in orchestras. I like the more transparent sound of smaller groups. I don't think orchestras match my temperament, and I don't think you get the care you get with a group like Kronos that I really work with intimately, with a lot of rehearsal time and discussion. When I talk to composers who've worked with orchestras, I find their experience to be really quite unpleasant. They spend hours and hours getting parts copied. They have very little rehearsal time. Many musicians in the orchestra are unsympathetic to the music, so they don't care how they play it. If you had an orchestra like the Kronos Quartet, yeah, I'd like to write for it. If there were an orchestra I could have a relationship with in music making, then I could see doing it. Lukas Foss wants me to do something orchestral, and I've known him for years, so I could imagine working with him closely with long-term rehearsals. But since I'm not around orchestras a lot, it's not something I think about much. I know it's a lot more prestigious, and you get a lot more visibility—that part of it is always enticing—but since I've never done it, at this stage of my life I don't miss it.

STRICKLAND: Your lifestyle—even where we are right now—doesn't indicate that you're going out of your way to storm Carnegie Hall.

RILEY [*laughing*]: I lived in New York from '65 to '69, and the time was well spent trying to let my work be known. But I didn't feel very good living there. I wanted to get back to California.

STRICKLAND: Where are you from?

RILEY: These foothills, a railroad town a few miles from here called Colfax.

STRICKLAND: Did you have a very musical family?

RILEY: My father's side was Irish but I didn't know them, since he'd left them in Ohio. My mother's side of the family was Italian, and most Italians are fairly musical. We had big family get-togethers with lots of music, and one of my uncles plays bass in a band, but there wasn't any particular focus on music. I kind of just took it up when I was young.

STRICKLAND: How young?

RILEY: Right from the beginning. I was all the time getting near the piano or singing songs, popular songs from the radio in the late '30s, "Pennies from Heaven" and those kinds of things.

STRICKLAND: When did you start formal musical training?

RILEY: I started violin when I was about five. After about a year the war broke out and my father joined the Marines. We left the town where we lived and I couldn't follow up on that, but at about eight or nine I took up piano.

STRICKLAND: Did you take lessons through your teenage years?

RILEY: It was very sporadic. I never studied very long. I much preferred to learn things by ear and just play with my friends in school. Although I played classical music, my real interest was playing popular music in groups.

STRICKLAND: La Monte had the same background of dance bands.

RILEY: I think that's why we were attracted to each other.

STRICKLAND: You met as grad students in Berkeley in '59.

RILEY: I did my B.A. at San Francisco State. I started a family early and grad school a year late.

STRICKLAND: It was an important meeting in the development of what's called Minimalism. I guess my next question is "Are you tired of the term?"

RILEY: Well, it isn't a subject I could speak at length on. It's valid because it's definitely caught on in people's minds as a particular area of music. But today I could write a symphony like Beethoven and they'd call it a Minimalist piece because my name would be on it. They call a piece like *Cadenza* Minimalist. I don't see the piece that way. If they put it unidentified beside *In C,* you wouldn't recognize it as by the same composer.

But I think the idea of presenting a certain limited number of musical parameters so that people can hear them is a valid musical idea, and that's what Minimalism is to me: repetition, long notes, things that people didn't ordinarily build a whole piece out of. La Monte's works of the *Trio for Strings* period were made out of long tones. And people didn't . . . I remember he was being *laughed* at. I remember when we used to go to college conferences composers would laugh La Monte off the stage, because nobody could take that seriously as music—only very few people.

STRICKLAND: He told me you, Terry Jennings, and Dennis Johnson were the only ones he felt really understood what he was doing, though others were supportive. In what vein were you composing before you went to grad school to study composition?

RILEY: I had a big interest in postserial music and also in Schoenberg and Webern, although I wasn't composing music exactly like that. I always did like their very interesting fluid rhythms. What I ended up doing was to distill the rhythmic part out of it and throw away the tone rows. I also think their sense of structure influenced me a lot. You never know just what leads you to the works that become your trademark. During that period, though, I hadn't discovered yet what I really wanted to do. I still don't know if I have! [*Both laugh.*] For me it's always a process of trying to work with something new. I didn't ever want to develop a style of music, although I was known for one. That wasn't important to me. *In C* was a step along the way. I didn't want to compose several of them.

STRICKLAND: What was it like to meet La Monte? What was he like back then?

RILEY: Like he is now! La Monte was masterful even in those days, much more masterful than any of my teachers. He knew what he wanted and very clearly demonstrated his musical ideas with no confusion. Very clear and very strong. He was good in jazz improvisation and very spontaneous both in his speech and in his music. He's rare. I think La Monte is one of the people of our time to take note of. His achievement has been great but not always in the spotlight, because he's always worked just for *music's* sake, *never* compromising commercially, which is rare. Most people *have* to. La Monte *refuses* to.

STRICKLAND: What was it like to hear the *Trio for Strings*?

RILEY: La Monte could put you in a spaceship. I used to perform some of his music. You'd be looking at the score, waiting through a duration of twenty-five seconds rest. I'd never done that before, you know? [*Both laugh.*] I mean, waiting for the next tone, which you're going to play for forty-five seconds—it was just like going somewhere in a spaceship! Time stopped, and I'd never had that experience. It's like an initiation. You're never quite the same afterwards. And his music has done that for a lot of musicians, more and more. I think in the future it'll have even wider impact.

STRICKLAND: How did confronting La Monte's music affect your own composition? Did you ever follow him into long tones?

RILEY: The 1960 string quartet I mentioned is the most directly influenced. It's funny . . . it's in C too, but it's all long tones. Some of the motives which later turn up in *In C* are in that quartet.

STRICKLAND: You ought to record it.

RILEY: Kronos has the score. They might do it sometime.

STRICKLAND: Even though La Monte originated the Minimalist style, he was still writing atonally. The most important things that you added were repetition and the re-embracing of tonality. He wasn't composing tonally at all, was he?

RILEY: He wasn't, but one thing I really liked in his early works, like *Study I* for piano—it's very, very chromatic, like something Stockhausen might write, but you'll have all these flourishes and out of them will come an open fifth, like a little tonal center. Or a ninth. A lot of the intervals that are in tune on the piano. It happens over and over again. Although he didn't understand just intonation yet he was instinctively going after the resonances of the piano. He had started to understand that tonality was very important, but there wasn't a climate for that yet.

STRICKLAND: But the next year you wrote the string quartet in C. What made you decide to choose that key—not only tonal but no sharps or flats?

RILEY: What I liked in La Monte and in jazz I distilled down to that simple form. I worked with him for years accompanying Ann Halprin, the dancer. And the things I liked most involved repetitions, so at that point I kind of split off into that area and found a greater satisfaction than I'd found in anything else. I started working with very primitive tape recorders in '58 or '59 making tape loops, studying the loops and their frequencies, and trying to manipulate them in different ways. I started to think about doing this live and wrote a string trio in '60 or '61 that is the first piece that uses tonal repetition, combining it with chromaticism. You have very simple repetitive motives going on and a lacework of chromaticism around it. That was the transitional piece for me.

STRICKLAND: You went to France in '61. How did you get involved with ORTF?

RILEY: I'd been living in France a while. I wanted to see what Europe was like, and I'd tried to get a grant in college, applied for the Prix de Rome and all those things. I never won anything, so I went to work in a bar playing ragtime piano at night and saved enough money in a year to get me and my family to France. I've played a lot in bars, and for me that's a much more real situation than the artificial realm of the standard concert with the people sitting out *there,* the piano onstage, the artist backstage nervously waiting for the lights to go down. Some drunk hanging on your shoulder . . . at least everyone's *here* all the time in bars.

I continued working in bars, clubs, and stuff in Europe. There were American bases there so I could make pretty good money playing in officers' clubs, being paid on the American standard. The playwright Ken Dewey had been invited by the Theater of Nations to do a play. He hired trumpeter Chet Baker and his group to play and me to be musical director. That sounds pompous because I was like a hippie traveling around, you know [*both laugh*]. Ken got me into the French Radio studio. It was the first time I'd ever been able to use a decent tape recorder. I don't know what they were . . . mono Ampexes, maybe, but fairly decent quality. It wasn't one of the big ORTF studios, just the Sarah Bernhardt Theater, but it was great for me. I'd been fooling around with an old Echoplex with Ramone Sender just before I left and had gotten this echo effect that I thought was quite unusual. I don't know if you've heard of that piece I wrote called *Mescalin Mix.*

It sounded just like an acid trip [*both laugh*]. I described the effect to the French engineer, a very straight guy in a white coat, who fooled around and ended up hooking two tape recorders together. Boy! When I heard that sound it was just what I wanted. This was the first time-lag accumulator.

STRICKLAND: I'm really dense technically. Can you explain the process to me?

RILEY: What you do is connect two tape recorders. The first one is playing back, the second recording, the tape stretched across the heads of both. As this machine records it feeds it back to the other machine which plays back what it's added. It keeps building up, and you've heard *Poppy Nogood* so you know what you get. Robert Fripp calls it "Frippertronics." He claims he invented it, but that was ten or fifteen years later.

I was in there for a week with the Frenchman, whose name I forget, and then Chet came in with the band. He'd just gotten out of jail in Lucca after being busted for possession. He hadn't been able to perform for a year and he was ready to play. I'd prepared a tune by Miles Davis, a nice modal tune called "So What"; don't know if you know it [*both sing opening*]. First I recorded the quartet, then I asked them to record their solos separately. Then I put it all together with the time-lag technique, plus the technique of just putting all the solos together, making canons out of the trumpet and other parts. I'd have ten trumpet parts, ten trombone parts, ten string bass parts. It's probably my first orchestral piece but I made it all out of tape. That piece, *Music for the Gift,* was when I really started understanding what repetition could do for musical form. That's the forerunner of *In C.*

STRICKLAND: You composed *In C* when you returned to the Bay Area.

RILEY: John Kennedy was assassinated, and they closed the clubs I was working in. It was to pay tribute to him, but it hit me, because I was just living from week to week and had to come back. I'd had a band and worked for floor shows—I was accompanist and bus driver for the floor shows. Fire-eaters, you name it . . . I played for everyone. I worked for a booking agency. It was a weird way to make a living, but I liked it, actually. It was a lot better than working in some store.

    We were traveling all over France, meeting really great artists, circus people . . . when I came back I began playing piano again at Gold Street Saloon in North Beach. I bought a Viking tape recorder when I got back and borrowed a couple of things. Morton Subotnick and Ramone Sender were running the Tape Music Center, and they offered me two solo evenings. That was just after I wrote *In C.*

STRICKLAND: The creation of *In C* could be described as an inspiration.

RILEY: *Music for the Gift* made me want to try a live piece that would have the same effect. I was working on writing out parts similar to those I'd written for Chet's group, but it wasn't working out. Then one night, riding the bus down to work at Gold Street, I just heard it—I heard the ideas, every motive.

STRICKLAND: There're fifty-three of them.

RILEY: Yeah, well, I didn't hear every one, but I heard the whole beginning with the modulation . . .

STRICKLAND: With the Pulse?

RILEY: No. Steve says he suggested that during rehearsals, and it might be true that he did, I don't remember. I think we did use it because we couldn't keep together without the Pulse. So after work I wrote down what I had and worked on it a little more to get the rest of the piece developed.

STRICKLAND: How did it feel?

RILEY: I knew that it was something hot, because I'd been trying to work these ideas out for a long time. When I finally saw it come together it was so simple that I wondered why I hadn't thought of it before. I was trying to do something much more complex. I was writing it all out in score, not the idea of just writing it all out on one sheet of paper.

STRICKLAND: You mentioned Steve Reich, who played the Wurlitzer in the premiere of *In C.* How'd you meet him?

RILEY: An old friend of mine, Bill Spencer, a jazz musician, had met Steve and told me Steve's group was performing one night down at the Mime Troupe.

STRICKLAND: This was a jazz group?

RILEY: No, it was Steve and a few other people. I can't remember, but maybe Jon Gibson was there. They were performing music that Steve had done for the Mime Troupe. I went to the first half and left. The next day at my studio in a garage up on Bernal Heights, where Steve also lived, though I didn't know it, there was a bang on the door, and it was Steve Reich. The first thing he said was, "Why did you walk out on my concert?" He was so *furious,* right? So I told him to come in. We sat down and got to know each other. I showed him *In C,* which I was working on, and he helped me a lot. He was really enthusiastic for the project. He wanted to *do* it.

STRICKLAND: Was he writing serially at the time?

RILEY: The thing I heard was improvisation, but very banging around and noisy. Wasn't anything like what he did after he met me. Definitely that impressed him. *In C* was his big entrance into this whole world, just like it was for me when I met La Monte.

STRICKLAND: Steve Reich invented the term "phasing." What about the process?

RILEY: Well, I don't think so, because I'd already done that . . . he had this piece he'd recorded in Union Square called *Brother Walter.* In Union Square he'd recorded—

STRICKLAND: *It's Gonna Rain.*

RILEY: *It's Gonna Rain,* right. He was driving a cab then. He played me the fragments, and then he started making a piece out of it. The first thing he tried before he heard what I was doing was sort of a collage piece. It's funny that if you listen to Brother Walter and hear [*sings*] "It's gonna *rain!* It's gonna *rain!*" it's like the first two notes of *In C.* It's C and E. I don't know if it's C and E but it's major thirds.

Not only that, but I'd made pieces with words and tape loops before that. And when you play two tape loops on the same machine they don't play at the same speed. What Steve did, because he's very methodical and clean in his work, was to make the phasing work very gradually and to make a process out of it. I made the tapes go backwards, forwards . . . it was fun, very funky. So I think his contribution was to clean all these things up and make kind of a method out of it, but what's important here is my invention of the form built solely out of repeating modules. When two identical modules are played simultaneously by either tape machines or live performers, imperfections in speed or pitch result in "phasing." I introduced the process into music composition; Steve correctly labeled it.

STRICKLAND: Like La Monte, Steve Reich had a jazz background, studying drums since he was fourteen. They've also both mentioned a Coltrane influence.

RILEY: La Monte introduced me to Coltrane's music at Berkeley. Most of the musicians around the table didn't think Coltrane was doing anything. La Monte and I went together to hear him play at Jazz Workshop. I heard him play with Miles Davis before that at the Blackhawk, but that experience wasn't as powerful. I went mainly to hear Miles Davis. What really impressed me was the next year when I heard John Coltrane with his own quartet in the "My Favorite Things" era. I don't think any musician could help but be impressed by John Coltrane. You really confronted something when you went to hear him play. The seriousness and the depth of his music would impress anyone.

STRICKLAND: There seems a clear connection to me between modal jazz and Minimalism, the slower harmonic movement in modal jazz as opposed to bop and the almost static harmonic rhythm of a piece like *In C.*

RILEY: John Coltrane himself, everybody was in a certain climate. We were just discovering Asia and Africa. Today it's available to everybody, and it's hard to imagine those days. Ravi Shankar had been over here once or twice. Essentially most of this stuff comes from India and Africa, the influences of modality and cyclic rhythm and repetition. It's *in* their music. So John Coltrane himself changed because he'd heard Indian music, but it opened up something bigger in him than any other jazz musician had confronted before that.

STRICKLAND: So it wasn't that Coltrane drew you into harmonic stasis. There was a common source.

RILEY: I think La Monte is more responsible. His *Dorian Blues* and so on were much more influential on me in terms of form than Coltrane's music. Coltrane was a great spiritual influence on everybody, just because of his power. The other thing I found interesting in his work was the permutation of motives in improvisation. He'd set up a four- or five-note chord and keep it vertical, permuting intervals of the chord. That was something I'd been fooling around with, but I think Coltrane did it better than anybody I'd ever heard up to that time. That's also done in Indian classical music. I don't know if he learned it there or just by intuition. His pointing out polarities in the scale and moving from one to another was very important for modal music development—because otherwise you're just going up and down the scale.

STRICKLAND: You picked up soprano saxophone around '65, like a lot of people. Was that Coltrane's influence?

RILEY: Also La Monte and the shenai of Bismillah Khan. I'd been working with Sonny Lewis, who's a tenor saxophone player. He played my first sax piece for me, *In A-flat (or is it B-flat?)*—with the tape distortion you couldn't tell what key it was in [*laughs*].

STRICKLAND: Is there any way all this'll get recorded?

RILEY: I doubt it. Tapes don't stand up. I pulled some out for my retrospective at KPFA a few years ago and some of the tapes are just . . . they weren't good in the beginning because I was using very cheap equipment. Lots of hum and stuff. I don't feel it's worth listening to. Maybe for some archivist or some music historian, but I don't feel by the time it's deteriorated that much it's worth saving. I'd just as soon take them all to the dump.

STRICKLAND: Straightforward answer! So you used soprano in '65 in *Dorian Reeds.*

RILEY: Both the soprano and the sopranino sound very shenai-like, more like double reeds than other saxophones. I felt the only way I could develop *Poppy Nogood and His Phantom Band* was to play the saxophone myself, because I didn't want to tell the saxophone player to do this or that. I felt it had to come out of my own musical spontaneity. I didn't see any choice but to see if I could learn the saxophone well enough to do it. I only learned to play the saxophone well enough to play this piece. I couldn't play *Cherokee* or anything like that [*both laugh*].

STRICKLAND: You weren't going to compete with Charlie Parker.

RILEY [*laughing*]: No, my goal was to play this piece. And I left the saxophone essentially when I played that piece. I never played saxophone with La Monte in the Theatre of Eternal Music, though that's been written mistakenly. I sang. I don't think that would've worked with his group, because he'd already given up saxophone himself. He already began to understand the harmonic series, the overtone system, and fractions and intervals, so he wouldn't have played saxophone in those days because he couldn't have done it to the precision he wanted.

STRICKLAND: You played with him in New York shortly after you composed *In C.* I was wondering if the title was an allusion to Schoenberg's statement, which shocked his true believers, revolutionary as he was, that good music remained to be written in the key of C major.

RILEY: Did he say that? I didn't even know he'd said that! [*Laughs.*] All these things have meaning. That has meaning to me. As I said, titles come to me often in dreams, just as the notes or melodies come. When I started singing Indian classical music later we began in C—we tuned the tamburas there, the key Pandit Pran Nath always sang in. So it's not a flow of coincidence but of events. Maybe when Schoenberg said that he was thinking *In C* was going to be written. I don't know what it was, but he knew something was coming. I think the connections are very important and we should reflect on them. Once I get the idea for a title I try to figure out what the title's telling me about the structure of the piece. What goes on in the subconscious is, I think, very important.

STRICKLAND: Back to titles again. What about *Shri Camel?* Is that the camel as Shri, the divine bearer of the burden?

RILEY: Shri means Lord in the sense of Mister or god. Shri is a yantra, a bunch of triangles coming out like this [*gestures*] as a meditation symbol. There's a Shri raga. When I was first doing the piece I used to think of a camel walking, the rhythmic ideas that came out of it. But I didn't want to just call it *Camel,* so I called it *Shri Camel* [*both laugh*]. The essence of divinity in camel.

STRICKLAND: That was your last record with Columbia in '80. How did they first decide to record *In C* four years after you composed it?

RILEY [*refilling stove with wood*]: David Behrman was working with John Mc-Clure, the director of Columbia Masterworks, as a producer. Another connection was Richard Maxfield, who was working there as a tape editor and telling David about all the new music around, "You should go and hear this." I don't remember if David took the music to McClure or if he heard it himself first.

STRICKLAND: La Monte about that time got his contract to record his singing with the ocean.

RILEY: Right. Steve Reich's *Violin Phase* was recorded then and released on Odyssey.

STRICKLAND: As you know, La Monte withdrew from his agreement with Columbia.

RILEY [*laughing*]: Yeah, I was right in on that!

STRICKLAND: You know what a sweet guy he is, but when you *mention* artistic control he's transformed into a tiger. When I spoke of you in this context, he said something like, "Well, Terry's just *nicer,* he's easier to work with . . . "

RILEY [*laughing*]: I liked John McClure a lot. You have to remember I was more or less totally unknown then. I was up in Buffalo with Lukas Foss on a grant when this was happening. I hadn't recorded yet on a major label, so when Columbia Masterworks said they wanted to record *In C,* to me it looked like the opportunity of a lifetime. Plus I was going to get to record it with musicians like Stuart Dempster, Jon Hassell, and David Rosenboom. To me it was ideal. The only problem I had was that they wanted to record the whole thing in three hours. Not a lot of time. In three hours you get three overtakes. That means for three hours we just sat there and blew our heads off. It was a very low-budget production, and the record's still out there on the stands, though they haven't sent me any royalties in quite a while.

STRICKLAND: Do you have other tapes of *In C* you wish you could put on record instead of or in addition to that?

RILEY: I don't have any tapes but I've been in performances of it which are quite different. We did one in Mexico City close to three hours long with something like eighteen vibraphones and marimbas. There've been some performances which have been definitely worth recording. The score says "for any number of instruments," and people have told me, "Yes, I played a solo piano version."

STRICKLAND: But it has such a collective feel to it.

RILEY: I envisioned it as a group piece. Kronos want to play it as a string quartet. The newest plan is to do the twenty-fifth anniversary performance in China with the Peking Orchestra. We'll go over in the fall to get that started. That'll be the next recording, and I think interesting, because we'll be able to do it in just intonation. The only thing that remains to be seen is if the Chinese can understand the system of playing because it's so democratic.

STRICKLAND: Are there any Chinese *jazz* musicians around?

RILEY: Yes. One of the groups I'm considering working with is called the Oriental Song and Dance Ensemble in Peking. They're all younger people and have a gamelan there and a jazz group. They're not the best classical Chinese orchestra according to reports, but they might be the best to do this. [*Note: The Celestial Harmonies recording featured the Shanghai Film Orchestra.*]

STRICKLAND: You mentioned just intonation, and that gets us to La Monte's using that in '64 with the first tape version of *The Well-Tuned Piano*. Were you composing in just intonation anytime around then?

RILEY: I discovered just intonation when I came to work with him in New York in '65.

STRICKLAND: Then in '70 you both became students of Pandit Pran Nath, who was singing in just intonation. How did you get to meet him?

RILEY: I met him through Shyam Bhatnagar, a disciple who had recorded him and brought over his tapes. La Monte met Shyam at Barbara Stacey's house around '67 or '68 and said, "You've got to hear these tapes!" It was extraordinary. We'd heard the Ali brothers, who were also Pandit Pran Nath's students.

STRICKLAND: What was the effect when you heard Pran Nath?

RILEY: It was very much like hearing Coltrane, this great spiritual power. You know how we all used to talk about "There must be some guy in a cave somewhere . . . "—I don't know why this was a fantasy of mine [*laughs*]. This tape was as close to that experience as anything I'd ever come up against. Hearing him sing, that *ancient* feeling, sounding like he was hundreds of years old. His music defied what I thought music had to have to make it exciting. But excitement wasn't what it had, it had a depth—Coltrane was exciting in another way, dazzling. With Pandit Pran Nath everything was stripped away but this ancient feeling. Shyam and La Monte got him a job teaching a class at the New School for Social Research. Shyam turned over all his students, so it got funded.

STRICKLAND: You went to India later and studied with him, but I wanted to ask you if it was primarily a musical or a religious apprenticeship. Or am I making a false distinction altogether?

RILEY: It's hard to separate them when you get your spiritual experience through music. Looking back on all my musical experiences, they've been spiritual experiences, even though that's maybe not the way I would have said it when I was fifteen or twenty. But that's been my experience with the Other, whatever you want to call it. Meeting Pran Nath, it wasn't just like meeting the exotic—he could've been in my own family. Like La Monte, who felt so close to me it was like meeting my spiritual brother, a great common bond of music that was understood. It was like a preordained family, meeting La Monte and meeting Pran Nath—it felt like gradually meeting your true relatives.

STRICKLAND: Do you consider yourself a Hindu now?

RILEY: No. Organized religion doesn't appeal to me personally.

STRICKLAND: Were you raised in it?

RILEY: As a Catholic. Irish-Italian, what else could you be? [*Both laugh.*] But it doesn't appeal to me to be a member of a religious group. I don't consider myself a Hindu, with their mantras and not eating meat. I don't see any reason to pick one religion over another.

STRICKLAND: Did you have a very strong religious sensibility in your family?

RILEY: Yes, I was an altar boy and I was very attracted to the Church.

STRICKLAND: As an altar boy did it occur to you to become a priest? It did to most of us, I think. I'm just wondering if there was a kind of Stephen Dedalus displacement from religion to art.

RILEY: No. I was in awe of some of the priests I was around. They were definitely role models in a certain way, and I could see them as being admired by the other people, but I never saw that for myself. Then you go to college and become cynical like everyone else and realize or swear that God doesn't exist. I think Pran Nath brought me back to a real spirituality. He was a real example to me of a high spiritual being.

STRICKLAND: Apart from the obvious Indian influence in your music there's also a strong Middle East influence, like Coltrane with Arabic *maqamat.* But you had that firsthand when you were living in Spain.

RILEY: And Morocco. That was, outside of Ravi Shankar, my first live experience of non-Western music—hearing musicians playing Moroccan folk music. I don't remember hearing Moroccan music earlier, but I do remember feeling this is the way music should be played. It shouldn't be played on the concert stage, read out of the book. I remember hearing the calls to prayer from the mosques—you know, those are my strongest influences with jazz and Indian classical music and Persian music—any kind of devotional music, which is true of a certain kind of jazz, in the sense that people give up their lives to do the music.

STRICKLAND: In the music you did in the '70s, the electronic keyboard solos, there's a lot of Middle Eastern influence. At least two of your album titles in that period referred to the dervishes. What was that about, the way the musical lines were spinning around?

RILEY: I'd been fascinated by the dervishes and Rumi all during my studies and felt a close connection with ancient Persian culture. I've been in Iran a couple of times and never felt when I was there what I feel when I dream about it. Somehow I was a little bit disappointed when I went there. I never got what I always imagined it to be. My Persia is an imagining. But I felt those keyboard pieces had a connection to the dervishes and the idea of transcending the body by spinning, whirling, repeating, losing body consciousness in devotion to the circle.

STRICKLAND: While you were doing these international concerts in the '70s you were teaching at Mills College full-time.

RILEY: Pretty full-time. I would take off now and then.

STRICKLAND: Was it because of your academic duties that you restricted yourself to solo work at that period?

RILEY: No, the reason I restricted myself to solo work is that I'm not good at telling people what to do. When I get together with a group of musicians the only way I can tell them what to do is if we can intuit together. I never have the right words to tell them what to do. It never comes out right. The way I make music is so moment-to-moment that I have to work with musicians who are intuiting it moment-to-moment. And there are very few musicians that I've been able to work with that way.

STRICKLAND: How improvised and how composed were your solo keyboard works?

RILEY: It's hard to say. I know people try to say ninety percent of this and so on. The things that are composed are the modes. But even those I might want to change. In Indian music there's a state called *uppaj*—I suppose you could spell it like "up-age" in English and it means almost the same thing—the state in which you transcend all the musical techniques you've learned and can play anything you hear; you're not restricted by a text or what you *think* you can play. I don't think you can get that in an orchestra—maybe it does happen in great orchestras at one point where every player is in perfect attunement in the moment. In Indian music it's starting with the raga, then forgetting the raga, which is just a vehicle to launch you into the higher moment. If you don't reach this moment, the raga's just an exercise.

STRICKLAND: Speaking of raga and *maqam,* you tend a lot toward modality—Dorian, for example—otherwise in your work.

RILEY: It's an attempt to establish mood—that's what mode is. You have to stay in a certain musical place enough to establish that mood, and once it's established this other thing can happen. Pandit Pran Nath, for example, is often able to add slightly different notes yet still somehow never leave the raga. Not consciously use them, but they'll come in because of a relationship he suddenly feels in that raga that no one's thought of before.

STRICKLAND: Charlie Parker often had arguments with his musicians about what notes could be played in a given key.

RILEY: There's Miles Davis, too, the way he'll record a piece immediately after writing a few chords out for his musicians. To me that's what music is. Of course, you can't have absolute beginners, you need people you can trust. *Crow's Rosary* I haven't really started yet, because I haven't figured out a way for Kronos and me to play together. I don't want to write a piece out where I have to play from the score, because I can't read music that way. They haven't very much experience *without* a written score, so in a sense I'm going to have to ask them to come my way a little bit. In a performance I really like to be able to switch directions, to go in any direction I hear the music coming. That's why I've played alone a lot. And I can't play from a written score. Music doesn't happen for me when I do that. I worry too much about what's on the page and that's a block to me.

STRICKLAND: In those solo albums you used a Yamaha organ primarily.

RILEY: I also had a Vox Supercontinental in *Persian Surgery Dervishes.*

STRICKLAND: In '82, when you did *Songs for the Ten Voices of the Two Prophets,* you suddenly switched from electronic organ to synthesizer.

RILEY: Chet Wood had developed the software or hardware to make it possible to tune the Prophet-V synthesizer. And since I'd been playing basically the same instrument for about six years, I thought it was time to move on to another.

STRICKLAND: You didn't last too long with it in terms of the discography. The next year you moved back to the acoustic piano with *No Man's Land* and *The Harp of New Albion.*

RILEY: I started playing electronic instruments because to have the same instrument wherever you're going to play is a real advantage. You know what to expect. A lot of places either don't have a piano or the piano's not very good, and you're faced with playing a concert on an instrument you don't like. In the '60s and '70s I was also really fascinated with the emerging technology. But as I pursued my study of Indian classical music I felt the need to do something similar for an acoustic instrument in my so-called creative music. There's a certain lack of breath, a breathing quality, in electronic instruments—the sound is sort of like light bulbs going on and off. Even though the tone is supposed to be so sophisticated, it's still rather dull and flat compared to acoustic instruments, especially the vibration of a string, which is one of the most beautiful phenomena in sound.

Around 1980 I bought an old upright and started to play and develop music on piano again. Of course I'd been aware of La Monte's *Well-Tuned Piano* since '64, but I'd also been playing both Indian music and electronic keyboards in just intonation. So I decided to tune the piano that way rather than in equal temperament. Finally we did the first performance of *The Harp of New Albion* in Cologne in '84.

STRICKLAND: But before that you'd written the *No Man's Land* score for Alain Tanner and recorded it on acoustic piano with Krishna Bhatt on sitar.

RILEY: I think I'd already started *The Harp of New Albion.* Krishna and I had played in just intonation, but he had some trouble with that because of the structure of the sitar frets, which wasn't what I would have expected. So we did *No Man's Land* in equal temperament. I don't dislike equal temperament, I just think it's too bad it's the only tuning normally considered. Alain Tanner came to a concert Krishna and I did in Geneva. I didn't actually know who he was. After we met he showed me a beautiful film of his made in Ireland, *Light Years Away* with Trevor Howard, one of the best films I've ever seen. That's what convinced me to do the movie score for him.

STRICKLAND: You rearranged a lot of earlier works for piano and sitar in that score. Did you find it as exciting to be adapting preexisting material as to creating new work?

RILEY: Well, Alain wanted those pieces, which he'd heard in concerts. Originally it wasn't planned as a recording but as a film score. I didn't mind the process, but we had very little time to do the album—in a few days we recorded, mixed it, everything. To start from scratch, we couldn't have done it in that time. We actually had a good time with it.

STRICKLAND: Was it as challenging or involving?

RILEY: Well, probably not. But if he wanted to give me six months to do something new, then we probably could have done it. I enjoyed the chance to record with Krishna finally. Around that time we had a new studio production called *The Medicine Wheel,* all new material composed in part with Krishna, which we're trying to get the release rights to from Radio Bremen.

STRICKLAND: That piece, *Cadenza,* and *Harp* form a series of works on Native American mythology. How did you develop that interest?

RILEY: The feeling came over me that this was *part* of me. I never studied Native American music but I felt a spiritual connection to that culture.

STRICKLAND: Does it have something to do with where we're sitting now?

RILEY: It could be, yes. It could be just the spirit of the land. I'm out in those woods daily and I get many of my musical ideas out there, walking or running. Those pieces started with that. I think our music has to come out of the land, not India. We can play Indian music, but we live here.

STRICKLAND: Will you do any more works in that vein?

RILEY: I don't know. That may be over for a while. But *Crow's Rosary* may be coming out of that.

STRICKLAND: Is the Crow the Indian or the bird?

RILEY: It's just the bird to me. The crow with a rosary is a beautiful image for me. Maybe he found it. [*Long pause.*] But after I dreamed the title I thought, "Maybe *Kronos.*"

STRICKLAND: A lot of people heard a new lyricism in *Harp,* particularly Side One in my own case. It's understated, spare, slightly exotic, and made me think of Satie—*Gnossiennes,* say.

RILEY: There may be an underplaying of motives and of feeling in common. The piano itself opened up lyrical possibilities because of the resonance of strings and their harmonics. I was able to give the music a different shape. The piano has a much greater scope of expressive possibilities than electronic instruments.

STRICKLAND: It almost seems to have permitted you a textural spareness. So in a way it's far more Minimalist than *In C,* though none of the new works is nearly as insistently repetitive. Is it Minimalist at all?

RILEY: I'm probably the last person to ask. People seem surprised that I don't feel a musical kinship with Steve or Phil Glass, though we're on good terms. More important to me than the Minimalist theme in my work is the interrelationship of motives. Both *In C* and the later works have a really strong developmental quality, a lot of variation and permutation of motives. This isn't theoretical; it's the way I hear. In *Harp of New Albion* many of the chords in the first, almost linear statement of the chorale later become horizontal elements, modes. I didn't do that consciously, but I looked at it later and could see how this chord became that section.

STRICKLAND: One question I've been asking everyone is what other contemporary composers you most admire.

RILEY: In Western classical music, Bartók and Debussy are for me the two great masters of the century. Outside of La Monte's work I don't think there's anyone today who really strikes me, although I don't really listen to much contemporary music. I listen to jazz piano, the greats like Art Tatum—who's like Mozart to me, unexplainable—and Bill Evans. Miles Davis is a musical shaman. Coltrane, of course.

I think most of the important things in American music happen in jazz. I don't think much comes out of the tradition of the composer writing in isolation and sending the score out to others to play. For a while the score became everything for classical composers, not what you listen to, and I think that was horribly misguided. I also like Bobby McFerrin's singing and Allaudin Mathieu's choir work very much.

STRICKLAND: Do you come here to compose at a certain time of day, work on a schedule?

RILEY [*laughing*]: Who works? I haven't worked for years! Of course I can go at a concept for twenty-four hours straight, but that's not working.

John Zorn

Photo by Michel Delsol, courtesy Elektra Musician.

John Zorn is the most familiar, or notorious, composer of the New York avant-garde to come to public notice in the second half of the '80s. He is also among the most wildly syncretic composers ever. To call his compositions episodic is to understate the case gravely: a typical Zorn piece may move from Brahms (on live strings or the turntable of Christian Marclay) to pneumatic drills to cartoon music to post-Ornette sax within half a minute. One might resort to the old cliché and say that Zorn throws in everything but the kitchen sink, were it not that he has thrown that in too, using it to blow duck calls into, in search of ever-more recherché timbral effects.

Both in New York in 1953, Zorn has been composing since his teens. After a stint at Webster College in St. Louis, he dropped out and began performing solo concerts on alto saxophone. In the Midwest he encountered the improvisational-compositional blend of the Black Artists Group (BAG) and the Association for the Advancement of Creative Musicians (AACM). On his return to New York he began associations with musicians as radical in their stylistic diversity as the city itself. Zorn's considerable achievement has been to embody his startling catholicity of taste in musical structures which are sometimes, remarkably, as compelling as they are outrageous.

His four Nonesuch recordings indicate his range. In *The Big Gundown* (1987) Zorn rearranged or exploded the already bizarre film music of Ennio Morricone, with South American percussionists and synthesizers, evil electric guitars, and the most provocative female vocalise since Donna Summer's Top-Ten moans a decade earlier. *Spillane* (1988), Zorn's most ambitious album to date, contains a mean blues suite with hilarious narration by guitarist Albert Collins, a sonic collage for string quartet, and the dark-hued tone poem of the title, an experiment in musical *film noir* and pop expressionism featuring the juxtaposed rhythms of machine guns, bump-and-grind combos, and the black eternal rain. *Spy vs. Spy* (1989) was a tribute to Ornette Coleman by Zorn and his band of that name; while in *Naked City* (1990) the eponymous combo, which borrowed its name from the old TV detective show, offers the hard of hearing and diminished of attention span vignettes of everything from Henry Mancini and James Bond to reprises of Ornette and Morricone, all resulting in what sounds like a musical walk down Memory Lane for survivors of nuclear apocalypse.

Zorn has roots in the American maverick tradition from Ives to Partch to Coleman. His fragmentation may be seen as exponential advance on Ives's block form, while his *ad hoc* instrumentarium makes Partch seem a conservative old craftsman. Even farther off the beaten track, Zorn has noted the influence of Carl Stolling and Scot Bradley, scorers of 1940s Warner Brothers cartoons, on his non-sequential, alogical structures. These include the chamber orchestra piece *For Your Eyes Only*, premiered in 1989 by the Brooklyn Philharmonic, and a work in progress commissioned by the New York Philharmonic for its sesquicentennial.

On the other hand, despite Zorn's blunt criticism of John Cage and his followers, his work in part represents an extension of Cageian practices. Christian Marclay's imaginative turntabling has roots in Cage's *Imaginary Landscape* pieces, beginning in 1939 with one for piano, percussion, and two record players and moving on to others for twelve radios, etc.—a debt acknowledged in a recent Nonesuch compendium of new electronic music. The deliberately random quality of Cageian anticompositions, as well as Cage's denial of the distinction between music and "noise," anticipates the form and content of Zorn's recordings and performances, albeit they are pervaded by later jazz and rock—and wit rarely in evidence in his precursors. Zorn has noted succinctly, "If you don't have a sense of humor in New York City, you die" and backed up the statement not only with his music but with threats to wear a yarmulke to sessions with allegedly anti-Semitic speed-metalists.

In game-structure pieces like *Pool, Lacrosse, Archery*, and *Cobra*, Zorn extends aleatory practice by composing nothing but the complex rules for the group improvisation he directs (when not being mutinied by his musicians—a practice permitted in the admirably democratic or quasi-anarchic schemata). This open-endedness of form is reminiscent of, though again far more radical than, the "action music" school of the New York avant-garde of forty years ago: Earle Brown, Christian Wolff, and Morton Feldman. They provided controlled-choice situations through indeterminate notation permitting leeway within established parameters of pitch, register, attack, and dynamics or charts delineating thematic or rhythmic motives to be developed—though rehearsals served to standardize the results (and co-opt the spontaneity).

Without themes or *any* predetermined content and *with* highly diverse and imaginative musicians, no two performances of *Cobra* are not only never the same but never recognizable to the uninitiated as the same piece. The skeptical are referred to the studio and concert versions of the work on the Hat Art double album, so far Zorn's best game on disc.

As of this writing, Zorn is planning a second string quartet for Kronos, and Nonesuch is considering the simultaneous release of three Zorn albums: one revis(it)ing film scores; a second of Naked City taking on piano miniatures of Debussy, Scriabin, and Webern; and a third of *New Traditions in East Asian Bar Music*, adapting Zorn's game-structures to what he envisions as a more "mellow" end (one adjective I told him had probably never been applied to his work).

We spoke on the floor of Zorn's East Village apartment in February 1988.

STRICKLAND: How far do you and Mickey go back?

ZORN: I've been reading Spillane since I was a teenager and watching the Mike Hammer movies, one or two of which actually have Spillane in them. But it's the whole world that attracted me, not one particular story or movie. The whole hard-boiled world of the detective—hard-edged sex and violence—for me is summed up completely by Mickey Spillane, just by the word Spillane.

STRICKLAND: The way John Lennon once said another name for rock'n'roll could be "Chuck Berry." Your record starts out [*laughs*] pretty unusually with a bloodcurdling scream.

ZORN: That's Carol Emanuel, the harp player. She does a lot of the screams.

STRICKLAND: Do the exaggerated sexist and violent elements in Spillane put you off, or are you treating them as camp?

ZORN: I'm dealing with it just as part of his world. It's part of the sleazy, dirty world the hard-boiled detective lives in and works in. It's just something that I dealt with because it's in the territory. It isn't anything that particularly bothers me. This is a dream world that this man has invented. It's more about sex to me than it is about sexism.

STRICKLAND: What made you decide to compose around the Spillane theme?

ZORN: I really don't know where it came from except New York. Like you, I was born and went to school in Manhattan and lived in Queens. From kindergarten I went to the UN school and had friends from all over the world. I suppose I can trace my connection to Japan back to that—I had a lot of Japanese friends then, and I live about half the year in Japan now. Anyway, Spillane was part of the New York experience, like being attracted to *film noir* as a teenager. I'm not much of a sleazeball, not much of a late-nighter. I don't go to bars, I don't drink or do drugs— but there's something about the mystique of the lone detective and his world that I've always been attracted to.

STRICKLAND: The detective has been called a contemporary version of the Medieval knight.

ZORN: I was just going to say the Japanese samurai, who's another example of that and part of another genre I was attracted to as a kid.

STRICKLAND: I can see a clear connection between the title work on *Spillane* and your earlier work, even the game pieces on Parachute, like *Archery* or *Pool.*

ZORN: That's nice to hear. I see the connection with the later works like the Godard piece and the Weill piece. I'm thinking specifically of the way I worked with my musicians in the studio, exploiting all their possibilities.

STRICKLAND: You're best known for musical structure involving a lot of juxtaposition, discontinuity. It's almost to me a dismemberment stylistically—you could call it a sparagmatic style, going back to the tearing apart of Dionysus. For example, in *Cobra* on Hat Art, you're listening to someone wail on the sax for a minute and then—

ZORN: Or ten seconds [*both laugh*].

STRICKLAND: And then ten seconds later you're listening to rock or Wagner. In Spillane you've got longer sections, but still the movement from strip-club music to country-and-western to blues, etc. So I was wondering if the picaresque style of the detective novel influenced your decision to work on this.

ZORN: That's the way I work, period. You can trace it back not only to *Archery* and *Pool* but to my very earliest compositional attempts when I was thirteen or fourteen, studying at school and with a tutor. The biggest influences I had were Stravinsky, who worked in block form; Ives, who also was interested in weird juxtapositions and discontinuity in a certain way; and what came off the tube, which I was brought up on. As a *baby* I was watching—to keep me quiet my mother used to put me in a basket in front of the tube.

STRICKLAND: Little did she know what would transpire.

ZORN: Her fault! Completely! Also just the crazy speeded-out world we're living in—and New York is a crazy mix of a place.

STRICKLAND: One would assume listening to your music that you'd be a hypertense, archetypal New Yorker, speeding away, zipping away.

ZORN: I *was* a hypertense person. I grew up! I think I'm an archetypal New Yorker. I was always kind of hyper . . . I was [*laughs*] a real asshole!

STRICKLAND: That's the archetypal New Yorker.

ZORN: Hey, your body gets old. I'm getting old, man. I can't keep up on that kind of level, but inside—I may look relaxed on the outside, but inside I'm still going at that rate. Everyone has a different metabolism. I eat as much as I want, really stuff myself, and never gain a pound. I've been 135 for I don't know how many years. The archetypal New Yorker has that kind of speed.

STRICKLAND: You compose the music. I have to describe it, which might be the tough job.

ZORN: Describing it *is* difficult. It's a music that draws on rock elements, blues elements, classical elements, ethnic folk elements, and the music is put together, as you say, in a very—"picaresque" is an interesting word—I would use maybe "filmic" way, montage. It's made of separate moments that I compose completely regardless of the next, and then I pull them, cull them together. It's put together in a style that causes questions to be asked rather than answered. It's not the kind of music you can just put on and then have a party. It demands your attention. You sit down and listen to it or you just don't even put it on. So it's put together in blocks and moves from one thing to the other really quickly and draws upon many elements or traditions.

STRICKLAND: You once compared your music to walking down the street in New York. I can tell you honestly that before I read that I once described your work to someone as like being in a New York subway station: the same diversity of different influences you suggested, but also there's a lot of mechanical sound in your music, as if the train pulls in once in a while. In the station you've got all these different types of musicians playing jazz sax or classical violins or Peruvian flutes. Part of the mix there is that you're blending a lot of [*makes quotation marks with fingers*] "high art" and "low art."

ZORN: This is something I really react strongly against, the idea of high art and low art. I mean, that distinction's a bunch of fucking *bull*shit. That's the kind of thing created to make it look like you listen to classical music while you're sipping champagne and with rock music you're boogeying with a bottle of beer and jazz you're in some dirty club with a shot of whiskey or some shit like that. That's a fucking bunch of *bullshit!* There's good music and great music and phoney music in every genre and all the genres are the fucking *same!* Classical music is no better than blues because this guy went to school and got a degree and studied very cleanly while the other guy was out on the street *living* it. This is the attitude I've been fighting against.

People who grew up in the '60s listening to blues, rock, classical, avant-garde, ethnic music—I think we all share one common belief, that all this music is on equal grounds and there's no high art and low art. Pop music has musicians creating lasting works of art and also schlock that's going to be thrown away the next day. And the same thing in the classical world—there's an incredible amount of bullshit being written.

STRICKLAND: Like what?

ZORN: I don't want to get into [*sing-song*] *name*-call-ing . . .

STRICKLAND: The average classical music fan will buy the next Bach Orchestral Suites recording that comes out to see if it's better than the dozen he's already got before trying something new. Now in the second work on *Spillane*, I thought you were doing a suite, but a blues suite.

ZORN: That's what it is.

STRICKLAND: Is it classical music?

ZORN: My study, my life, the world I dealt with, the traditions I felt connected to, my heroes Harry Partch, Steve Reich, Ives, Stravinsky, Varèse—all these people I see as a line and I see myself at the end of that line. But people of our generation have been exposed to more music than any other in the history of the world because of the recording boom. As a kid I listened to my father's jazz 78s, blues, pop and rock on the radio—I was really into surf music—and at eighteen or nineteen I started studying jazz saxophone. *All* of these musics made me who I am. Today you're able to buy music from all over the world at the first record store you see. This is the music that results. In a sense my music is rootless since I draw from all these traditions; I don't hold to any one camp.

Cinema's a younger and less jaded genre, so Scorsese can make *Taxi Driver* one year and a comedy or documentary the next and no one says, "Hey! this isn't a Scorsese film—he's supposed to make . . . " They don't say he's a comedy-film maker or a horror-film maker, they just say he's a film maker. The new generation of music makers works similarly, drawing upon different genres in works that sometimes have a little more orientation towards classical—like when I write for Kronos—or jazz or blues, like "Two-Lane Highway." What makes composers interesting and individual to me is not *what* they've got but *how* they deal with it.

STRICKLAND: Okay. No one ever heard of you. No one ever heard of Albert Collins or anyone else. They pick up the record and play it. Do they say, "Oh, it's a good blues record" or "Oh, it's a good classical record" or just "What's goin' on here?"

ZORN: They'd say, "Hey, what's goin' on?" with every piece on the record. That's the point.

STRICKLAND: I heard the different rhythms in "Two-Lane Highway" almost as a Baroque suite—here's the allemande, now the courante . . .

ZORN: I don't use classical models, I try to create new forms. "Spillane" is a new form, though connected to Strauss tone poems.

STRICKLAND: So what distinguishes your treatment of Albert Collins from standard blues?

ZORN: First of all, as you said, it's a suite, one which explores many different places, not as quickly as "Spillane" because Albert needs more time to stretch out—so I'm not going to give him just eight bars of blues and then take him somewhere else. The compositional arc is the first thing I put down, the arrangement of five areas he plays great and five he's never dealt with before, such as playing a duet with another guitarist, or in an organ trio, or over an E-minor drone with a kind of Morricone riff-oriented bass line. I created a compositional flow unlike the normal blues structure.

Some of the younger black musicians on the session were upset and reacted by saying that I was ripping off the blues, that I was a cultural imperialist—this whole aggressive, militant stance that really intimidated me and depressed me. Albert did not feel that way, his managers did not feel that way, and I thought I was using my experience of the blues in my own way. I thought I was giving the blues a different structural basis. For me structure is what it's about. I created a very different structure for Albert to stretch out on.

STRICKLAND: How much of the piece is notated?

ZORN: This is the kind of music that's best not written down on paper, so I left a lot of room for improvisation. But the arc of the piece, the structure of the piece was written out. I knew *exactly* where the piece was going.

STRICKLAND: Chords? Keys?

ZORN: I wanted to use classic blues chord sequences, twelve-bar blues. Key sequences I had decided. I knew what bass lines and rhythms I wanted. I put stuff on tape and played it to the musicians. In "Spillane" there was written music, but a lot of it isn't notated in any conventional sense, because we're dealing with musicians that improvise, work in a personal language that defies notation from the word go. If you write it down you're taking something away from that spark. They don't want to sit there looking at a page. I explained what I wanted and ultimately I think Albert and the other musicians felt more comfortable that way, because everyone was on an equal level.

STRICKLAND: The final work on *Spillane* is "Forbidden Fruit." I'd heard last summer you were doing a string quartet based on the Fallingwater home designed by Frank Lloyd Wright. Did that become "Forbidden Fruit"?

ZORN: Yes, in a certain sense. I was interested in the idea of translating architecture into music. Like Xenakis's drawing upon ideas from Le Corbusier. The Fallingwater building was approaching its fiftieth anniversary. It's a beautiful building. I wanted to do a piece that was more pristine, that didn't have the greasiness of "Spillane" or the hot live quality of the Collins piece, something that dealt with the classical world, which of course is very dear to me—as is the blues world—in a very adventurous way.

I began to write the piece for Kronos, Christian Marclay on turntable, and the Japanese vocalist Ohta Hiromi, who was there in connection with Frank Lloyd Wright's obsession with the Far East. So I worked on the piece, and worked and worked and worked, and for one reason or another it just wasn't going the way I had hoped. I didn't think I really could do justice to the building. The connections weren't as concrete as in "Spillane," where a car crashes and I could say, "This is the car crash," and anyone can say, "Yeah!" Here I was dealing with a room in a building, and I'd say to someone, "This music is that room in that building," and they'd go, "*What* the *fuck* are you talking about?!" It was just too oblique somehow, and I couldn't justify it to myself. So I chucked the idea and decided I would do a series of variations, just pure music, and maybe that could be the most pristine thing I could do, the way Schoenberg would write a string or wind quintet.

So I began working on that. Halfway through, one of my heroes, Ishihara Yujiro, the Japanese film star, died. It was really a shock. These are all [*gestures to several shelves of tapes*] Japanese video tapes, and I must have about twenty of his films. I wanted to create a tribute piece for the forthcoming record, so I began to revise the set of variations I had written to include a further set of variations on the first film he had made, which could be translated as "Fruits Gone Wild"—a very sexual connotation. "Forbidden Fruit" had that sexual connotation in English, though it's not a literal translation.

What I had was a set of maybe twelve musical themes—all the players staccato, all the players performing glissandos, or *col legno*—twelve themes and twelve variations on those themes, which is what I would call harmonic counterpoint, where each of the four musicians is given a different theme to play. First violin plays glissandos, second plays pizzicato, viola plays maybe *col legno*, and the cellist improvises. I worked out twelve different combinations of variants on those twelve themes that combine them harmonically so that they're working simultaneously. Then I added twelve scenes from the movie and orchestrated them as if I was writing the music for the sound track.

Then there are twelve tributes to quartet composers—a tribute to Bartók, Elliott Carter, Beethoven . . . and there are twelve sections that I completely notated in my own style. So there are the themes, the variations on the themes, the movie stills, the written music, the tributes, which kind of work with the written music, and the improvisations with Christian Marclay.

STRICKLAND: One interesting element in your work is the use of quotation, Mozart, for example, in "Forbidden Fruit."

ZORN: It's an arrangement of a C-minor Mozart piano sonata [*both sing opening*]. I wouldn't have used one of his string quartets—that's too much.

STRICKLAND: How'd you like working with Kronos, who don't come out of an improvisational tradition?

ZORN: They were very excited with the way I was working. It was very hard to get them together, but when we finally figured out logistically the three days we could go into the studio it was great. It took exactly three days, we were right on schedule. It wasn't like "Oh, I can't improvise." I gave them a situation that I knew they could deal with—it couldn't go wrong. It was like a fail-safe system. Maybe if I gave them a one-minute improvisation, that would be too much for them at this point, so each section was three to six seconds long. I'd say, "Go and improvise with Christian on turntable. Go and do whatever the hell you want. I don't care what it is." They'd say, "How long do you want us to do it?" "Six seconds." They'd go, "Oh! Well . . . okay! We can do that!"

I also had written sections where they played incredibly well. The kind of precision they deal with was a whole new level. I'm a perfectionist, but these guys were ridiculous! They'd do a take and it'd sound great to me. "Okay! That was *it!*" I'd see them all nodding their heads. I'd say, "Okay, great, great!" And then I'd click on to what they were saying. It'd be "Yeah, I fucked that up really bad." "Sounds great to me!" "No, we gotta do it again. That G-flat was a *lit*-tle sharp." It was incredible.

STRICKLAND [*laughing*]: And their public image is so devil-may-care.

ZORN: Man, they're precise! They're a composer's *dream.* They're gonna play the shit out of your music, no matter *who* you are. They're gonna figure out what you're all about and *play* it and do it right. They're amazing.

STRICKLAND: How many splices are there in those ten minutes? Or is the figure too astronomical to estimate?

ZORN: There are *no* tape splices! I never work with tape splices. Even with "Spillane" there are no splices. And this is the reason for my success in this area. People have done tape work for years. There are *no* interesting tape pieces, period—because they're always using tape splices and the ear gets tired of that. It's too sharp a change.

STRICKLAND: You admire Steve Reich. What about his early tape pieces?

ZORN: Well, yeah, they're wonderful pieces. He's a great, great musician. But what I do is done live in the studio. We'll rehearse the first six-second segment, put it on tape, roll the tape back to the top, rehearse the next section, then roll the tape again and get ready for section two while we listen to section one. As soon as section one is over I give the cue, they come in with the next section and we punch it in. We have A and B tracks. This way there's always a slight overhang, slight decay—as A is fading out B is already in there. There's a kind of organic glue, as if the sections were growing one out of the other instead of chopped up and pasted together. At the end of one day of work usually I have about three minutes of music.

STRICKLAND: After eight hours of work?

ZORN: After ten hours. We complete three minutes of music—but "complete" is exactly the right word, it's complete. Everything, the echo, the EQ—everything is done right then. Now we can go on! It's like through-composing a piece of music.

STRICKLAND: To rephrase the earlier question then, how many fragments are there in the ten minutes and twenty seconds of "Forbidden Fruit"?

ZORN: "Fragments" is a better word. There are sixty, one per section.

STRICKLAND: Getting back to quotation, what's the function of the "Für Elise" in "The Big Gundown" or the Wagner in *Cobra?* There's a comic element there.

ZORN: It's not comic at all. In many way Ives used quotations to comic effect, but you're really dealing with emotion. Like signposts. "Für Elise" to me is not comic at all. It's nostalgic, a very tender moment.

STRICKLAND: I was thinking more of the Wagner in *Cobra.*

ZORN: *That's* hilarious!

STRICKLAND: What's the point of using Wagner hilariously?

ZORN: It's just another tool. It's something that's out there, part of the world that's out there. I didn't say, "Use Wagner." Christian Marclay wanted to use it. Everything he does is quotations because his instrument is the turntable and he's using records as his material.

STRICKLAND: Is it a way of deflating the pomposity of Wagner by transposing it to an alien context?

ZORN: No, I'm not interested in anything like that. That particular piece was chosen by Christian right then. He wanted to use it, he used it. I had nothing to say about it. In *Cobra* the musical materials are completely up to the performers. I have nothing to say about it. I make no musical decisions. I set the situation up, I set the rules up. *They* make the decisions.

Getting back to "Für Elise," it was used by Morricone in the original sound track. He plays with it, makes variations on it. Why did he use it? Go ask *him!* The *Route 66* theme in "Spillane" I used as a kind of icon of the detective world.

STRICKLAND: What's your compositional process like? It seems programmatic, but in a very unusual way.

ZORN: I write every day, fragments. [*Takes out notebook and indicates several notations, all short musical phrases.*] Sometimes I'll put, like here, "nostalgic" or "mysterious . . . romance . . . tension." But when I create a piece, [*takes out inch-thick pack of flashcards*] I work visually. I write things down on cards. This is a new piece I'm working on about China [*reading from cards*]: "Legend of the Mountain . . . Chinese drums and flutes . . . thunder . . . rain and thunder . . . balladeer pipa in the castle . . . cat transformation . . . birds in the trees." And sometimes I'll write down [*reads*] "high strings," blah blah blah. Each section relates very specifically to a theme. I'm using a visual kind of node to inspire me because I was brought up on TV and love movie sound tracks. So in "Spillane," as you suggested, each section relates to an adventure in the picaresque detective novel: he goes to a strip joint to relax or goes to a country and western bar and gets the shit beat out of him.

STRICKLAND: Actually, I thought your distillation of the detective novel was a lot better than any of the Spillane books [*Zorn gives long high shriek and smiles*], which I liked best when I was twelve looking for the dirty parts by the rack at Woolworth's.

ZORN: Yeah, yeah, yeah! The dirty parts, yeah! Actually, though, it was a distillation of *all* the books. Those scenes are in almost every one of his books. It's the epitome of the hard-boiled detective world. And the ending is the apocalyptic ending of every one of his books.

STRICKLAND: You've got that great rain section at the end, which of all your work might be the most—maybe tender isn't the word . . .

ZORN: Tender's the word. I cry when I hear that section. That section is about Mike Hammer done with whatever he's done, killed whoever he's killed, lied wherever he's lied. Now he's alone again walking down the street in the rain smoking a cigarette with his trench coat on, walking away from the camera into oblivion. It's in every Western . . . it's the archetype, and ultimately if you can get to the archetype you can't lose.

STRICKLAND: It's not just tender, like a lyrical piano piece. It's also menacing. It's in a minor key, right?

ZORN: Yes. Most of the things that I write are in minor keys. I hear minor. But Wayne Horvitz told me it's because I write on this little Casio and on a Casio minor chords sound good [*plays*] but major [*raises the third*] sound like shit! I need a good keyboard, there's no doubt about it.

STRICKLAND: Other examples of the odd kind of programmatic work you do is the game pieces. Along with *Spillane* or spaghetti Westerns you've got records called *Lacrosse, Pool, Archery*, and *Cobra*, all based on game structures. Now I don't know these games too well. What's the relationship between the sport archery and the composition?

ZORN: There's no relationship specifically. The pieces have game structures but not those of the games in the titles. I tried to pick games that had names that had another meaning. Architectural archery, a pool of water, a snake. The connection between the game pieces and the later works which are more composed is what I'm doing with the musicians physically. I'm setting them up in situations where they can produce a certain kind of fast-moving structure—that's my sound, that's what I live for. I'm really trying to milk something new out of them and that's what all improvising musicians want—to play their best, play something they haven't done before. The live concert is not a record, it's a game, a play of personalities. It's not just music, it's an event. Sports, I think, is the same way. You don't want to put the World Series on video tape and then watch it over and over again. You know what the outcome will be. Although some people do that.

STRICKLAND: I've watched a video tape of the Mets' final inning in the sixth game of the '86 Series at least twenty times.

ZORN: But how many other games do you watch?

STRICKLAND: Very few and only sections, never a whole game.

ZORN: Live is what it's about in sports or improvised music. Maybe there's one or two or three improvised concerts a year that you can put on tape and watch. They shouldn't be put on tape. Looking back on the records I've made, I don't feel I made a mistake. I'm happy with what I've done, but these situations weren't made for record—you had to *be* there!

STRICKLAND: *Corbra* is by far my favorite of the game-composition discs, though I'm not sure if I can separate the music from the cover, which is one of the greatest ever.

ZORN: Kiriko Kubo, the designer, is incredible. I'm glad you like it.

STRICKLAND: In *Cobra* we've got a studio version on Disc One and a concert version on Disc Two. But again we're not talking about two different versions of the *Concerto for Orchestra* or even a jazz standard. You agree that we could call *Pool* "Archery" and *Archery* "Lacrosse" or *Lacrosse* "Cobra" or whatever. But is there any continuity in the two versions of *Cobra*? Could we call the concert *Cobra* "Pool" or "Archery" or "Lacrosse"?

ZORN: The piece stays the same in concert as in the studio.

STRICKLAND: How?

ZORN: Because the rules are the same.

STRICKLAND: What are the rules?

ZORN: Wow! If I was to go into that, man, we'd be here all day. To put it as simply as I can, there's a set of eighteen cards, each card standing for a different set of relationships among the players. When I give downbeat number one, which I call Pool downbeat, it means, "People who are playing, stop. People who are not playing may come in if they wish." The Runner downbeat means, "Only people I point to can come in. Everyone else, stop."

STRICKLAND: Come in playing what?

ZORN: Whatever the hell they want! I don't talk about information. Content is left to the performer. So I have a whole series of different relationships, like trading games—when the card comes down you can do duos with whoever you want, etc. The cards act as dividers to set the improvisations up into little sections, so that it works the way "Spillane" works, in blocks. But what happens in those blocks is completely up to them. How those blocks are ordered is completely up to them. *I* don't make decisions, saying, "Now it's this, now it's that." The musicians make signs to me telling me what they want to happen and I just act as an intercom device.

STRICKLAND: What kinds of signs?

ZORN [*touching index and middle finger to nose*]: "Nose Two." On the score the section that says "Nose Two" is "Pool," for example.

STRICKLAND: "That's the game I want to play right now. Give me a chance."

ZORN: Right. I hold up a sign that says "Nose Two" and give a downbeat and everybody plays Nose Two. Then someone looks at me and gives "Ear One." I hold up a card that says "Ear One"—everybody knows what that means, so we play Ear One.

STRICKLAND: Nose Two or Ear One have no thematic content. They're just structures—I play and Joe plays but Sally and Jim don't play?

ZORN: This is going to be very complicated. Is this very important for your article, to talk about this?

STRICKLAND: I would just like to get some idea—all the articles talk about your games but never explain anything. I think it's important so we know what you're doing.

ZORN [*takes out score of* Cobra; *in one column there is a series of cues, Ear One to Four, etc., beside each one the name of a game structure*]: I'm interested in working in blocks, but the problem is I have a dozen improvising musicians, each of whom has his or her own style. They don't want to be told what to do, they want to play their fucking *music*. But at the same time I've got to create a structure that makes it my music as well. So I don't tell people *what* to play but create a structure that tells them *when* they play.

STRICKLAND: I understand that, but I don't get the distinction between Ear One and Nose Two.

ZORN: Ear, Eye, Nose, Head are just ways of making cues.

STRICKLAND: Right. So what happens if I cue you [*puts index finger below eye*] that I want Eye One?

ZORN: When you want Eye One [*moves finger from left column to right*], you want "Cartoon Trades." Then I hold up the sign that says "Cartoon Trades."

STRICKLAND: Aha, good! The sign says the name of the game, not "Eye One." Now is there any relationship between "Cartoon Trades" and cartoons, which you've mentioned as another big influence?

ZORN: No. "Cartoon Trades" just means one player plays one sound and passes it to another player.

STRICKLAND: I go doo doo doo doo and the next guy goes ding ding ding ding.

ZORN: And the next guy goes dat da dat da dat and the next goes Whaaaaang!! and the next goes Boom! And this structure continues until the next downbeat, so no one can sneak in. Except then we start talking about the Guerrilla Systems [*indicates another pair of columns on the right side of the page with graphic symbols (squiggles etc., indicating hand gestures) and corresponding game-structure notations*]. These are ways of fucking up the structure. Then people can sneak in a downbeat, people can become guerrillas and have squads, get people to imitate them, capture people, switch them . . . so it really becomes a game that's fun to play. It creates real excitement onstage. The musicians are into it. They want to create a situation where they can be in control, where they're the guerrilla leader with their squad telling this guy to stop and this guy to play.

STRICKLAND: So it might be the saxophonist and I temporarily against the tuba player and the electric guitarist. That clarifies it.

ZORN: And each piece has a different set of rules. Similar elements may crop up but the situations will be very different.

STRICKLAND: So now you've temporarily given up all the games.

ZORN: No, only the game titles. I still use the game structure, but the most recent piece is called *Hsu Feng*.

STRICKLAND: What does *Hsu Feng* mean?

ZORN: It's the name of a woman. That woman. It's the name of a Chinese actress. [*Points to several photos of her around the room.*] I'm still doing the games but now I'm not calling them sports but Chinese actresses. *You* figure it out! [*Both laugh.*]

STRICKLAND: When I heard you play Ornette Coleman in October you had *Hsu Feng* advertised in the papers.

ZORN: It just wasn't ready. If it'd been five years ago I would've done it anyway. "Not ready? No problem!" [*Laughs.*] Now I have to be a little more careful. Now if a piece isn't perfect I'm just not going to do it, because it's very delicate. For example, if I have the players chosen and one guy says he can't do it, if the chemistry isn't right, I won't go ahead. Ten years ago, "Sure, go ahead, push, keep going!" Now I feel I'll just do one or two a year.

STRICKLAND: You ended up playing Ornette in a quintet introduced as WRU.

ZORN: It's from a series of Ornette compositions in the early '60s based on works of Freud. *T&T* was *Totem and Taboo*. I forget what *WRU* meant. [*Note:* Der Witz und seine Beziehung zum Unbewussten, *translated as* Wit and Its (*or more commonly* Jokes and Their) Relationship to the Unconscious. *The band was renamed Spy vs. Spy after the* Mad *magazine comic strip.*]

STRICKLAND: When did you start playing alto?

ZORN: When I was about twenty. I started playing piano when I was about nine or so, playing by ear. I took guitar lessons when I was about eleven, playing Beatles shit. When I got to be fourteen I knew I wanted to be a composer and started taking composition classes.

STRICKLAND: Your records are as likely to be found in the jazz as in the classical section. There's also a strong rock influence in your work. Did you ever play in rock groups?

ZORN: Not really. I began working in that style when I became friends with people like Arto Lindsay, Anton Fier, Bill Laswell, people who were dealing in that world. Because I liked them and their music very much I became attracted to that world and realized I'd hear a lot of great musicians there. I became open to using them in my music as well, and they began asking me to play in their music, and that's how the work with the

Golden Palominos and Bill Laswell's group happened. It became a real conversation between the two worlds.

STRICKLAND: I thought Arto Lindsay's texts for "Spillane" were terrific.

ZORN: He did a great job.

STRICKLAND: In the past couple of years you've gotten a lot more acceptance. Earlier you drew some colorful but not always flattering critical comments. How did you feel as a composer when your music was described as, what was it, a rhinoceros caught in barbed wire?

ZORN [*laughing*]: Oh, you remember that one! It was an elephant—no a *constipated* elephant caught in barbed wire. Or "a horde of army ants gone duck hunting." [*Both laugh.*] I think it's great. I've got a copy of Slonimsky's *Lexicon of Musical Invective*. It's one of my main sources of inspiration, and through those years if I didn't have that book I probably would have really been depressed. But critics have their job, they do their job. It's not easy music, it takes time. It took ten years and I'm very happy that I kind of did it the hard way. I went through a lot of bullshit to get here and paid my dues. Even the ones who said it was just boring crap, the same old jam session of special effects, were dealing with it the best way they could, which was completely lame. I know it's not boring crap [*laughs*]. I know it hasn't existed before and they just don't know what the hell they're talking about.

STRICKLAND: Talking about the army ants gone duck hunting, in the early and mid-'80s you used a lot of very weird duck calls and bird calls as instruments [*laughs*]. Wasn't an attempt to get back to nature?

ZORN: No, I just wanted some kind of raucous, ugly sound.

STRICKLAND: You used the adjective "ugly," and I wonder if in fact some of your music isn't just that. You're often imaginative enough to incorporate these sounds into a context that's esthetically satisfying, but if you played a section of those calls *out* of context, I'd say, "Come on, put on another record!"

ZORN: I don't think they're ugly. I find them beautiful. It's like Thelonious Monk's title "Ugly Beauty." People used to think his playing was ugly; now it's recognized as classic.

STRICKLAND: You left New York for a year and a half, coming back in '74.

ZORN: I was studying at Webster College in St. Louis, and it was exactly what I needed to do at that time. I needed to be exposed to the black jazz scene in Chicago, AACM, and BAG in St. Louis: Anthony Braxton, Leo Smith. BAG was mixing improvisation with set structures in a very interesting way then.

STRICKLAND: So that made the trip West, or Midwest, worthwhile. How did you find the New York scene when you came back?

ZORN: I dropped out of Webster in '74 and went to the West Coast and played and met people like Phillip Johnston, who works with the Microscopic Sextet. Then I came back to New York in late '74, went back to the West Coast, and came back here in '75. I was performing in my little apartment on Lafayette Street, meeting musicians one by one. The downtown improvising scene didn't exist at that time. I met all the musicians I work with one by one over the years, and they all helped me grow as a musician.

STRICKLAND: What else was going on then that attracted you?

ZORN: Hmmmmmmmmmmmmmm . . .

STRICKLAND: The Minimalists were strong downtown, and virtually *only* downtown.

ZORN: That was very big, the SoHo scene. Glass was performing in galleries, La Monte Young, Reich. They were really inspiring to me. They were doing something diferent and showing the classical world that you didn't have to write music for the usual ensembles. You could create a band and travel like a rock group the way Philip Glass did, and it was still classical music. Reich was drawing upon influences from Africa after having studied there, which was very inspiring to me. They were also working in a collaborative way with their groups. They'd bring music in and if it didn't feel right on the saxophone [Jon] Gibson would say, "Can I make this into a such and such pattern instead?" "Yeah, go ahead, do it!"

The jazz music scene was beginning to get some new blood at that time. Henry Threadgill was working with Air, and he's someone I admire very much as a composer. The punk thing at CB's was very exciting.

STRICKLAND: You've mentioned a few already, but what other contemporary composers do you particularly admire?

ZORN: I think John Adams's sense of orchestration is brilliant. Orchestration is something I pride myself on. I always had a particular talent for it and I love it. For me it's a matter of mixing electric and acoustic instruments. John Adams can deal in the traditional world and create a new sound. I think it's beautiful what he's doing. I like the way Steve Reich's compositions move, but I think there's a real danger in giving fast sixteenth-note patterns that are meant for mallet instruments to winds and strings. It can turn to mush very easily, and there's a real danger in that, but I think he's done a lot of really great music. More than Glass, whose orchestrations just suck the bird, forget it. I like the young composer Aaron Kernis. He's a great, great talent. Scott Lindroth, Henry Threadgill . . . Wayne Horvitz and Elliott Sharp are doing really interesting things. Yuji Takahashi's great.

STRICKLAND: What are your recording plans for Nonesuch?

ZORN: The Ornette band is recording a record in April for release in September. I want to do a romantic piece next, called "Live and Let Live," which should be out early next year. I have a list [*takes folder from shelf*] of people I want to work with, but I haven't contacted anybody yet: a Chinese pipa player who's living here in New York, Nana Vasconcelos, Robert Quine, some rock people like the bassist from Live Skull, Hüsker Dü, Prince, Gidon Kremer, Tom Waits. I'm working on a hobo piece as a tribute to Harry Partch, and I hope Tom Waits will be interested.

STRICKLAND: Have you thought of doing any orchestral work?

ZORN: The Brooklyn Philharmonic called me up and want me to write something for next year. I'm going to write a chamber piece. No improvisation, entirely notated. Every note—because that world is not *about* improvisation. I'm not interested, like Cage, in giving a symphony orchestra a bunch of little pictures from Thoreau and seeing what they come up with. I'm interested in getting the best out of these players and inspiring them, which means finding out who loves to play virtuosic music and who doesn't and writing specifically for that group.

STRICKLAND: One last thing I want to ask you about is the genesis of the opening section of "The Big Gundown." It's mentioned by Robert Polito briefly in his notes to your first Nonesuch album, and the story of its coming to you in a dream intrigued me since I write about Romantic poetry and it recalled Coleridge's experience in "Kubla Khan."

ZORN: Coleridge, yeah! I normally can't remember my dreams too well, and I don't otherwise have that kind of musical dream as far as I can recall. My dreams are very filmic. It's almost as if I'm watching myself in a movie. I see different shots and angles. Often very weird architectural structures—I'll go into a building and it'll be a maze or a giant cube. Very large and complex structures. I think that's from my interest in musical structure. I woke up from the dream you mentioned drenched in sweat, remembering each image very vividly, like cockroaches crawling on my body. It was a horrible nightmare, but there was music accompanying each separate image. I don't exactly know where that dream came from.

STRICKLAND: And you incorporated all that music into the opening of the title cut on *The Big Gundown*.

ZORN: It was the first five minutes until the Brazilian percussion comes in.

STRICKLAND: This is fascinating, and I hate to invade your private—

ZORN: It's not private at all! [*Laughs.*] I just wish I could remember it all. Being in the middle of the desert completely parched. There was a scene flying in the air and seeing the moon really close. It was a wild dream, man. If I listened to the piece I'd probably remember [*laughing*] all the different images, but I don't think I *want* to remember some of those images!

Photo by Steve Prezant, © 1989 CBS Records Inc.

Philip Glass has been as successful in extending the audience for classical music as in his stylistic innovation in works ranging from the miniature to the mammoth and from the frenetically rhythmic to the lyrically demure. Born in Baltimore in 1937, he took up violin at six and began flute studies at the Peabody Conservatory at eight. After studying philosophy and mathematics at the University of Chicago, Glass studied composition at Juilliard and had many of his works performed and several published. After graduation he went to Paris for what became a musical re-education with Nadia Boulanger. Hired by director Conrad Rooks to notate Ravi Shankar's *Chappaqua* film score for Western musicians, Glass encountered in the additive process and cyclic structure of Indian music major influences on his mature style. These are apparent in the music he composed in 1965 for a performance of Samuel Beckett's *Play* and in his 1966 *String Quartet*, neither of which has been recorded to date.

Returning to New York in 1967, Glass joined in what he described as a "generational search" in the downtown Manhattan music scene. He composed prolifically and performed with the Mabou Mines Theater and musicians who in 1969 became the Philip Glass Ensemble. Glass recorded for his own label, Chatham Square Records, and supported himself by working as a cab driver, plumber, mover, and studio assistant to sculptor Richard Serra. Through the late '60s Glass's works represent an often engaging but relatively simplistic form of Minimalism as the composer experimented with radically bare-boned harmonic and contrapuntal structures in works like *Music in Fifths* and *Music in Contrary Motion*. In 1971 he began the work which culminated his period of extended *études*, the four-hour compendium of rhythmic experiments entitled *Music in Twelve Parts*. Glass performed it at Town Hall in 1974, in his first uptown concert, leading his ensemble from the Farfisa keyboard as usual.

Glass came to broader notice with the 1976 Metropolitan Opera production of his futuristic collaboration with director Robert Wilson, *Einstein on the Beach*. It exposed the conservative operatic audience to the Minimalist style while attracting a younger crowd to the Met's sacred portals for the first time. The work proved a popular and critical success, and the authors were invited to stage a third performance. The economics of production, however, were such that, even if it sold out, as the first two performances had, a third one would have raised "the Einstein debt," soon a Soho *cause célèbre*, from $90,000 to six figures. In his book *Music by Philip Glass* (New York: Harper and Row, 1987), the composer relates that, ensconced in his cab more firmly than ever after the *Einstein* acclaim, he was advised by a passenger who had noticed his medallion that he had the same name as a famous composer.

Einstein proved to be the first in a trilogy of character-operas, followed in 1980 by *Satyagraha* (dealing with Gandhi's early years in Africa) and in 1983 by *Akhnaten* (dealing with the fifteenth-century B.C. pharoah). The three were staged together in Stuttgart in June 1990 to great acclaim. Glass collaborated with Wilson again in the Rome and Köln sections of *the CIVIL warS* and with Doris Lessing in *The Making of the Representative for Planet 8*. He is currently planning further collaborations with both. In addition, Glass has scored the theater piece *The Photographer* and one of the two acts of the chamber opera *The Juniper Tree*; the films *Mishima, The Thin Blue Line*, and *Mindwalk*; and the first two installments in a projected cinematic trilogy by Godfrey Reggio, *Koyaanisqatsi* and *Powaqqatsi*. He composed the inaugural and valedictory music for the 1984 Olympic Games in Los Angeles; the song cycle *Songs from Liquid Days*, with texts by pop composers Laurie Anderson, David Byrne, Paul Simon (for whose "The Late Great Johnny Ace" he composed an elegiac coda), and Suzanne Vega (for whose "50-50 Chance" he arranged the strings); dance pieces commissioned by choreographers Molissa Fenley, Jerome Robbins, and Twyla Tharp; a violin concerto for Paul Zukofsky; and various other performance works and pianistic miniatures.

Glass's remarkably prolific output has led to sometimes justified charges of superficiality: the double album *Dance 1-5* is best accompanied in the absence of dancers by a Saturday morning vacuum cleaner. On the other hand, Glass elsewhere manages, more successfully than anyone else today, to create a pristine lyricism out of primitive figuration—or in the case of the *Satyagraha* reincarnation area, merely a repeated Phrygian scale. Literary critics as diverse as T. S. Eliot, Jorge Luis Borges, and Harold Bloom note that our experience of a later poet's work changes our experience of his precursors', so that when reading Shelley we may be struck, proleptically, by the way he was "influenced" by Yeats. It is difficult now to hear the opening figures of the Mozart K.595 concerto without momentarily acknowledging the composer's "debt" to Glass's string arpeggiation.

Glass continues to work primarily in theater but still tours widely with his ensemble. Shortly before our interview in April 1988, he was in the headlines for a Metropolitan Opera commission to celebrate the 500th anniversary of the discovery of America. The opera is tentatively entitled *The Voyage*, with the second act focusing on Columbus. In fall 1989 Glass went on a one-month tour playing his solo piano works, including "Witchita Vortex Sutra," an erstwhile accompaniment to the poem by Allen Ginsberg; and in April 1990 he and Ginsberg gave the premier of *The Hydrogen Jukebox* in Philadelphia.

I arrived early at the door of Glass's brownstone, but I was soon greeted by the composer, who crossed the street with face shaded by a borrowed Boston Red Sox cap. We spent the rest of the afternoon talking in his den.

STRICKLAND: Has opera become your life's work?

GLASS: I try to do a lot of other things, without the constraints of the house and so on.

STRICKLAND: What are you working on now?

GLASS: The sequel to *Koyaanisqatsi* is being released this month in New York and Los Angeles. You know, these things are such a gas! If it goes well, it will go into more general release. *Koyaanisqatsi* had a very slow start and ended up being around all the time. Films of this kind don't follow normal distribution expectations. It took five years to get the second part of the trilogy done, and about half that time was spent raising the money.

STRICKLAND: I got an advance of the album and was quite surprised by *Powaqqatsi*, which is in such a different vein. *Koyaanisqatsi* is one of my favorite works of yours.

GLASS: Thank you. The difference was obviously intentional, although things *can* happen accidentally. The music reflects the drastic difference in the two films. *Koyaanisqatsi* was filmed in North America, most of it in Four Corners, where Colorado, Utah, Arizona, and New Mexico meet, and a bit in Los Angeles, San Francisco, and New York; *Powaqqatsi* in South America, Africa, and Asia. In a general way it's a portrait of those parts of the world.

STRICKLAND: Apart from geography, *Koyaanisqatsi* was a quite apocalyptic vision and *Powaqqatsi* seems much more subdued. The apocalypse is a tough act to follow?

GLASS: You might say that. There's another act following this one though, *Naqöyqatsi*, which is as different from the first two as the second was from the first. We've begun working on it. With the first two it was almost the same difference as between *Satyagraha* and *Einstein*, the lyrical opera after the apocalyptic.

STRICKLAND: I thought *Akhnaten* was much more lyrical than *Satyagraha*.

GLASS: More lyrical? I think of it as the tragic opera. I think of them as apocalyptic, lyrical, and tragic in order—but look, don't take that as . . .

STRICKLAND: Is *Powaqqatsi* still dealing with the conflict of technology and nature?

GLASS: It has more to do with the influence of Northern on Southern culture. Godfrey considers the South to represent more traditional ways of living. Most of the planet lives there, actually, and about eighty percent of the world lives in villages. Most of the world is not living the way Americans live. So to that end I traveled with Godfrey and incorporated a lot of indigenous instruments, and that gave the music a much more rhythmic sense—a lot of native percussion. I also used a singer from Egypt and an African kora player.

In May—now this will interest you as an English professor—we have a chamber opera I wrote for twelve instruments and three principal singers based on "The Fall of the House of Usher." Are you interested in Poe?

STRICKLAND: I gave a paper on that story years ago!

GLASS: You'll be very interested then—of course, I hope you would be anyway. Arthur Yorinks and I did it together. Act One treats the very strange relationship between Roderick and Madeline Usher. Act Two is mainly a treatment of the House itself.

STRICKLAND: Critics have suggested that the House is the cause of their disease as well as a reflection of their disorientation.

GLASS: I didn't do a literary study of it, but I'm a literate person and I follow my own instincts as well as knowledge of a lot of Poe's work. I did the music for a stage version of his "A Descent into the Maelstrom" a few years back. My feeling was that Poe's piece was full of forbidden possibilities . . . incest, necrophilia . . . but possibly the most horrifying is one that comes up in the Greek myths, infanticide. When someone commits suicide, their children can survive them; when we kill our parents, the same; but when we kill our children, it's the most complete form of death.

STRICKLAND: Killing the future.

GLASS: The future. Of suicide, patricide, and infanticide, I think infanticide is the most horrible because it's the most final. And the House represents to me the family of Usher.

STRICKLAND: The title's been analyzed as a pun—"the House" being both the family which ends and the physical edifice which collapses.

GLASS: Exactly. For me the House means the lineage of Usher, all the Ushers that ever were, and finally the line ends with the children, and it's the House that kills them. There's music for the House that begins in Act One and seems to be subliminal, unimportant music. In Act Two it suddenly becomes the foreground of the piece.

STRICKLAND: A little bit like the transformation of the flute line in Act One, Scene Two, of *Satyagraha* into the final aria.

GLASS: That's right, going from background to foreground. The other important element is the visitor. We gave him a name, William. It could have been Edgar or any name. His importance is that the only access we have to the piece is through the visitor—without him there's no one to tell the story.

STRICKLAND: But there's always been a question as to his credibility. I interpreted Roderick, Madeline, and the narrator as the triangle of Romantic artist-magician, Muse, and auditor, who's finally taken over by Roderick's own visionary madness.

GLASS: I would also hope that there would be interpretations of our interpretation. For one thing, Madeline never says a word in the story or the opera, but she sings wordlessly, onstage and off. The second act begins with the burial, a wonderful scene. You see, there's a whole thing about Roderick's screwing down Madeline's coffin lid, which is a very significant thing. After all, why do you screw down a coffin lid?

STRICKLAND: That was my question in the paper!

GLASS: Because obviously he murdered her!

STRICKLAND: Exactly!

GLASS: Right! [*Claps hands, jabs interviewer's knee.*] And he suspected that perhaps she might not stay dead—and in fact she comes back to avenge the murder. Now the *reason* he murders her—and we'll see if this agrees with your interpretation—is that—this is a very strange idea, but to me it's emotionally true, and for a theater composer that's what to look for. It doesn't matter—pardon me—if that's what Poe exactly meant.

STRICKLAND: Sure! We don't know what Poe exactly meant anyway [*laughs*].

GLASS: The reason that he murders her is that he realizes the House is going to destroy them and offers his sister as a sacrifice to it. If she dies, perhaps he'll escape. He does it thinking this will stave off the inevitable, his own death. It goes back to the blood-sacrifices of the American Indians.

It's a very primitive idea, that we sacrifice a cow or an animal to save ourselves. In other words, Roderick *betrays* Madeline. Her anger and revenge is at her betrayal more than her murder. But what I do at the very end, which is something Poe couldn't do, is that after the fall of the House the brother-sister music begins to appear again. It's very, very interesting, this whole subject [*laughs*]. That's how I view it.

STRICKLAND: I saw the murder as the attempt of the deranged artist to murder his art, his Muse, to escape his own diseased imagination.

GLASS: That seems absolutely legitimate. My interpretation worked for me because it enabled me to make the House the ultimate culprit.

STRICKLAND: The House as described in the story can also be interpreted as the whole dark-Romantic visionary tradition, Roderick's and Poe's *artistic* family. Anyway, there are dozens of conflicting interpretations.

GLASS: But the great thing about being a composer is that you can write an opera about yours.

STRICKLAND: Beats a conference paper!

GLASS: Well, could be. But my ideas don't strike you as . . . [*sotto voce*] off-key?

STRICKLAND: Not at all.

GLASS: The defect of my interpretation, which I will admit, is that it gives too little room for the witness. An earlier theory I had was that the primary relationship was between the witness and Roderick, a homosexual relationship threatened by Madeline. Roderick, to prevent Madeline running away with the visitor, kills her. But I decided that was too ornate.

STRICKLAND: It does seem kind of baroque.

GLASS: I felt it was not as interesting as what I ended up with.

STRICKLAND: I agree. Sounds a little like Freudian criticism in the '30s.

GLASS: Films have taken that approach. I liked the way the House became a spirit of fierce and motiveless retribution in my later version. Anyway, that premieres on May 18th at the American Repertory Theater in Boston—designed and directed by Richard Foreman—then May 31st at the Kentucky Opera. It'll run about thirty-five performances in Boston. Then on July 7th at the Houston Grand Opera we've got the premiere of *The Making of the Representative for Planet 8*, after which it goes to the English National Opera, then Holland and Germany.

STRICKLAND: That's your first time setting a full-length opera in English.

GLASS: That's right. I was reading Mrs. Lessing's work and decided it was something I wanted to do. This was in about 1984. She was not completely willing to do it at first, but I persuaded her and in the end she became my co-author. We share the credit as co-authors without distinguishing because we worked on it together. That work took three years to finish. It's designed by Eiko Ishioka, who did the *Mishima* sets. The other forthcoming piece is the mixed-media *1000 Airplanes on the Roof,* which is for my ensemble, one actor, and visualizations by Jerry Serlin, who uses projected photography. David Hwang, the Chinese American author of the Broadway play *M. Butterfly*, did the text to an idea of mine. He's a very brilliant writer.

STRICKLAND: You're an awfully busy man. I'm catching you now between Florida and Canada.

GLASS: I do about seventy concerts a year. I keep the ensemble going. I've been lucky in that I've had more or less the same people in the group, so it's been easier for me to keep it together than for some of my friends. I've always had keyboards and wind players. It's been together twenty years and we're able to work in a very personal way. And this year I'll be able to use the ensemble in *1000 Airplanes*. Let me tell you what it's about.

It's a monologue in which the actor describes a series of encounters he has with extraterrestrials—it's about UFO abductions. It grew out of a series of discussions I had with Doris Lessing on the subject of memory. We were talking about our capacity for forgetting. Whole societies just forget tremendous events. I became very interested in this whole social and personal amnesia. She challenged me once and asked, "Do you remember the influenza epidemic of 1919?" I said, "No, what's that?" She said, "That's exactly my point!" Two and a half million people died—more than died in the First World War. I suddenly was completely shocked that we actually forget such things.

We remember the Holocaust of the Second World War only through the greatest effort. It takes a whole religious group to remind us. The twenty million people who died in Russia are *almost* forgotten, and we've already begun to forget the number of people who died during the Cultural Revolution in China. Interested in the subject of memory, I noticed that in my encounters with people and my reading in the area that those who've had these encounters with UFOs have the *greatest* difficulty remembering them. And the greatest problem is not that there have been so many undocumented cases but that there have been so many where the people involved are not willing to talk about it.

STRICKLAND: Have you been concerned with this subject for very long? Have you had this type of experience?

GLASS: Well, most people—you know, I'll tell you another thing, about forty-eight percent of the people I talk to have. An *amazing* number have. But that's not important. What's important is that it becomes the occasion to do a piece about memory, about our inability to remember terrifying experiences. It's about repression, in other words—the way we personally repress things that challenge our notions of order. It's part of the progressive displacement of man in the universe. We start off being the center of the universe with the Sun turning around us. Then it turns out we're going around the Sun. Then it turns out that our solar system is part of a larger galaxy. Then it turns out that our galaxy isn't even a very important one. So with each *stage* of this we seem farther and farther from the main events.

So people have fierce reactions to the subject of UFOs. I was talking with Jerry and David about this and said that the terrible anger that people felt towards those crackpots Galileo and Copernicus and their ideas is very similar to the anger that people feel towards those who claim to have had contacts with extraterrestrials. The challenging of man's position in the universe is one of those things we accept with *great* difficulty.

But the subject has lots of different *foci.* Another has to do with communication. Doris Lessing addresses herself to this in *The Making of the Representative for Planet 8,* and that novel and opera are very much about the relationship of one person to his culture. One of the questions she asks in the opera is "When you dream, do you imagine those dreams are uniquely yours?" In other words, to what extent are our experiences, even our dreams, unique?

STRICKLAND: It's a Jungian question.

GLASS: That may be the *least* of it! What if we take it literally? [*Laughs.*] It's a very interesting question, and in a certain way *1000 Airplanes on the Roof* continues it, using encounters with nonhumans as a pretext.

STRICKLAND: Speaking of forthcoming projects, the news of your commission from the Met to do *The Voyage* made my local paper, which has very minimal—if you'll excuse the word [*Glass laughs*]—classical music coverage.

GLASS: It got to be big news, didn't it? Well . . . [*laughs*] I think it's big news! This will be coming up in '92. You know what it really means? It means a lot of things but . . . this year every opera I've written is being performed somewhere. And this happened without my meaning it to. At a certain point, my agent said, "Do you realize the amount of paperwork we're doing?" and we sat down and counted the works. *Satyagraha's* being done in Seattle, *Akhnaten* in Brazil, *Einstein on the Beach* and *The Juniper Tree* in Germany, *The Fall of the House of Usher* in America, *The Representative* in several countries. The only opera that isn't receiving a full production is *the CIVIL warS,* and that's being partially done as a concert in Bonn. It's really remarkable that this has happened so quickly.

STRICKLAND: Well, you deserve it. You certainly paid your dues.

GLASS [*laughing*]: I did that. About "deserving," it's not for me to say. But the shocking thing is that before 1980, apart from *Einstein,* which Bob Wilson and I produced ourselves, I was never in an opera house! Eight years later I have all these operas being produced and a commission from the Met. It's changed so quickly because obviously the time was right for it. John Adams can write a successful opera like *Nixon in China* now. Anthony Davis's *X* was in my opinion a marvelous, marvelous work, and I think he's a great, great theater talent.

STRICKLAND: Are there other contemporary composers you especially admire?

GLASS: A lot, but I'm going to avoid that question in a way, rather than leave someone out. Two names have already come up in the natural course of our conversation because I'm interested in theater. I'm looking around and seeing in the last decade a movement from people saying "Opera is dead" to realizing not only is opera very much alive but there are producers seeking out and helping to develop these younger talents.

STRICKLAND: Let me ask you a funny question. Have you heard the new TV commercial for Kellogg's Special K?

GLASS: I've heard about it. Someone else mentioned it to me.

STRICKLAND: I happened to hear it for the first time last night and was struck by the coincidence. As I recall it's got pulsing strings alternating chords with some wind punctuation, very much in your style.

GLASS: Generally speaking, these people are fairly clever. By the way, I don't do commercials. This also happens to Laurie Anderson and others. What you're hearing is a what we call a "knockoff" in the business. You can imitate the style but not the content.

STRICKLAND: Steve Reich once said he thought he could sue *Adam Smith's Money World* for its theme music.

GLASS: In the past I've had some discussions with attorneys about this kind of thing. In one case I actually collected. For the film *Breathless* they literally took "Opening" from the *Glassworks* album and used it without permission. They knew what they were doing. They had hired another composer, and he didn't deliver a score on time. I knew the director, and he told me they had a week to come up with a score—so they did what we call "needle-dropping" in the business. They *knew* that I'd be after them. They had a delivery date with the bank and figured it was cheaper to pay the damages to me than either hire another composer or be in default with the bank. They had permission to use a portion of my music and ended up using it as title music, doing it very differently than they had suggested. We collected. I got paid. It wasn't a particularly pleasant experience. Had they asked me to do it I would have said no—I didn't like the movie—so in fact they were right. Of course it was completely immoral, but they knew damn well what they were doing.

Now about the commercial people, the funny thing is that when you confront them they pretend that they're doing you a favor by making you more acceptable. I'm *quite* beyond needing that, however, so it's all rather disingenuous.

STRICKLAND: I'm not trying to be your *consiglieri* against Kellogg's [*Glass laughs*], but I mention this and *Money World* as examples of how this once-weird music has now pervaded society. You mentioned international opera houses, but now we're talking about TV cereal. Glenn Gould said something similar about atonality, that it reached some acceptance through horror or suspense films. You know, someone goes mad and there's an atonal burst or tone cluster.

GLASS: But it kind of stopped there. People *think* of atonality as music from a horror movie now. It never found a wider usage unfortunately—or fortunately, whatever you feel about it. *Our* language as such is no longer shocking. I just came from Florida, where our audiences tend to be ten or fifteen years older than the norm. Older people are coming to our concerts now and they're not so shocked, partly because they've been conditioned.

It's not the way any of us would like to have done it. We can't collect from these people, but the only good thing about it is that the language is no longer *so* esoteric that audiences flee from it or throw things at us as they used to.

STRICKLAND: This leads to my questions on the rumors, possibly legends, about your career. Many see it as an archetypal success story of the struggling pioneer who finally achieves acclaim. First of all, is it true, as critic friends tell me, that people literally used to throw tomatoes at you?

GLASS: No. Actually, it was eggs. [*Interviewer breaks up.*] But really, there's a big difference. Eggs don't hurt. They just kind of mess up your clothes. But tomatoes . . .

STRICKLAND: How long did this go on?

GLASS: The last egg thrown at me, I think, was in 1979. I happen to remember because we were doing *Dance* with Lucinda Childs, and I was standing next to one of the dancers and saw some yellow on his leg and thought one of the gels had fallen off the lights. And the poor boy was totally horrified. No one, evidently, had ever thrown anything at him before. And then I saw a woman in the aisle, hurling these—[*momentarily bemused*] isn't it . . . ?—and some ushers carried her away. There were worse things that people used to throw.

STRICKLAND: Did this happen frequently?

GLASS: It went on. We were always in some danger of that happening. If not, people would scream at us or . . .

STRICKLAND: Why do you think you provoked this extreme reaction? Why would someone go out and buy eggs to take to a concert to throw at you instead of staying home and watching TV?

GLASS: That's a good point. Obviously you don't go to a concert with eggs unless you think you *might* want to throw them. You probably don't just happen to have eggs in your pocket. It was a political statement. There was a political statement to make and someone went there to make it. Recently a friend of mine said to me after a performance of *The Light* at Carnegie Hall, "You've finally reached the status of Callas. People would buy tickets to her concerts just to boo. There are people who came tonight and stayed only for the pleasure of being able to boo at the end of the piece." That was only about three months ago. We don't get eggs anymore.

STRICKLAND: Did all this bother you?

GLASS: No, these are musicosociological questions. I can afford to laugh about it. I can afford to read critics that don't like me and laugh.

STRICKLAND: But how did you feel when you were fifteen or twenty years younger, not so well known but having eggs thrown at you?

GLASS: You know, I never minded the controversy. Never bothered me. I kind of enjoyed it. Recently Virgil Thomson was asked on his birthday, "How does it feel to be 90 years old?" He said, "Well, it beats the alternative." [*Both laugh.*] And when people ask me, "How do you like being controversial?" . . . well, it beats the alternative.

In fact, Maestro Dohnányi, who did *The Light* extremely well with the Cleveland Orchestra, discovered, I think for the first time in a long while, the pleasures of doing a truly controversial work where the audience gets up and some of them scream and some of them cheer. I was with him at a number of these performances, and he was clearly stimulated by it. And that didn't happen when he did a new twelve-tone work by some young German composer and people sat there and snoozed. As I said, consider the alternative.

At this point the records sell well, I've got a commission from the Met—I can hardly feel that my career has been destroyed by critics. It would [*laughing*] not be fair to say that. If anything has happened it's that there's developed a pretty pronounced schism within the critical community itself between the pros and cons, who tend to quarrel with each other.

STRICKLAND: To what extent do you think you've converted the audience, and to what extent is it a matter of refining or developing an initially primitive style over the years? It's a long way from *Music in Fifths* to *Akhnaten*.

GLASS: That's true. The style continues to change. For example, when we sat down you even said to me, "I was very surprised to hear *Powaqqatsi*." And you didn't say you liked it. You said, "I was surprised."

STRICKLAND: To be honest, I don't know if I like it as much as *Koyaanisqatsi*.

GLASS: And I didn't ask you because that's not important. Maybe in a year from now you'll like it more or you'll like it less. [*Note: Less.*] Doesn't matter. The point is that you heard a piece of mine and it's not simply "another Philip Glass piece." And at this point if I said to you, "I'm going to play you a new piece," you could not honestly anticipate what it would sound like. That's an achievement in itself. I think it's partly because as a theater composer I have the great advantage of working with subject matter that to a large extent informs the work. I also work collaboratively, and my collaborators to a large extent inform the work. I change projects, collaborators, medium, scale—so it should be hardly surprising that the work would change also. It's been partly a conscious effort on my part to do that because it interests me.

Anyway, it might be safer for you to wait to see the film of *Powaqqatsi*. It's a little difficult to judge from the record.

STRICKLAND: You've mentioned the native percussion in *Powaqqatsi*, which surprised me, along with the decreased reliance on repetition. The percussion in *Akhnaten* was very effective, I thought. Was it the first time you used it?

GLASS: The first time since about 1963.

STRICKLAND: The funeral of Amenhotep III was quite raucous and sounded a bit like a punkers' sock-hop [*Glass laughs loudly*]. A little B-52s there. Is there also a question of decorum here? Is it too raucous for a funeral?

GLASS: My conception of earlier Egyptian culture was a very militaristic one, and I wanted to represent that character. In addition, the purpose of the funeral music was to alert the gods that Amenhotep III was dead. If you read *The Egyptian Book of the Dead* you discover the great fear of the Egyptians was that the Pharoah would die and be forgotten. The gods wouldn't notice.

STRICKLAND: So the percussion was a way of waking them up.

GLASS: Exactly.

STRICKLAND: Are the contrasting light timbre and rising phrases of the piccolo in that scene meant to represent the Pharoah's soul ascending?

GLASS: It had no special function. In general, though, it was important to make the funeral as odd as it sounds. It's one of the first clues we have that this is going to be an unusual work, when the funeral turns out to be a raucous, drum-rattling march. That gives us a clue that the whole order is going to be changed. So it's a prelude in a way.

STRICKLAND: *Akhnaten* is my favorite work of yours, particularly because the orchestration makes, say, *Satyagraha* look quite pallid by comparison.

GLASS: *Satyagraha* was a transition piece. I'd done *Einstein* for my ensemble, and *Satyagraha* really imitates the sound of the ensemble in orchestral form. It doesn't have a sound of its own. So with the third opera I was actually addressing for the first time the idea of orchestral identity. *CIVIL warS* is another very orchestral sounding piece.

STRICKLAND: Acoustic rather than electronic instruments dominate *Akhnaten*, which is also true of *Powaqqatsi* as opposed to *Koyaanisqatsi*. Is this a new movement in your work?

GLASS: That would *appear* to be so. However, the latest piece, *1000 Airplanes,* is almost entirely electronic. I'm even using a wind synthesizer for one of the flute players. At the same time as I was writing a very acoustic piece I was also writing a very electronic piece.

STRICKLAND: You have no preference?

GLASS: None. The subject matter dictates to me what I need to do.

STRICKLAND: I was thinking of the contrast between the funeral music in *Akhnaten* and the electronic ensemble version released on *Dancepieces*.

GLASS: Of course it's the same music, but the earlier version I did for the ensemble so that we could have it to tour with.

STRICKLAND: Comparing the two, I don't think the electronic *Dancepieces* version even comes close.

GLASS: I would agree with you that the ensemble version is pale compared to the orchestral. It hasn't the same nobility. However, in its defense, let me tell you that when we go on the road to play in Clearwater and Tacoma and the places we do, these are places that will never see *Akhnaten*. And the impact in a concert is actually terrific. You'd have to see that piece in the context of a live ensemble concert to see that it functions very well. There's another orchestration—of *Glasspieces*—that Jerry Robbins does, without the voices, which is actually not [*sotto voce*] particularly good.

STRICKLAND: On last year's TV show from The Kitchen you redid a 1979 piece, "Mad Rush," on piano rather than electronic organ.

GLASS: How did you like that?

STRICKLAND: I thought it was great!

GLASS: I've just written three more—no, five more—piano pieces at the same time as I've been developing the synthesizers for my ensemble, so I tend to work in very different idioms at the same time.

STRICKLAND: Continuing with *Akhnaten,* the centerpiece is the Hymn to the Sun, where you used the vernacular.

GLASS: That's the one text we attribute to Akhnaten himself perhaps. At that moment it's as if we were suddenly in the mind of Akhnaten. Up to that point we've been hearing Egyptian, a language we don't understand.

STRICKLAND: My problem with this is that, as you noted in your book, the higher the voice the harder to understand. And though Paul Esswood is singing beautifully in English, I can't make out the words all that clearly in his countertenor.

GLASS [*laughing*]: So it's not so different from the rest!

STRICKLAND: You also have the chorus singing Psalm 104 in Hebrew offstage. Was that meant as a physical correlative of the historical distance of the Hebrew monotheism foreshadowed by Akhnaten?

GLASS: In a way. What I was most interested in is that Akhnaten had sung his hymn alone, communicating to his God, and hopefully—apart from the fact that you couldn't understand the words—it would enter our minds the same way. I raise a very controversial point, that the Old Testament derived from earlier sources, principally Egyptian. This is a controversial idea and not a particularly popular one, but one that's hard to deny when you compare the texts of the Hymn to Aten and Psalm 104. It's very hard not to see that one came from the other. I was drawing attention to the continuity between the world of Akhnaten and the Judeo-Christian world.

STRICKLAND: Akhnaten was the first monotheist out of the closet.

GLASS: We always talk of Greece as the cradle of civilization, when actually it was Egypt. The Greeks themselves turned to Egypt, Herodotus, and so forth. They would visit and learn from it.

STRICKLAND: You had in Achim Freyer's Stuttgart production a very hieratic presentation of the work, which seemed to me better suited to the text than the more intimate, expressive, slightly grotesque approach of David Freeman in Houston.

GLASS: I agree with you. I think it was the more successful. However, there's going to be a third one this winter, which I'm hoping will be even closer. I felt always that the central image of *Akhnaten* was the funeral, and even though I urged both directors to make it the overriding image of the piece, it failed to be sustained after the first act. I wanted each act to end with the return of the funeral image.

STRICKLAND: You mentioned that you saw *Akhnaten* as the tragic opera, *Satyagraha* as the lyrical, and *Einstein* as the apocalyptic. In terms of traditional forms, I saw *Akhnaten* as the Requiem, *Satyagraha* as the *Heldenleben* or *apothéose*, and Einstein as the dream play.

GLASS: That's not a bad way to look at it. The value of your point of view on *Akhnaten* is its focus on the subject of death—the death of his father, his own death, the preoccupation with death that Egypt had. But when I was writing these things I didn't think in terms of any of these categories. It was years later that I began to formulate it in this way.

STRICKLAND: All the operas in the trilogy are connected to films that came later, not only *Satyagraha* with Attenborough's *Gandhi*, but the endings of *Einstein* and *Akhnaten*. Have you noticed this?

GLASS: No!

STRICKLAND: Have you seen *Sid and Nancy*?

GLASS: No.

STRICKLAND: See it and think about the end of *Einstein,* where the phantasmal bus approaches the two lovers. In *Sid and Nancy* they ride off to death in a cab. And when you see *The Last Emperor,* when the protagonist returns to his palace, which is now a tourist site, you might be reminded of Akhnaten's ghost in the ruins of Tel-el-Amarna. One thing I love about your operas, by the way, is how you always manage to conclude in such a fitting and moving way. But I wanted to ask you a technical question about the end of *Satyagraha*. The reincarnation aria has been described in a couple of national magazines as an E-minor scale, when really it's a straight Phrygian.

GLASS: That's right. If it were E minor it would be E to F-sharp instead of F. I'm sorry that got out.

STRICKLAND: The question that leads to is how modally oriented is your work. Minimalism has been publicized as a return to tonality. I wonder if it's not even more retrospective, going back before tonal organization—

GLASS: To modality. That would be true of that aria, but modality as a main harmonic element would only be true of that piece. If you look at *Akhnaten* you're really dealing with something more to do with polytonality. The real meat of *Akhnaten* is in the ambiguity of tonality. It's another answer to the century's question of how do we go beyond tonality. In my case the answer wasn't atonality but rather polytonality. It offers for contemporary ears a more interesting possibility, and that's the direction I've obviously developed in. But that would not be true of *Satyagraha*.

STRICKLAND: Which period of classical music are you most drawn to?

GLASS: My most thorough *studies* were done in Bach and Mozart with my teacher Nadia Boulanger, who trained us *relentlessly* in their works. Bach was her main subject matter, secondarily Mozart.

STRICKLAND: When you listen to music do you tend to gravitate to them?

GLASS: Not necessarily. Maybe not at all. I studied them so *endlessly* with her that I'm not so inclined to do it now. A friend came in the other day to visit me. I was making dinner and listening to the Rachmaninov Third Piano Concerto, and he said, "My God, you're listening to Rachmaninov!" I said, "Yes, indeed, one of the great composers of the twentieth century." He was surprised, but composers tend to have less categorical ideas about what good music is than other people. Maybe what I'm interested in in that piece is the extension of melodic lines that he was able to contrive.

I was just talking at some length today with a colleague of mine about the structural ideas in the Sibelius Fourth. I was talking recently about Lou Harrison's work, a somewhat older contemporary whom I very much admire. I feel at this point in my life—thanks to the training I had from the age of eight to twenty-eight, when I finished my formal studies—that the world of music is very much a book that's open to me. Boulanger also concentrated very heavily on the Renaissance period. Palestrina and Monteverdi were other great composers that we studied with her. She didn't do much after Mozart.

The rest I did on my own anyway. I was studying twelve-tone music when I was fifteen and Charles Ives at the same age. So contemporary music was something I didn't need an instructor for in that way. But I feel that all periods are open to me and I'm oriented very positively towards all of them. So I don't have preferences, I have predilections at any given time to listen to one music or another.

STRICKLAND: To get back to early music and your first opera, in the opening of *Einstein*, the first Knee Play, you have a numerical chant. Was your idea a post-Einsteinian version of Gregorian chant?

GLASS: Not really. To tell you the truth, the numeric chanting was my way of teaching the chorus the music. At the time it was a way of learning the changing meters. And by the time they learned it I suggested to Bob that we simply retain it as the text.

STRICKLAND: Just a pedagogical device.

GLASS: Exactly.

STRICKLAND: What about the quasi-canonic overlapping of text by Lucinda Childs and Sheryl Sutton in that section? And elsewhere you have *different* texts recited simultaneously. Were you aware of Glenn Gould's radio documentaries, which he saw as a form of contrapuntal new music using speech?

GLASS: Collage is one of the main techniques of *Einstein*. Bob is a very intuitive creator and was really more responsible for the placement of texts than I was, though I was certainly complicit. I knew Gould's documentaries, but Bob didn't. I consider Glenn Gould one of the great musical minds of our time and Bob Wilson one of the great theatrical minds of our time. That they should come up with the same idea is not at all surprising. [*Note: The technique of simultaneous recitation of different texts was anticipated by the storytelling of the ¡Kung bushmen of the Kalahari as well as the 1916 performance of "Poème simultan" at Cabaret Voltaire by Dadaists Tristan Tzara, Marcel Janco, and Richard Huelsenbeck.*]

STRICKLAND: *Satyagraha* was the first opera in which you didn't perform. How did it feel to be sitting there as composer rather than composer-performer? Did you ever feel like jumping into the pit?

GLASS: I felt *much* more vulnerable than when I was playing. Since I'd been playing in public since I was ten, I felt much more comfortable *in* the performance, playing. I found watching it to be sometimes excruciating. However, I've gotten used to it and I can sit through them now. It was a very difficult adjustment at first.

STRICKLAND: One rumor still persists about *Satyagraha,* that the Utrecht Symphony, tired of playing your repetitive lines, "mutinied" in Rotterdam and had to be ordered back by the Dutch government. Christopher Keene repeats the story in Michael Blackwood's documentary on the making of *Akhnaten*.

GLASS: Not true.

STRICKLAND: No truth to it whatsoever?

GLASS: No truth at all. Christopher wasn't even there. In fact, Christopher was not even in Holland at the time. I can't *believe* it. Bruce Ferden, the conductor, was very upset about that. He called me up and said, "Do you realize what Christopher is saying? This simply didn't happen. There were a few people who were unhappy and I asked them to leave and they left and never participated in the performances." *That's* true. But Bruce was very upset because he thought the word might get around, and so I clarified it in my book out of deference to him. Well, Christopher will tell that story to his dying day. Because Chris *likes* a good story!

STRICKLAND [*laughing*]: We all do. That's why the legendary tomatoes will keep on flying [*Glass laughs loudly*]. You've said that Minimalism was over by 1974. Any reason for that date?

GLASS: Yes, because from that point on I was engaged almost entirely with working in theater. I'd always worked in theater with Mabou Mines, but at that point it became almost entirely my line of work, and my feeling was that the esthetic of theater is additive rather than reductive, which in this context is almost counterproductive or counterindicated.

STRICKLAND: When did you abandon atonality? In Paris?

GLASS: The Juilliard compositions were already tonal. My atonal period was over by the time I was eighteen. The earliest piece of mine that is still played is the string quartet from '66—the Kronos Quartet has it. That's the earliest piece of mine which represents the music that I'm doing now.

STRICKLAND: Will it be recorded?

GLASS: I don't think so. I mean, I doubt it. But there's a solo violin piece called *Strung Out* from '67 that's recorded and that would represent that very early period of highly reductive Minimalism that I was involved in. That would be the earliest piece from that period.

STRICKLAND: Your main influence, as you mention in the book, was your exposure to Indian music through Ravi Shankar in Paris. To what extent did you feel affected by, say, what Terry Riley was doing or Steve—?

GLASS: I'm glad to bring it up. When I came back to New York I would say there were roughly thirty composers working in a very similar style. It's highly unfortunate that the larger community isn't—Frederic Rzewski was one, and Terry Jennings was another, and Charlemagne Palestine was another, and Tom Johnson was another. Meredith Monk was a *very* important composer from that period.

STRICKLAND: Still is.

GLASS: Philip Corner was another, David Behrman was another, Jon Gibson was another—I'm just mentioning names almost at random. If you'll recall that period, it was a very intense generational search—a lot of people were doing this music. Unfortunately, the media has concentrated on a handful of people and I think it's not been fair—it's not just that it's not been fair, it hasn't reflected the variety and vitality of the music that was being done. Phill Niblock is another one. It's *frustrating* in a way because I object strenuously to this kind of reduction of history to a shorthand for the convenience of a newspaper editor. Maybe you don't have this problem—when the editors say to you, "Look, the public doesn't want to know about all that. Just give me the main outlines." But in fact the reality of the music of the late '60s and early '70s was very dynamic and everybody was involved with everybody else's music. I hope someday there'll be a reevaluation of the whole period because there's so much music that's almost been forgotten. Dickie Landry is another composer worth listening to. A guy named Richard Munson is another one. Louis Andriessen and a whole bunch of other Dutch ones, English ones.

What was so *exciting* about it was that there was all this *music!* People weren't waiting around for the new performance of Terry Riley's *In C.* Because there was music going on *every night!* It's only in retrospect that "Well, this piece happened and then . . . " And this whole scramble for—to be the—I think it's silly.

STRICKLAND: To be the what?

GLASS: To be the originator of a style. When the thing that's particularly sad is that [*sotto voce, almost melancholy*] the style turns out to be not very important.

STRICKLAND: How so?

GLASS: I think that Minimalism in its formative period is not the music that's going to endure. I think the music that will endure was written later.

STRICKLAND: That has to do with my question earlier as to whether you converted the audience or your style.

GLASS: I think the style developed. You take somebody like Anthony Davis or John Adams and they're both influenced in their own ways by that generation of composers. Meredith Monk is a wonderful composer whose music is not acknowledged because people insist on concentrating on a handful of composers.

STRICKLAND: She's following you to the Houston Grand Opera.

GLASS: Is she? Good! Oh, it'll be wonderful! I mean, I hope it will.

STRICKLAND: Speaking of future operas, can you tell me anything about *The Voyage*? Do you know much about it yet?

GLASS: I've already written a four-page synopsis. It's in three acts and the middle act is about Columbus. The other two acts deal with other figures.

STRICKLAND: How do you react to the criticism that your operas are not so much operas as pageants or a series of tableaux?

GLASS: Well, opera never interested me very much to begin with [*interviewer laughs*]. It doesn't really matter to me. When people say opera they think of the tradition of Italian opera, and it's really a nuisance to have to be part of that anyway. So I don't really care. In fact, we talked earlier about four new works, only one of which you might really call an opera anyway, *The Making of the Representative*. I prefer the term "music theater." It gives me much more range and tends to include everything into one larger category.

STRICKLAND: Don't you think the structure you've chosen for *The Voyage* invites the "pageant" or "tableaux" characterization of the work?

GLASS: I don't care. It doesn't really matter. I think, for example, it'll be very hard to look at *Usher* that way. However, it doesn't really matter. Who cares?

STRICKLAND: What else can you tell me about *The Voyage*?

GLASS: I don't want to say much more about it. I want to leave a lot of the surprise for 1992, and I'm afraid to talk about it. We're so far in advance of the piece, don't you think?

STRICKLAND: Sure. Do you know who the other historical figures will be?

GLASS: Yes, I do [*laughs*], but I'm not going to tell you. [*Both laugh*.] But they're not necessarily historical characters.

STRICKLAND: Will theater continue to be your principal focus?

GLASS: I'm working with Bob Wilson on a new work based on the *Thousand and One Nights*. We're starting that this year. Doris Lessing and I will be working on a piece called *The Marriages between Zones 3, 4 and 5*. And I have another three ideas, all music theater of one kind or another. So I would say . . . hmm, yeah, I don't know . . . I still find time to write a violin concerto now and then, but really and truly, what I really do is theater. The most distinctive thing about me in terms of my fellow composers of my generation is that I was the theater composer.

STRICKLAND: Some find this a problem in your records, insofar as what's meant as a musical accompaniment or complement to a stage representation has to stand by itself and at times doesn't do so successfully.

GLASS [*laughing to the point of losing his breath*]: You can't win them all!

George Crumb

© Sabina Matthes.

George Crumb was born in West Virginia in 1929. He studied at Mason College, the University of Illinois, and the University of Michigan, where he was awarded the doctorate. He has taught at the University of Colorado and since 1965 at the University of Pennsylvania, where he is currently Annenberg Professor of Music. Crumb has produced a wide range of highly acclaimed and at times fiercely derided compositions. He has been awarded grants from the Koussevitsky and Guggenheim foundations, a Pulitzer Prize in 1968 for *Echoes of Time and the River*, awards from the American Academy of Arts and Letters and the International Rostrum of Composers, and in 1989 the Gold Medal of Prince Pierre de Monaco for lifetime achievement in composition. He has also been the recipient of some of the snidest criticism of our time.

Crumb came to public attention in the 1960s with works for various instrumental and vocal configurations: solo piano, soprano and percussion with assorted instruments, baritone and electric ensemble, and orchestra. Notable among them are the electric (in both senses of the word) string quartet *Black Angels* (1970), in which, like La Monte Young in his roughly contemporary Andy Warhol film-scoring, Crumb requested that the volume be raised to "the threshold of pain"; *A Haunted Landscape* (1984) and *Echoes* for orchestra; numerous settings of Lorca's poetry, from *Night Music I* (1963) to the recent *Canciones para Niños;* keyboard works entitled *Makrokosmos I-IV* (1970-1979); and more lyrical works featuring amplified flute, *Vox Balaenae* ["Voice of the Whale"] (1971, with cello and piano), and *An Idyll for the Misbegotten* (1985, with three drummers).

Crumb is undeniably among the most eclectic of composers, drawing upon a wide range not only of influences but of direct borrowings from earlier composers. In an often grippingly effective technique of quotation, he juxtaposes modal Christmas carols with sharp dissonance and Bachian counterpoint with atonality. He has explored the ritualistic/theatrical elements of musical performance in numerous works in a manner some find liturgical and others burlesque. Almost hermetically, he has entitled works simply with the initials of musicians, scored his compositions as works of graphic art (spiral galaxies, crosses, circles, double stars) with painstaking calligraphy, and, updating Bach's technique of motivic signature to later technology, written xylophone parts that tap out his name in Morse code.

Most important, Crumb has experimented with a broad range of harmonic systems and timbral effects. He has adapted traditional classical instruments and imported others from Asia and Africa, as well as from the barn and the nursery. His players blow winds into concert grands, achieve multiphonics by playing *col legno sul* (and *sotto*) *ponticello*, and raise and lower struck gongs into vats of water in attempts to expand the palette of sonorities. Crumb is probably best known for his works for voice, many of which feature his longtime collaborator, the late soprano Jan DeGaetani. They similarly explore extended-vocal techniques in pursuit of an expressiveness that transcends traditional expectations. If the overtones of Meredith Monk's extended vocals often recall both early Minimalism and Stockhausen's incantatory *Stimmung,* Crumb's more relentlessly chromatic and percussive-tympanic vocals bring to mind the contemporary European *Klangfarbenschule* and the more lacerated world of Stockhausen's *Momente.*

While his juxtaposition of tone colors, dynamics, and even harmonic systems is anything but Minimalist, Crumb shares with composers so denominated a frequent if never so relentless use of repetition and a sense of stasis created by drones and suspended harmonies. A passing resemblance to the work of La Monte Young, in particular—certainly not due to direct borrowing by either—may be connected to their mutual debt to Bartók and Webern. In addition, both communicate a sense of transcendence by means of negating normal concepts of duration. Crumb's more event-full scores are, however, texturally and at times even timbrally more akin to some of the electronic composition (one medium in which Crumb has never worked) of composers like Varèse.

Crumb's compositions continue to be performed internationally on a regular basis. Published exclusively by Peters, they have been recorded on numerous labels. The Kronos Quartet chose *Black Angels* as the title piece for their fourth Nonesuch album, released in July 1990.

On a warm morning in July 1988 the composer met me at the train station in Media, a Philadelphia suburb, and we spent a few hours together in the den where he composes. Crumb's manner is as considerate of others as it is self-effacing, and after going out of his way to help me catch a train back to Philadelphia farther down the line, it never occurred to him, I'm sure, *not* to wait with me at the station until the belated train arrived.

STRICKLAND: I think you're best known as a colorist. Have you always had an instinctive interest in exploring sonorities?

CRUMB: Yes, it goes back quite a way. When I was in college a big influence on my music was Béla Bartók, whom I think of as one of the early colorists—in a way, I think, in the Debussy tradition. He picked up quite a bit from Debussy, and I picked up quite a bit from both of them. To take it back a step, I think Debussy marks a turning point in the way composers think about timbre, and I've always thought that a work like *Afternoon of a Faun* is quite as revolutionary in its own way as, say, *Le Sacre du printemps*. It's an astonishing work, and I think the very new thing there is making timbre a very exalted part of the music.

STRICKLAND: When were you first exposed to Bartók and Debussy?

CRUMB: A little bit in my teens in my home town, Charleston, West Virginia. Even down there [*chuckles*], even in that period, the '40s, you might hear things like *Mikrokosmos*.

STRICKLAND: Was that the first Bartók you heard?

CRUMB: Yes.

STRICKLAND: I ask, of course, because of the connection to your four works entitled *Makrokosmos*.

CRUMB: That was a little bit of homage, I guess.

STRICKLAND: Two early works of yours are titled or subtitled "Night Music." I'm wondering if there's a connection here to another composer, Mahler, and his Seventh Symphony.

CRUMB: There are similar subtitles in Bartók: "musique nocturne" in the

Out of Doors suite, I guess. I think that's his homage to the two *Nachtmusik* movements in the Mahler Seventh, which are really just uncanny. And there are other night music works of Bartók that aren't labeled as such, the insect music and two or three of the late works.

STRICKLAND: The quartets and insect music had a strong effect on a work like *Black Angels*, no?

CRUMB: A string quartet I wrote as a student in Ann Arbor was like recycled Bartók [*laughs*]. The influence was immensely strong. That quartet couldn't be considered representative now, of course. I really didn't find my own way until 1962, after I finished school.

STRICKLAND: What about *Variazioni*, which dates from 1959?

CRUMB: That is sort of transitional.

STRICKLAND: It seems to me quite distinctive.

CRUMB: I would say there are *glimmers* of my voice, but perhaps also an array of influences: Berg, Schoenberg, Bartók, and even Dallapiccola.

STRICKLAND: I can feel a continuity between *Variazioni* and an '80s work like *A Haunted Landscape*. You, obviously, are more intimately involved with them, and I wonder if you find that to be the case.

CRUMB: Sure, I'm more intimately involved with them, but I wouldn't have your perspective on it from the outside. I sense, though, that there is some continuity. Even in that transitional work there are certain little elements that carry on in my representative style, which began in 1962 with *Five Pieces for Piano*. And I don't think my style has drastically changed since then, which might be bad, I don't know. It could be good or it could be bad, but I sense an organic relationship in all of my music.

STRICKLAND: We're talking about a quarter century—'59 to '84—from *Variazioni* to *A Haunted Landscape*. Do you feel there's any particular new direction in your recent work?

CRUMB: I sense that I'm further elaborating seeds that were already planted in earlier works. I think I'm that type of composer, the type of a Debussy or a Mahler. One can speak of *the* symphony of Mahler. I think one can speak of the total work of Debussy as being of a piece, in contrast to other composers who experience significant stylistic breaks, so that one can speak of their first, second, third style, etc.

STRICKLAND: With Mahler, or with Bartók and Debussy, was it essentially sonority that attracted you?

CRUMB: No, that was just one element. Perhaps even more important was the way they introduced a new problem in their music—how to combine all kinds of musics one wouldn't normally think of as belonging together.

STRICKLAND: The folk element in Bartók . . .

CRUMB: In Debussy you have the French *clavecin* tradition, the music hall, the pop music of the time, even some jazz, Eastern music, Spanish influence—even Medieval organum. All of this is somehow magically synthesized in a style of great power and personality. The same with Mahler and Charles Ives, even Bartók—the way he combined so many systems: atonality, chromaticism—a relentless dissonance that's even more incisive than anything in the Viennese composers—tonality, modality, whole-tone configurations, all of these things.

STRICKLAND: Being from West Virginia, you've incorporated your own folk elements with banjos and musical saws and mandolins.

CRUMB: Those sounds were very familiar to me living in that area.

STRICKLAND: Was it a conscious effort on your part to integrate folk influences into a classical music context?

CRUMB: These are sounds that I remembered in later years, subsequent to my living there, when I was so much interested in developing sound as an expressive element. The banjo is close to some Asian instruments, so there are cross-references too.

STRICKLAND: The Japanese biwa or shamisen.

CRUMB: I'd heard a lot of Asian music both live and in recordings, and perhaps that stimulated memories. I lived in Charleston, after all, till I was twenty-one, studying at a little school there called Mason College before moving on to Champaign-Urbana and Ann Arbor.

STRICKLAND: How much twentieth-century classical music were you exposed to in Charleston?

CRUMB: Those were the pre-LP days, but I would have known what was on the radio and available in the record library.

STRICKLAND: You knew Debussy, Bartók, Mahler, those people back then?

CRUMB: Mahler I did not know. That was really in Ann Arbor. I guess I probably would have heard *Das Lied* or the Fourth Symphony on the radio, but it didn't make much of an impression if I'd heard those works. Those were then the only two pieces that were performed with much regularity before the big Mahler revival.

STRICKLAND: In what other way has your background nourished your music?

CRUMB: Composers inherit an acoustic that during their formative years molds their ear. Living in the city, the seashore, the desert would be different from living in an Appalachian river valley. I have always thought the echoing sense of my music is distilled really from the sense of hearing I developed there.

STRICKLAND: I've never lived in a river valley—unless you count the East River—

CRUMB: You couldn't hear the echoes there! [*Both laugh.*]

STRICKLAND: Can you explain to me the acoustic effect of that topography?

CRUMB: Well, it's . . . it's [*voice drops*] haunting, you know. Say on a quiet summer evening, sounds from the other side of the river waft over, you see, because there are hills on both sides. You can sometimes hear sounds from the mouths of the river. It's a special characteristic.

STRICKLAND: You mentioned organum in the context of Debussy. In your own work, for example, the basses of *A Haunted Landscape* and the wine glasses of *Dream Sequence,* you have prominent drones and sustained tones. I'm wondering if they come from the Charleston acoustic or the Notre Dame school as filtered through Debussy. Steve Reich and La Monte Young, by the way, hear "La Cathédrale engloutie" as organum.

CRUMB: I would agree with them. The source, I think, is clear there. But I think my drone is an outgrowth of the concept of reverberation, a single tone in the piano or crotale or other instruments. One low note on the piano rings out for quite a while. This fascination with long notes may have led me to the idea of using drones. There may be some Eastern influence there—Indian music. At Penn we used to have some Indian musicians teaching sitar and tabla. Their room was across the hall from mine. I'd be teaching students and these sounds would be wafting over. I think they really entered my head.

STRICKLAND: You started teaching at Penn in '65. When did the Indians arrive?

CRUMB: Just about that time. Harold Powers, who's now at Princeton, was in the department, and his field was ethnomusicology, and it was through him that they came for a couple of years.

STRICKLAND: Along with organum another somewhat later Medieval influence seems to be isorhythm. You use it in the "Myth" section of *Makrokosmos III* and Book III of *Madrigals*. Have you had a special interest in the music of Machaut, Dufay, or Dunstable?

CRUMB: I would say I'm not even well educated in that music. I have a very brief acquaintance with it. A few works sort of bowled me over like, say, the Notre Dame Mass and its harsh, vivid sounds as opposed to later periods, where the sound was more elegant.

STRICKLAND: Do you tend to listen to music of a certain period?

CRUMB: Well, I rarely go out of my way to hear music nowadays. When I'm involved in a concert I hear the other works, or if I'm driving to Penn I hear what's on my car radio. It's a matter of chance [*chuckles*], whatever they happen to have on.

STRICKLAND: You don't spend a lot of time listening to records.

CRUMB: No, it's funny, I don't. I tend to read the scores like a book rather than put on a recording. I have a very large score collection. Reading the score is somehow more private, more intimate—*without* the sound. I generally read anywhere from Bach to now.

STRICKLAND: Bach and others have been incorporated into your own music by means of quotation. It's a very strong element in your music. What inspired this technique?

CRUMB: I always find it very hard to answer this question. Why Bach? Why a little bit of the *Hammerklavier*? Well, the *Hammerklavier* I think of as metaphysical music, about as metaphysical as music can ever get.

STRICKLAND: Is the quotation conceived of *before* you begin your own composition? Would you say, "I'll compose something now and incorporate the D-sharp minor fugue"?

CRUMB: I can't remember honestly. The ideas may come very early on in the sketches. I think I always knew I'd use that little bit of the *Hammer-klavier* one day . . . because it *meant* so much.

STRICKLAND: Perhaps I'm being overly analytical, but do you ask yourself when you decide to incorporate a quotation, "What is the function of this?" or is it simply intuitive.

CRUMB: Well, it's intuitive, but trying to articulate it, I would say that quotation can produce different effects: nostalgia for a past world, or a strange spanning of time—by juxtaposing something that was written two centuries earlier with something new.

STRICKLAND: Has it ever happened that you've wondered at a given point, "Should I quote this now or something else?" Do you have alternatives, or is it always that *this* fragment belongs here now?

CRUMB: It's the feeling really that only *this* serves the emotional function of the piece. There's an interesting story in connection with that. The first version of *Makrokosmos* quoted Rachmaninov's D-flat music from the *Paganini Variations* and was first played with that quote. Then it came to recording and publication and there was difficulty in getting clearance, legal hassles concerning rights. It would have been an impossibility. At the time I thought it was public domain, but not so [*laughs*].

So I was forced to find a substitute. It had to be in D-flat major, first of all, to suit the structure of that piece. It had to be music that expressed a kind of decayed elegance, something not as exalted as an excerpt from Beethoven, something *awfully* attractive but slightly flawed. It *had* to have that quality. And I searched. And the pianist David Burge—he was faced with recording—would send me this and that of Chopin and suggested the D-flat Nocturne of Chopin. That didn't work, because the music is too good! [*Both laugh.*] An incredible piece of music. And it's transcendental music. I wanted something more effete and decayed, and I hit on the *Fantaisie-Impromptu*, which I'd played as a kid. And it worked. But I still hope one day we can revert to the Rachmaninov.

STRICKLAND: So there *was* a choice there, enforced. Each case of quotation is *sui generis*.

CRUMB: In the case of *both* the Bach and the Beethoven I wanted a metaphysical quality. It was part of my conception in *Makrokosmos*.

STRICKLAND: There's also the quote from Debussy's *Syrinx* in *Idyll for the Misbegotten*.

CRUMB: It's a bit of an ecological piece and *Syrinx* evokes the woods.

STRICKLAND: You've often set or alluded to literary works in your music: Whitman, Wolfe . . . we'll get to Lorca in a minute—you'll never escape him if you live to be a hundred [*Crumb laughs*]—but is *Idyll* an allusion to O'Neill's *Moon for the Misbegotten*?

CRUMB: No, only the title must have suggested itself to me. There's really no connection. I *like* O'Neill. Nor is there any substantive connection with Wolfe's *Of Time and the River,* which I haven't actually even read. But the title was very beautiful.

STRICKLAND: Let's forget about O'Neill then [*laughs*]. In the title the misbegotten are the human race. Why are we misbegotten?

CRUMB: People are almost illegitimate now, upsetting the natural scheme of things. They represent a danger to so many other forms of life. And in that sense we've passed from legitimacy to illegitimacy, occupying a place where, if we continue like this, we jeopardize at last even our own existence.

STRICKLAND: Then why, instead of, say, a jeremiad for the misbegotten, are you offering us an idyll?

CRUMB: The idyll is nature music. There was a phrase—I probably read it somewhere—"a broken idyll" or "a flawed idyll." The idyll is something naturally perfect, and here we have a flawed idyll, but nonetheless an idyll, in my mind.

STRICKLAND: You mention summer in the section notes to *Idyll,* and another work, which you subtitled *Makrokosmos III,* is called *Music for a Summer Evening.* What do you associate with summer?

CRUMB: Well, summer, hmm . . . the world of natural sound is so much more evident in the summer—all the bird voices, the insects. Up here we're so shut in during the winter months from all the natural environment of sound.

STRICKLAND: I ask because much of your work is so eerie in general that if I were to subtitle your work as a whole I might call it *Music for a Winter Midnight.*

CRUMB [*very softly*]: Thank you.

STRICKLAND: In fact, I'm just a bit surprised to find you as mild mannered and relaxed as you are. Your music is not. There are times when I find it very scary, to be quite blunt about it.

CRUMB: I think composers are everything they've ever experienced, everything they've ever read, all the music they've ever heard. All these things come together in odd combinations in their psyche, where they choose and make forms from all their memories and their imaginings. I think there's a lot of music that has a darker side and maybe some of this music influenced me. Chopin definitely has it in certain works, some of the piano preludes . . .

STRICKLAND: But isn't that—there's maybe a Romantic morbidity to that, but it isn't the demonic and eerie quality that I find in your music.

CRUMB [*half-questioningly*]: Uh huh.

STRICKLAND: Is that the Mahlerian influence?

CRUMB [*sounding surprised*]: Maybe so. Maybe that's Mahler, the night music in the Seventh Symphony, which is very spooky music—even though the melodies and themes themselves are disarmingly amiable. There's an undertone. I feel this with Mozart's music, the hard irony that's underlying all that surface. I think all vital music, even when it's overtly cheerful, always *implies* the darker side of life.

STRICKLAND: I certainly agree with you about Mozart, though there's no unanimity among listeners. Now a work recorded with *Idyll* on your last New World album is *Vox Balaenae,* which also deals with nature, the voice of the whale. Had you heard the records by Paul Winter and Paul Horn, among others, where they play winds with whales or dolphins?

CRUMB: I'd just heard the tapes of whale songs released by the New York Museum of Natural History, I believe—was Roger Payne supervising that? I haven't heard the recordings you mentioned, just the actual tape of the whales singing.

STRICKLAND: The work has a mosaic and geological structure.

CRUMB: I think much of my work has a mosaic structure. The geological periods there serve as titles for a set of variations in the middle of the work. I forget now just how that came, except that I wanted to suggest in the titles a kind of measureless time. I thought there was a little of this obsession with time in the music.

STRICKLAND: There's a greater sense of spaciousness in that piece than I find in a lot of your work, which to me has a more threatening quality. At the end you even move into timelessness with the sea nocturne subtitled "For the End of Time," in which you transcend the periods you've delineated musically. That's obviously an allusion to Messiaen.

CRUMB: Borrowed from Messiaen, of course.

STRICKLAND: Is he a stylistic influence on the work as well?

CRUMB: I think there's one little section in one of the variations that is a trifle Messiaenic. I admire much of his music, I find it intriguing, but I doubt it's had as much influence on me as earlier composers we've discussed.

STRICKLAND: Messiaen is, of course, closely associated with sacred music, and I associate you with that very much, perhaps more than most people do. Your work is not merely "spiritual" in a nebulous sense but often specifically religious in allusion. Is your religious background—which I don't know—a strong influence on the way you see the world and reflect it musically?

CRUMB: Well, I don't think so, even though there are numerous biblical allusions. I had the traditional Presbyterian background associated with West Virginia, but early on in my reading I became interested in religion in the nonsectarian sense. Other religions, Asian religions and so forth.

STRICKLAND: You have so many religious allusions even in your titles and sectional notes—references to Saint Francis, Pascal, Rilke. Even the *Idyll,* despite its lyrical title, has a subtext which is really quite apocalyptic. Others among your works are more patently eschatological. *Black Angels* has a strong Gnostic-Manichaean feel to me, and you set up the apocalyptic aura by quoting the *Dies Irae* fairly early in the work.

CRUMB: That's the purest strain, I guess, of that particular element.

STRICKLAND: Does your imagination seem to gravitate towards the apocalyptic?

CRUMB: Well, I hope I'm not obsessed with it. You know, our music reflects the currents of the time. There have been many events in the twentieth century thus far that would, I suppose [*laughs*], instill a certain appreciation of the apocalypse.

STRICKLAND: You began that work in the late '60s and you allude to the Vietnam War in the Haydnesque "in tempore belli" notation of the score. Was the primary external influence on the work social rather than religious *per se*? The title is *Black Angels*—that is, devils.

CRUMB: I think Vietnam was an obsession in my music at that time. *Black Angels* also taps into certain elements of the musical tradition: Berlioz and certain dark pieces of Chopin, even though there's no religious apparatus in his titles.

STRICKLAND: Berlioz also quotes the *Dies Irae* in the *Symphonie fantastique*.

CRUMB: In fact I quote some of *that* in another work.

STRICKLAND: Other religious works include *Lux Aeterna* and *Star-Child*—where you allude to the Slaughter of the Innocents. Michael Walsh once wrote something I think is quite true: "In George Crumb's universe the Black Angels are never very far away." [*Crumb nods almost grimly several times.*] You agree with that.

CRUMB [*quietly*]: Uh huh. But I would think of religion as just one more cultural inheritance. Now—more than in earlier periods—everything is alive for us that ever existed in the past, plus all that earlier periods didn't know anything about—archaeology and so forth. Apart from what religion might mean to any particular person, it also has an enormous purely cultural presence.

STRICKLAND: I'm a bit surprised to hear this. From my own experience of your music I would have pictured you to be much more committed religiously. Are you—and please don't answer this if you don't want to, it's really none of my business—but are you a theist?

CRUMB: Oh, yes, I think I am, but it's divorced from any particular creed.

STRICKLAND: You're not a church-going Presbyterian at this point.

CRUMB: Oh, no. I think the world is a large place and all the religions—there's some spiritual energy that's burning all over the world that takes different forms. I can see it in music. I can say music is equally religion. Certain scientists, you know, have this almost religious dedication to finding their truths. The new astronomy to me is inventing a new religion.

STRICKLAND: There's a strong ritual element in the performance of your music. Is that in any way an inheritance from your religious upbringing?

CRUMB: No. No, that [*laughs*]—I don't know the precise source. Catholicism has much more ritual than West Virginia Protestantism. In Eastern religions the ritual element is much stronger. I had the traditional Sunday-school Bible-class training. My father, who was a musician, had lots of books that shaped my thinking early, not putting down any single religion but interesting me more than purists might be in the multiplicity of religions rather than their exclusiveness—though I'd never speak disparagingly about that, which is noble in its own way. I was equally interested in all of them, which might be a form of *un*commitment, but I didn't think of it that way.

STRICKLAND: What led you to the ritualistic trappings in your music—having musicians wear masks, assume the lotus position, light candles, wear visors, strike cymbals while assuming "portentous ritual postures" in *Of Time and the River*? It isn't the normal way one sees classical music performed—you know, "Put on your tuxedo, get out there and play!"

CRUMB [*laughing*]: No. The simple answer is that in the works of those years I wanted to introduce a theatrical element. The normal way of performing music was becoming too fixed, stuffy, routine. My processionals, for example, are not only symbols, they're an *acoustic* event. If the musicians are moving in space, that affects the sound.

STRICKLAND: It recalls the Spanish *saeta* tradition of processionals with impromptu arias to sacred images carried on floats.

CRUMB: I think I've seen that on film. It's very beautiful.

STRICKLAND: Some people find your ritualism very effective and have suggested this town be renamed *Mixed* Media, Pennsylvania, in your honor. Other people find all these shenanigans a little vaudevillian. How do you feel about that criticism?

CRUMB: What I'm really concerned with is music in itself and through itself. This sort of external apparatus may have a relation to the music, but I'm traditional in the sense that despite all this I think of the music as fulfilling itself. It should be completely expressive on the record player, when you see nothing. After all, Debussy could have called *La Mer* "La Terre"—doesn't make any difference, except that in his mind there were those associations. The sounds of the sea could also be accepted as sounds of the wind in the trees and all that. You have to call a piece *something*.

STRICKLAND: You're not that strongly committed then to the whole programmatic element.

CRUMB: No, but I wanted in those performances to heighten perhaps the balletic element that all music has. To me, to play a string quartet is to perform a kind of choreography. Even a quiet, as opposed to an emotional, pianist plays his instrument like a dancer. I love to see a performance rather than just hear a recording. Everyone is entitled to react in his own way, however.

STRICKLAND: Let's just spend another moment on the critical reactions to your work. You seem a very mild-mannered person, yet your music has evoked wild superlatives and severe invective. On the one hand it's described as—you'll be glad to hear this one—"extraordinarily haunting and intoxicating magic" [*Crumb looks gravely embarrassed*]. Another critic has said that—please don't punch me in the nose!—virtually all your music has "nauseated" him and that you're "not fit to lie with the hogs."

CRUMB: Oh, I'd love to have that for my collection! The really *bad* reviews, I just love those. I haven't seen that one—people must have been trying to spare my feelings. Peters did a recent book on my music, and they should have *that* one in there! I'm really delighted—a reaction that strong—at least they're not *ignoring* the music [*laughs long and heartily, recovers*].

I'm fairly philosophical about it all, because no matter how we try, the ultimate fate of our music is really out of our hands. A composer cannot promote himself. It doesn't do any good. The music has to stand on its own. And who knows? That's up to some later generation. And maybe there's nothing being written today that has the power to carry into the next generation. But we don't know that ourselves.

STRICKLAND: Another manifestation of the mixed-media element in your work is the graphics of your scores, such as the ones here on the walls. They remind me a little bit of both Medieval illuminated manuscripts and Baroque pattern poems like George Herbert's "Easter Wings" or "The Altar."

CRUMB: In early music too you have *Le Chansonnier cordiforme.*

STRICKLAND: Was it just the visual attractiveness of the spirals and so on that drew you to this?

CRUMB: Actually, I had a visual image of these particular pieces. I call it symbolic notation as part of the whole concept of the composition. In some cases the forms represent visually what the music is doing aurally. A circular score might *sound* circular, like a wheel going around.

STRICKLAND: It also imposes certain exigencies on the performers. But you'd say that the patterns are primarily esthetic and conceptual rather than functional.

CRUMB: That's right. Symbolic. Although in a piece like *Eleven Echoes of Autumn*, practically speaking, the circles there, the broken arches separate that music visually from the other music which is written out in the traditional way. They fortify the separation.

STRICKLAND: A recent, nonpattern score called *A Little Suite for Christmas* is a work I admire. I think the quotation from the Coventry Carol is very beautiful. But the work is not nearly as festive as I, at least, expected, more ruminative. What was your approach to Christmas?

CRUMB: I allude to Giotto's paintings, which I like very much, and the almost childlike simplicity of those works. A lot of music that was in *Night Music I* was originally sketched for a work called *A Christmas Suite*. It was just an idea in the back of my mind for all those years.

STRICKLAND: Some of the more recent piano works have been stylistically sparer than the earlier pieces. One critic has suggested this might be a response to Minimalism.

CRUMB: Uh huh, somewhat maybe. As an idea Minimalism is useful, I think, like anything else. I think all good music is minimal in the sense of being economical. I react a little against the repetition *ad infinitum* when the harmonic spectrum is rather narrow.

STRICKLAND: Well, as someone who prefers scores to recordings, you wouldn't have a whole lot of fun reading the same broken chord sixty-four times.

CRUMB: No, but the style can be effective, as in John Adams's *Phrygian Gates*, which is very colorful and seems to have a little more harmonic substance than some of that music.

STRICKLAND: That's because it has the gates as well as the Phrygian [*both laugh*]. Which contemporaries you do especially admire?

CRUMB: Luciano Berio is kind of a favorite of mine. I mentioned Messiaen. I'm sure I owe little things to them, though my most important influences go back earlier in the century. Berio's music always has that Italian lyricism, and technically it's always beautifully made. I admire Stockhausen's earlier *Refrain*, which also employs symbolic notation.

STRICKLAND: What about American composers? You use the inside of the piano continually in your work, attach objects to instruments, and so on. I think of Cowell and Cage naturally.

CRUMB: By '62, when I wrote *Five Pieces*, I knew about Cowell and Cage and their efforts but hadn't actually heard any of the music of either. Strictly speaking, I've never used the Cageian prepared piano, affixing nuts and bolts to the strings. The prepared piano *à la* Cage is really a very beautiful sound, but it was more personal for me to find my own way.

STRICKLAND: Apart from adapting instruments—putting paper on harp strings, a chisel on the piano wires—you have a very unusual instrumentarium: Oriental instruments, toy pianos, etc., along with the American folk instruments.

CRUMB: I'd come across them in my background or hear them used in works of other composers, or percussionists might show me all their new things, and I'd remember that—like a repertory of timbral aspects. One day I'd want that sound and use it.

STRICKLAND: In *Ancient Voices of Children* you've got an interesting tonal as well as timbral adaptation, tuning a set of mandolin strings a quarter tone low. You seem to have an ambiguous, maybe love-hate, relationship to tonality in general.

CRUMB: I *love* tonality. I feel that what happened with Schoenberg and others was in a way an aberration and not an entirely successful one, philosophically or simply musically. My ear rejects that sort of symmetry. Melody itself is based on asymmetry, and therefore our inner ear is asymmetrically constructed. That's another reason I admire composers like Bartók, who avail themselves of all the rich new possibilities while retaining the tonal principle as the *spine* of the music.

STRICKLAND: Well, one of the most cryptic statements that you've made, I think, is in the "S. E." section of *Makrokosmos III,* which you say "might be described as more or less atonal or more or less tonal." That's kind of hedging your bets, isn't it? You don't feel militaristic about either position?

CRUMB: No. I think technically atonality is a valid addition to the vocabulary, but the movement to strict Serialism, going the next rational step, didn't appeal to me at all. But all those new possibilities, new chord structures, new modes of introducing tension, are important for the musical vocabulary.

STRICKLAND: Was your graduate training at Illinois and Michigan in Serialism?

CRUMB: No, there was no special emphasis. Many of the students were getting into serial composition—this was the mid and late '50s. I was bemused by this more rational mode of construction. I tried it and never could make it work. In *Variazioni* the theme happens to have all the twelve notes, but it's not a genuine serial work.

STRICKLAND: But even that nonserial use of the tone row is ambiguous, do you see what I mean? You just have no martial feeling about the issue.

CRUMB: No, not at all, no more than Debussy would have had if someone had asked him, "How committed are you to whole tones?" Debussy would probably say, "Oh, it's a valuable addition to the vocabulary. I'll move in and out of whole tones. Whole tones will be followed by diatonic functional harmony. That'll be followed by modality" [*laughs heartily*]. I feel the same way! You can create almost a prismatic sense by going from one to the other. I'm not a purist at all. I'm very sloppy about these things.

STRICKLAND: All through the '60s you worked on texts of Federico García Lorca. You wrote somewhere that it had largely developed out of your experience of the conclusion of the "Balada de la Placeta," where the poet declares he'll voyage far beyond the mountains, seas, and stars to ask Christ to give back his ancient childlike soul.

CRUMB: That was the core of *Ancient Voices of Children* specifically. I first encountered Lorca as a student in Ann Arbor. A classmate and fellow composer set "The Boy Wounded by the Water" in English. I thought it was a very striking composition and that got me interested in Lorca, which I had in a bilingual . . .

STRICKLAND: The Penguin with the green cover? Or the New Directions?

CRUMB: I own both of those. I can't remember which I had at that time. I think both. Now I also have *Complete Works* that someone presented to me.

STRICKLAND: What led you to spend *so* much time setting his texts?

CRUMB: I think every composer looks for the poet whose works spark musical ideas, and you feel that empathetic resonance between the words and your music. I admired the simplicity of the language. Though I don't speak Spanish, I can read it fairly well.

STRICKLAND: The demonic quality in Lorca—what he calls *duende*—is also very present in your music.

CRUMB: There's also the constant combination in his work of the darkest of possibilities with a feeling of joy. Philosophically that's the way I view the world, as immensely beautiful and immensely tragic at the same time.

STRICKLAND: In those works—to return to the question of colorism—you're involved with extended-vocal techniques with Jan DeGaetani, who's virtually screaming at moments, whispering, and so on.

CRUMB: I guess I felt the poetry demanded something in addition to normal *bel canto* singing. It was so intense at times, so intimate at times it needed a much more primeval mode of singing.

STRICKLAND: So it was really Lorca that led you to explore or expand vocal sonorities. Were you aware of what Meredith Monk was doing around that time?

CRUMB: No, although I must say I think we pick up all sorts of influences subconsciously from jazz and—my youngest son is quite a collector of rock music, and I'd heard these sounds in the house, all the Beatles things, and I'm sure things from popular traditions have found their way into my music. Definitely Eastern music—as a student in Ann Arbor I'd heard Chinese opera and modes of singing that had nothing to do with *bel canto.*

STRICKLAND: I can't hear rock in your music.

CRUMB: There are nuances in the voices there. They can become *parlando,* shout, and so on.

STRICKLAND: Hmm. You do similar things in *Apparition.* What led you to set Whitman's "When Lilacs Last"?

CRUMB: Jan DeGaetani had asked me for another work, and I felt I had temporarily no more to say about Lorca, though in recent years I've set his *Canciones para niños.* Yet the little English poetry I knew was somehow more elaborated, autonomous, sufficient to itself, as opposed to the inviting simplicity of Lorca.

STRICKLAND: The one thing I don't like in that work is the vocalise "Invocation to the Dark Angel." It just seems to me to border on the bathetic. The end of the section, when the extended vocal almost seems to exhaust itself, to me is unintentionally comical.

CRUMB: I would agree with you that it's the weakest section of the piece, for whatever reason. Maybe it's conceptually ill advised. I wanted something very dramatic to announce the following poem, "Come, dark deliveress." But it doesn't quite strike the right note. It sounds a little hysterical. Something is not quite right there. I do agree with that.

STRICKLAND: Do you have a favorite among your works?

CRUMB [*without hesitation*]: Yes. It's one of the Lorca settings, *Songs, Drones and Refrains of Death.*

STRICKLAND: You prefer that to the better-known Lorca settings of *Ancient Voices?*

CRUMB: That's better known, but of all my compositions *Songs* seemed to remain closest and most faithful to the original germ of the idea.

STRICKLAND: The dynamic range in your vocals, as elsewhere in your music, is enormous. How do you feel about digital technology? Do you find it liberating in terms of expanded dynamic range in sound reproduction?

CRUMB: I do. My music has always cried for that. In the old technology the engineer would get beautiful things on tape that would all have to be compressed down to here [*looks through thumb and index finger*] when it was there [*stretches out arms*]. The compression of a single sforzando crotale stroke in my music just ruined everything. The range goes from a whisper that the microphone won't even pick up to the needle going off the edge. This new technology is a godsend. A good many of my works are being re-recorded. Even the reissues of the old analogue tapes on CD are still better than the original LPs.

STRICKLAND: Do you have any negative feelings about digital technology?

CRUMB: My first exposure to CDs was some years back when a friend played me the opening of the Mahler First. Those harmonics were never pure before. Then he played the conclusion of the *Pines of Rome* with a huge blast [*laughs heartily*].

STRICKLAND: Converted you. Looking ahead now, are you going to continue the *Makrokosmos* series of piano works?

CRUMB: No. There's a new work for two amplified pianos which carries over a lot of the *Makrokosmos* ideas. It's written for German-speaking performers and called *Zeitgeist*. I project it as the first of a set of three compositions, unless I run out of ideas. So far it's only been played in Europe and needs, I think, some strenuous revision before I'll be quite happy with it.

STRICKLAND: Any other projects?

CRUMB: I'm beginning to sketch a work for David Starobin, a contemporary guitarist who's sent me some works written for him by Elliott Carter and others.

STRICKLAND [*pointing to acoustic guitar propped* against shelves]: That's why that's here?

CRUMB: I can't play it at all—it's my son's—but I want to get to know the sound. I'm thinking of an ensemble work featuring guitar prominently.

STRICKLAND: Anything orchestral? I really admire *A Haunted Landscape*.

CRUMB: I'm glad you like it, but I have to do some revision on that before it's published in conventional form. I have to get back to orchestra for the National Symphony. The commission is informal at this point. But I have numerous other notations in my notebook—you know, "One day I would love to do this or that." [*Laughs.*] I want to do kind of a ballet—a real dance piece, something relating to the South Seas idea. I won't get more precise because it's all a little nebulous.

STRICKLAND: Grass skirts?

CRUMB [*laughing*]: I've never done a work specifically for dance, although a lot of my music has been choreographed. I would love to do a solo cello work in some form. My early solo sonata is a student work. These are just a few ideas and there are lots of others, but I wouldn't speak in detail about any of them because projects abort. I work [*almost mournfully*] very, very slowly. It's a very slow process.

STRICKLAND: But you've produced consistently: You've never been really blocked for long.

CRUMB: I guess, but . . .

John Adams

Photo by Deborah L. O'Grady, courtesy Elektra Nonesuch.

John Adams was born in Worcester, Massachusetts, in 1947 and raised in Vermont and New Hampshire. He received B.A. and M.A. degrees from Harvard University before moving in 1971 to the Bay Area, where he has lived ever since. After a year of warehouse work he obtained a teaching post at the San Francisco Conservatory of Music, which he retained until 1983. He has served as New Music Advisor and later Composer in Residence to the San Francisco Symphony, which has premiered and recorded several of his works under Music Director Edo de Waart.

The 1973 triptych *American Standard*, written under the influence of Cornelius Cardew and his Scratch Orchestra, displayed Adams's interest in both American hymnody and Cageian aleatorics—and in a later incarnation, with the addition of the 1976 tape piece *Sermon* to the centerpiece of the triptych, electronics and Reichian tape techniques.

Adams came to wider attention in the late '70s with the piano solo *Phrygian Gates* and the septet *Shaker Loops*; both were premiered in 1978, recorded the next year, released the next by 1750 Arch Records, and reissued by New Albion in 1986. *Phrygian Gates* extended the modal experimentation of the first generation of Minimalists, while *Shaker Loops* managed to combine the modularism and additive process of Riley, Reich, and Glass with Stravinskian dynamics and dissonance, and Sibelian *tremolandi* with hoe-down fiddling.

Despite roots in swing jazz and hymnody, Adams may be the most traditional of the Minimalists in his absorption of European influence. He has described himself variously as "a Minimalist who is bored with Minimalism" and "more a postmodernist than a Minimalist," though he applied the latter term to himself during our conversation. His large-scale choral work *Harmonium* and his orchestral work *Harmonielehre* illustrate the influence of Mahler and early Schoenberg (after whose 1911 treatise the latter work is named), as well as, again, Sibelius and Stravinsky. Between the two works, however, Adams composed the controversial *Grand Pianola Music*, in which he stood elements of the European tradition on their heads by juxtaposing them with snippets of popular forms *à la* Charles Ives in his more jocular moods.

Among American composers Ives may ultimately prove as important as Reich in Adams's work. Adams has conducted *The Unanswered Question* frequently (once for release on Nonesuch), and that more meditative side of Ives bears strongly on his *Tromba lontana* and other works. Adams imaginatively fused brass ensemble and synthesizer in *Light Over Water*, a dance score similar in its combination of brass and electronics to Ingram Marshall's *Fog Tropes*, which Adams helped develop from its found-sound Ur-text and has conducted both for New Albion and Nonesuch.

In 1941 Aaron Copland wrote, "For a long time there has existed a strong desire for somebody to write a real American opera." This statement implicitly and problematically dismisses Gershwin's *Porgy and Bess* (not to mention *Show Boat*, which like *Porgy* and the later *West Side Story*, has moved from Broadway to the opera house in recent years). The desire may not have been fulfilled until Anthony Davis's *X* and Adams's *Nixon in China*, in which American classical idioms were applied to the first American operas to deal with contemporary public events and figures. (Einstein was more a pretext than a protagonist in the Glass-Wilson *Einstein on the Beach*, which the composer rightly prefers to regard as music theater rather than opera.) *Nixon in China*, a collaboration with director Peter Sellars, librettist Alice Goodman, and choreographer Mark Morris, premiered in October

1987 at the Houston Grand Opera after unprecedented publicity for what was, after all, a rookie performance by the composer. While eschewing the tableaux structure of Wilson's theater of images, it remains highly episodic, an atmospheric prism of extended vignettes in structure, thus in tone ultimately almost as disengaged emotionally as politically.

Afterwards Adams again gave voice to the more rambunctious side of his sensibility with the witty *tour de force Fearful Symmetries*, in which Ellington is filtered through Stravinsky's *Ebony Concerto* and Gershwinian-Bernsteinian theatricality through punk-rock rhythmic insistence. It was paired on disc with a spare and at times even stark setting of Whitman's *The Wound-Dresser*, probably the most accomplished text setting in Minimalism and Adams's most moving composition to date.

Adams conducts both works on the album and continues his association with various orchestras, notably the St. Paul Chamber Orchestra, of which he has been Creative Chair since 1987. A second opera, *The Death of Klinghoffer,* opened in Brussels in March 1991, shortly after the war with Iraq, to tight security and qualified acclaim.

We spoke in September 1989 in a Berkeley coffee shop until it closed for the evening, then concluded our chat in a self-service luncheonette.

STRICKLAND: How do you feel about conducting as opposed to composing?

ADAMS: In the case of the *Wound-Dresser / Fearful Symmetries* disc, I got to know the Orchestra of St. Luke's as the pit band for *Nixon in China*. They're a chamber orchestra which has been very active in New York for the past ten years, a young orchestra, very flexible and very quick to comprehend what I want. We work together very harmoniously. I'd conducted the original *Shaker Loops* and *Light Over Water*, but I'd say this was the first substantial conducting I've done on disc. I have, however, been conducting all my life. It's a very beautifully balanced relationship, because composition is a very introverted and hermetic, at times even claustrophobic activity, and conducting is of course just the opposite, very extroverted, other-oriented, also very physically liberating in a way, very eurhythmically satisfying. I couldn't conceive of doing the two things at exactly the same time—I need to shift gears in my psyche over three or four days—but now I alternate frequently between the two activities.

Last year I did four weeks with the St. Paul Chamber Orchestra, where I'm called Creative Chair—a novel designation insofar as the orchestra, acknowledging the growing specialization in music, instead of having one "philosopher-king" as music director has three specialists now: Chris Hogwood for early music, me for twentieth-century music, and a generalist, Hugh Wolff, who deals with the standard repertoire.

I'm also developing a very good relationship with the London Sinfonietta, and I'll be doing their two opening weeks in November. I work with St. Luke's a lot and do a yearly concert with the L.A. Phil.

STRICKLAND: Which works have you been conducting?

ADAMS: My own in almost every program, but also what I consider a very wide range of twentieth-century music. I've always had a particular interest in Schoenberg—can't quite explain the connection between that and my own style—and I've done works by the other Minimalists, a lot of Steve Reich, works by younger American composers I'm interested in promoting: Aaron Kernis, Paul Dresher, Scott Johnson, the premiere of a work by Michael Torke last year, some Birtwistle, the Górecki Harpsichord Concerto. Conducting and composing for me have a sort of symbiotic relationship, each feeds the other. Conducting also pays the rent very well.

STRICKLAND: More so than composing?

ADAMS [*without hesitation*]: Oh, yes.

STRICKLAND: You've recently been leading a chamber-orchestra version of *Shaker Loops*, which was first recorded as a septet and later in an orchestral version. Which setting do you prefer?

ADAMS: I think the septet has a raw terror that can't be duplicated, but the rather fat orchestral version is nicely sensuous in the middle movement. I think I prefer the version with about twenty players as a combination of both.

STRICKLAND: That piece derived from a now obscure work of yours called *Wavemaker*.

ADAMS: It was a string quartet which grew out of the tactile patterns of *Phrygian Gates*. It crashed and burned, it was malformed. I withdrew it after one performance at the Cabrillo Festival but learned a great deal from my mistakes and turned the piece into *Shaker Loops*.

STRICKLAND: You mentioned Steve Reich. Would you say he's your major influence among the first generation of Minimalists?

ADAMS: Of those composers Reich means the most to me because I think he's the most sophisticated. His pieces are more painstakingly put together and there's more going on in them. I think Glass often presents a fresh and even shockingly new idea, but my basic problem with Philip's music is that there's never more than one thing going on at a time. He never seems to challenge himself with creating more than one layer of music, hence the music gets very tiresome very quickly. At a key point in my development Reich's music had a great deal of meaning for me, and I've always been very open about acknowledging that, unlike a lot of composers who reach a certain level of notoriety and don't want to admit influence. They want to rewrite history or something. I don't. I think that certain pieces of Steve's, particularly *Music for 18* and *Tehillim* and *Music for Mallet Instruments* and *Drumming* were very critical in helping me develop my own style.

STRICKLAND: In *Fearful Symmetries* I find Glass in the broken chords of the synthesizer halfway through and the flute arpeggiations somewhat later, both accompanied by beat punctuations in the winds. In *Nixon* I found the same influence in the storm in Act Two, while the arrival of the plane in the first scene is, weirdly enough, both Glassian and Wagnerian with its fanfare and drone. Did you take Glass as a model when you accepted, initially somewhat reluctantly, Peter Sellars's proposal for *Nixon in China*?

ADAMS: I was reluctant about the project because I wanted to do a more serious, more mythic opera, and the comic possibilities of Peter's subject seemed much more evident. As for Glass, the only Minimalist opera I'd ever seen was *Satyagraha*, and I thought that worked very well because the plain, spare, repetitive musical language which was so *extremely* simple was so perfectly appropriate to the theme of passive resistance. But I could only bear to listen to the piece once or twice. I just can't hang in there.

These citations you bring up are often held up to me, and I've become a little bit defensive. A lot of Glass fans thought I was an opportunist who'd plundered his great discoveries. But you can't work in a simple language like Minimalism or any other strong artistic style without these similarities. I think I can say without any qualification that despite whatever affinities, conscious or subliminal, may exist, my music is radically different. If anything it suggests a very strong evolution away from what Glass has done, and that's the way things ought to be. I'd be delighted to see younger composers developing upon what I've done myself.

STRICKLAND: Do you have any particular affinity for La Monte Young's work?

ADAMS: No.

STRICKLAND: What about Terry Riley? I'm reminded of his *In C* in the opening of *Light Over Water*.

ADAMS: I've performed *In C* several times in the last fifteen or twenty years and each time been more restless. It's influenced me, along with Steve's pieces, but it's almost as if the work is more important for what it could have been than what it was. It's real, pure, simple Minimalism and my mind is just not able to slow down . . . I demand more from musical experience.

STRICKLAND: Would there be Minimalism as we know it today without *In C*?

ADAMS: As Tolstoy says at the end of *War and Peace*, it wasn't Napoleon—history would have invented someone if he hadn't been there. The times demanded the kind of musical revolution that Minimalism brought about. It *had* to happen. When you look at a score by Ferneyhough or Boulez, you realize that kind of complexity couldn't go any further. There *had* to be a violent reaction against it.

STRICKLAND: What were you composing before you joined the Minimalist club, the name of which none of the members seem to like anymore? As a grad student at Harvard were you composing atonally?

ADAMS: No, I never wrote atonal music. Schoenberg is part of my musical patrimony because my main teacher, Leon Kirchner, was his student. Fortunately I was at Harvard at a time of great academic laxness, the late '60s. There was not a tremendous weight upon us as students to compose in a certain style or form. I always had a tonal orientation. I think one's predisposition towards tonality or another system of organization is an organic thing—it isn't just a choice, it's something you were born with. I wouldn't even call it an acquired taste. You experience life tonally or you don't. And it's been such a profound aspect of my being it's never seriously occurred to me to compose in any other way.

STRICKLAND: Why did you come west after Harvard?

ADAMS: I was in Cambridge for six years, two as a graduate student. The normal thing at that time was to have your *Wanderjahre* in Europe, Paris with Boulanger or Italy with Petrassi—but I'd already become profoundly disenchanted with the European hegemony in contemporary music. I detected something very authoritarian and possibly even a little bit phony about the European avant-garde that was in full flower at that time—the Darmstadt school, Berio, Stockhausen. I'd discovered John Cage philosophically if not embraced him musically, and I was interested in an *American* musical language. I was very strongly influenced by jazz since my parents were both amateur jazz musicians. So I knew I didn't want to go to Europe, but I wanted to get the hell out of Cambridge.

The idea was to go west for a year and see what was happening in the Bay Area—I had one friend out here, the composer Ivan Tcherepnin, who, ironically enough, went back to Cambridge the year I came out. My first year was very confused and vague. I spent most of my time in warehouses packing clothes off to the Sears Roebucks of the world. Then by pure chance I landed a job in the San Francisco Conservatory in 1972 and taught there for ten years while establishing myself as a composer and very gradually finding my own voice.

Cage had a profound philosophic more than esthetic effect—teaching me to question what we were handed as standards and canons of taste and methods of procedure. He also made me feel very sanguine about technology and its relationship to music, and I thought California was a good place to explore that. I think I was right. I've been very much in tune with technological advances in music. You wouldn't think, listening to my music, that I'm a heavy techno-freak—which I'm not—but my experience with synthesizers has deeply affected my composing. In the mid '70s I actually taught myself enough electronic engineering to be able to build a synthesizer.

STRICKLAND: Has it affected your orchestration, which is the most sophisticated in Minimalism?

ADAMS: When you work with synthesizers you learn about sound in a way you just *don't* as a composition student involved with earlier music— you learn to analyze, to listen in a very critical way to the attack of the sound, the areas of resonance in its band width, whether a sound is fat or skinny, strident or liquid.

STRICKLAND: But is it difficult to translate the timbre of synthesizer programs into the traditional instruments you largely work with?

ADAMS: Once you're sensitized by that study you can look at the great masters like Strauss and Debussy, Ravel and Stravinsky and Mahler and realize they understood those aspects of sound by firsthand empirical knowledge. Unfortunately most composers today have so little empirical experience with orchestras or instruments this whole aspect of sound is simply abstract and they really don't know how to orchestrate, to take a group of instruments, put them together, and make them *sound* good. I've had that experience since I was a kid but it's been complemented by my experience with electronic instruments.

STRICKLAND: What about the jazz influence you noted? The first-generation Minimalists have mentioned it to me—especially modal jazz.

ADAMS: My primary influence was Duke Ellington. My grandfather owned a dance hall in central New Hampshire called Irwin's Winnepesaukee Gardens, which played host for I think thirty years to all the big bands. When I was a kid my father took me up to hear the Ellington band. They were on the road God knows how many consecutive evenings and probably felt totally burned out, but it didn't matter. The experience of standing in front of that band and hearing them was just one of those indubitably primal experiences which I never got over.

STRICKLAND: There's someone else who could orchestrate!

ADAMS: Exactly. It was his concept of sound, and also the power of his sound—phenomenally powerful without amplification. I'd also mention among the white band leaders Benny Goodman when he wasn't compromising—my father was a clarinet player, and that was my first instrument. As I grew up I got very interested in bop and would take Charlie Parker solos down by dictation, then Coltrane and Miles Davis. I was intrigued to learn from a friend recently that Toru Takemitsu listed his three great influences as—I hope I get this right—Debussy, maybe Ravel, and George Russell, who wrote *The Lydian Chromatic Concept of Tonal Organization* on the modal theory of music. But I find that when jazz became modal around '60 it lost some of the brilliance of its earlier modulations. I still prefer early bop or late swing for the wonderful color of those modulations based on songs.

STRICKLAND: Not being attracted to atonality, were you at all interested in Ornette Coleman or late Coltrane?

ADAMS: I think late Coltrane had less to do with musical structures or languages than states of emotion or consciousness. It was part of the late '60s. I find a terribly reactionary swing taking place now, since many of the developments of the late '60s, including those which involved marijuana or psychedelics, were very important and helped redirect our values at least momentarily. I think some of those developments were quite important, musically and otherwise—[*laughs*] and you as a student of early Romanticism ought to know that.

Similarly, given my interest in opera as reflecting contemporary myths, I wonder if a subject for our generation might not be the recent resurgence of materialism. One might write an opera about the fall of Ivan Boesky. America continues to live out myths that are often very destructive: material success, the Drug War—here we go using martial analogies again! Remember Nixon's "War on Cancer"? Now Bennett's our "Drug Czar."

STRICKLAND: We're all Cossacks. There was Carter's "moral equivalent of war" and Johnson's War on Poverty. [*Note: Shortly after this interview President George Bush declared "war on couch potatoes."*]

ADAMS: But in fact the war's not on drugs but the have-nots, as it's always been. Ever notice on the news that it's always the ghetto that's being raided, always blacks that are shown smoking crack? Now, admittedly, drug use is higher in the inner city, where a lot of desperate people have nothing to live for, but still . . . there's a resurgence of racism, and I truly lament the demise—and let's hope it's temporary—of the liberal spirit in American life.

STRICKLAND: Uh-oh, you said the L-word.

ADAMS: Of course I did—and I'll never forgive Michael Dukakis for rolling over like a dormouse when he should have fired right back. But he couldn't have saved it, it's just the times. If you really want a war on drugs, spend the money on education and information. Look how the gay population reacted to AIDS information—the problem hasn't been solved, but the situation has certainly been ameliorated. Of course you also have to give people the opportunity of a life worth living. If your life isn't worth living, why *not* take drugs? If you can't make a living otherwise, why not *sell* drugs? But no, let's spend all our billions on building jails and intercepting drugs at the border. Forget it. Never worked and it never will.

STRICKLAND: Getting back to the '60s, is there a rock influence on your work?

ADAMS: Yes, very strong but very subliminal, for instance in my pulsation and slow harmonic rhythm. I loved rock but never played it. I didn't play an appropriate instrument, not being comfortable enough on keyboards to attempt it.

STRICKLAND: What's the earliest of your works you want to acknowledge?

ADAMS: For a while I wanted to set the tone of my *opera* by citing *Phrygian Gates* from 1977 as my first mature work.

STRICKLAND: How important is modality otherwise in your work?

ADAMS: Modality, apart from denoting a scale, conventionally implies a static use of it, as in modal jazz. *Phrygian Gates* is the only piece of mine that takes that as a given. My naturally restless disposition as a composer already caused difficulty because I immediately imagined a piece in which modes would *oscillate*—two radically different church modes, the

Phrygian, which is very nervous and unstable, since it starts on the third degree and so opens with a half step, and the Lydian, which begins on the fourth degree and so has a raised fourth—very stable and yet ecstatic, used in a lot of New Age music, which is supposed to induce bliss and ecstasy. The oscillation of modes was combined with the conception that each hand would be a wave form, the two intertwining. It's the only piece of mine that was, to use the vocational term, precompositionally designed. I felt there were very arbitrary moments in the piece where things happened because they had to—according to my plan.

STRICKLAND: It doesn't feel forced to me.

ADAMS: Well, it feels it to me. I'm open about these things. Stravinsky didn't mind criticizing *The Firebird* despite the fact it's a masterpiece and he made millions of dollars off it [*both laugh*]. But I only criticize *Phrygian Gates* to explain why I didn't go on composing that way. I felt the natural sense of rightness and balance within me was so intuitive and internal that I didn't need to make decisions in advance. In the next piece, *Shaker Loops*, a lot more is left to intuition.

Now that I'm a little older and more relaxed I can also acknowledge some earlier pieces. I wrote a piano quintet as a graduate student which I'm ready to release with a little revision. It has obeisances to Berg, Schoenberg, and Bartók, but has a power and originality that look forward to my later works. I also wrote a tape work called *Heavy Metal*—before it became such a popular term—a setting of some passages from William Burroughs's *Nova Express* for speaker and tape. The first piece that's still available is *American Standard*, an experimental triptych from 1973.

STRICKLAND: We have only the central section on disc.

ADAMS: There are two good reasons for that. The outside panels were not very successful. And the third section was a trope on Ellington's "Sophisticated Lady," and I was very naive about copyrights in those days.

STRICKLAND: What's left, *Christian Zeal and Activity*, is a favorite of mine, along with *Harmonielehre*. I don't mean to slight *Nixon*, but I'm not an opera fan.

ADAMS: Neither am I.

STRICKLAND: I'm not a Nixon fan either, which I'm sure also prejudiced me. For example, in the PBS production I found the audience's applause for Nixon's arrival very off-putting—it was clear they weren't applauding your music or the set but Nixon himself. I mean, of all the people to choose—his China initiative may have been wonderful, but Nixon has *so* many other black marks against him I thought you were asking for trouble—[*laughs*] at least with me.

ADAMS: I think I can speak for my co-authors in saying that we were totally unable to control the circus that went on in the ridiculous PBS presentation, where they hauled in Walter Cronkite to read an idiotic introduction to each act. I apologize for that. But the most important thing I have to say about the opera is that my Nixon is not the historical Richard Nixon, he is every President. I take him to be an archetype of an American head of state—maybe not even necessarily a head of state, just any emotionally undeveloped man who finds himself in a position of tremendous power. It's a particularly American figure we've developed. If you take that as a given and try to forget the Nixon of Checkers and Watergate, I think it immediately becomes a more interesting opera. My Nixon has as much relationship to the real Nixon as Shakespeare's Julius Caesar does to the Roman emperor.

STRICKLAND: But he was writing sixteen centuries after Caesar's death. I found the suspension of disbelief harder with a living figure.

ADAMS: Well, what's to be disbelieved? Do you think we're honoring him? I don't think he's honored or damned. He's treated in no predictable way—there are moments when he's quite ridiculous and moments when he's very pathetic.

STRICKLAND: But is there any moment where we see Nixon the cunning conniver?

ADAMS: Definitely that happens in the ballet. I think his treatment of Pat is very interesting.

STRICKLAND: I didn't buy the ballet, frankly, but let's drop—

ADAMS: The ballet was, at least musically, conceived as a piece that might have been written by a committee [*both laugh*]—that's how they composed often during the Cultural Revolution. That was my starting point.

STRICKLAND: So your Nixon isn't Tricky Dick but an archetypal American, archetypal man of power who's somehow imaginatively deprived.

ADAMS: "Imaginatively deprived?" Hmm . . . *I* said he was "emotionally undeveloped."

STRICKLAND: That's Blakean sociology on my part, perhaps.

ADAMS: Let's include them both then—"imaginatively deprived" is quite wonderful, actually. Anyway, I use the term archetype because opera, if it's to be successful, has to function on a mythic level. Otherwise it's utterly ridiculous to have these people running around the stage screaming at the top of their lungs. But for me as an American today the myths aren't King Lear or Odysseus but historical figures and events, cultural focal points often blown up by the media into a mythological dimension, in the way that Andromache meant something very specific to the Greeks. I think that's enough to do me for a lifetime of work.

STRICKLAND: Getting back to *Christian Zeal and Activity*, Michael Steinberg referred to the "dream polyphony" of the score. Is this achieved just by holding voices in the hymnal harmonies and overlapping them with the next?

ADAMS: My phrase was "the homophonies had been liberated"—high-blown language! In any hymn the voices tend to move in blocks, so I went in and unhinged the hasps and let the four voices float in a dreamlike space so that they only rarely come together, and the effect was very beautiful.

At moments it almost sounded like some unwritten Mahler Adagio. I didn't mean it to, but it just ended up sounding that way.

STRICKLAND: One critic referred to the contrast between the dreaminess of the music and the "dogmatic tirade" of the Evangelist. I didn't find it—

ADAMS [*sotto voce*]: He didn't listen very carefully.

STRICKLAND: What was *your* attitude toward the Evangelist?

ADAMS: I don't have an attitude. I chose it because it was outrageous and also very musical—as Southern Evangelists often are. And I thought his story of Jesus healing the withered arm had a real poignancy to it. Without attempting to amplify that poignancy I did—simply by randomly chopping up the tape without any premeditation—following Burroughs's technique of cut-up.

STRICKLAND: There's one problem with that insofar as the fragments at one point intersect as "Take up your bed and walk/God"—as if God were in the vocative.

ADAMS: I never heard it that way. What's interesting about the cut-up technique is that any eventuality, as Cage is fond of saying, can obtain. It can move or it can irritate you.

STRICKLAND: The music was composed independently of the text, called *Sermon*, which was combined with it three years later. Was *Sermon* conceived as an addition to *Christian Zeal*?

ADAMS: I was going to do a performance of *Christian Zeal* in New Hampshire and wanted a new text. When I did *American Standard* I originally wrote in the score of the second movement that any other media connected to the subject were welcomed into the performance.

STRICKLAND: You could dance to it—

ADAMS: Yes, or you could show a movie or do this or that. The first time I did it I just took a tape off a radio talk show of an obnoxious late-night radio host arguing with a preacher over the Bible. The two of them were just *hopelessly* foolish, and I didn't touch the tape at all, just left it as it was and played it. That actually appears on another recording of the same piece on Obscure Records. This was very much under the influence of Cornelius Cardew and the Scratch Orchestra.

STRICKLAND: The only other piece associated with them I know is one I love by Gavin Bryars—

ADAMS: *Jesus' Blood Never Failed Me Yet*?

STRICKLAND: Yes. What was Cardew all about?

ADAMS: Cardew at that time had made a very aggressive about-face against Darmstadt and European Serialism. He became very left-wing in his politics and when I met him here he was a totally, hundred-percent, by-the-book Maoist. He had just previously spent a lot of time in England with a group of young people—some musicians, others art students—and developed the Scratch Orchestra, a kind of People's Orchestra where anybody could play or compose—a kind of free-form, Norman O. Brown, pie-in-the-sky tribal activity, and of course most of the pieces that resulted were pretty awful, but some of Gavin's and Cardew's music had a wonderful freshness and playfulness about it that attracted me a great deal.

STRICKLAND: But there was no specifically religious orientation to Cardew's work? Your *Christian Zeal* and Bryars's *Jesus' Blood* just happened to appear?

ADAMS: Well, Gavin's a sentimental old slob just like me, so the two of us hit it off very well.

STRICKLAND: Is your religious background—which I don't know—important to your work?

ADAMS: Sure. I'm a totally lapsed Episcopalian from New England. My father had no interest in church religion. My mother was brought up a Catholic and sort of half-heartedly converted to Episcopalianism and later Unitarianism, but I think her Catholicism was the most profound and subversive element in her and probably my emotional makeup. As you know, once it's in the family it's there. You can hate it and kick it and spit on it—as James Joyce did—but it's *there*. I was a very earnestly religious young boy, even though I haven't gone to church in the last twenty-five years. I acknowledge the power of music to contact our innermost emotions, which I believe are religious.

STRICKLAND: A lot of quasi-religious emotions are also offered in musical form these days. How do you feel about seeing your records in the New Age stacks?

ADAMS: Usually they only put *Light Over Water* there—it's got a white cover! With some notable exceptions, most New Age music is soporific and basically tries to put its listener into a kind of gelatinous trance.

STRICKLAND: One work that won't put its listener in a trance—how's that for a segue?—is *Fearful Symmetries*. What was the impulse for the piece?

ADAMS: Well, I'd just finally gotten free of *Nixon in China*, which dominated my life for two years, and was in Rome with my family convalescing.

STRICKLAND: Did you find it that much of a strain?

ADAMS: Well, yes, it was extremely hard work. I can't even begin to describe to you how time-consuming and exhausting it is to write an opera—you just don't have help doing it, as with a movie. Just dealing with the huge public interest in the work was very exhausting.

In Rome I was getting an itch to write a new piece, but all that came out was this ridiculous eight-bar phrase that was so square, almost like a figure from a rock or pop tune. I decided instead of hating it I would embrace the beast. Obviously this next piece was going to be about maddeningly symmetrical phrases and their relationship, so I went with it, which I've learned is the only way to continue to survive as an artist, to go with your impulse, no matter how perverse it may be.

STRICKLAND: You've compared it to *Grand Pianola Music*, which is not one of your best-loved works, including by me, but I didn't find *Fearful Symmetries* either fearful or as raucous or bizarre as I expected. Even the half-step modulations were, as my illegible notes say, "pleasantly cacophonous." It wasn't as . . .

ADAMS: Confrontational as *Grand Pianola*? I meant "fearful" in the sense of a silent movie, like . . .

STRICKLAND: Tying the girl to the railroad tracks?

ADAMS: Exactly! By now people aren't as easily shocked by me. *Grand Pianola* really did shock them and make them think I was a charlatan. I'm very fond of that piece, by the way, and I've just made a new recording that Nonesuch will release in another year or so. I think that work will be more appreciated in time than it is right now.

STRICKLAND: The problem is the third movement, which parodies the excess of Beethovenian bravura and gospel, etc., but comes to share their bombast. As Coleridge said of Wordsworth, it's hard to write a poem in the voice of a garrulous narrator without making the poem itself garrulous.

ADAMS: Could be. It's funny that the word "problem" always comes up with *Grand Pianola*. It indicates the mind-set that most people have when they're dealing with contemporary music. Just because a work doesn't fulfil the listener's expectations or fit into a preconceived musical subset . . . in any case, I don't see it so much as consciously parodic as a Trickster piece. There's an element of parody there, I suppose—but primarily it's that I happen to be drawn to certain . . . *things* in our culture, Beethoven or Evangelists or gospel piano. I didn't design the piece in a didactic sense, certainly not in a parodic sense. There was a connection between gospel piano and Beethoven, and without saying, "Gee! I'm going to write a piece and fuse these two elements together and it'll be a big laugh," I just let it happen. The work is not constructed tendentiously—any more than certain literary works with a sense of the picaresque or the wild that we enjoy without being able to analyze them—so I can't pinpoint exactly what it "means."

STRICKLAND: If you do, it's no longer a Trickster piece.

ADAMS: Right.

STRICKLAND: *Fearful Symmetries* makes reference not to Beethoven but to Gershwin, maybe theatrical Bernstein . . .

ADAMS: A very important element in my music is my relationship to popular culture. I think most great art has a very close relationship to popular culture. In *Faust* or *Don Quixote* or Shakespeare or *Ulysses* we can find a wonderful intertwining of quotidian experience with the artistic gesture. What's happened in twentieth-century art in general, but particularly classical music, is that it's gone in a very wrongheaded direction and become very self-referential. Systems of musical grammar become developed that are virtually solipsistic and have no relationship to the *lingua franca*, musical or emotional. People have written of this referring to Noam Chomsky and linguistics, but it seems quite obvious to me that once an art form becomes self-referential it's bound to die. I see in the serial composers, Babbitt, the European avant-garde, that their music *is* inaccessible and tends to be music about itself or similar music.

I've taken a huge amount of stimulus from popular culture and music, whether it's jazz, rock'n'roll, or gospel, and I do it in a way many purists find promiscuous. You know—"It's okay to take these influences and smooth and shape them into a sublime experience, whereas Adams just throws 'em in the soup pot." But I think that's what gives my work its vitality and impact, and I think it's what drives my critics crazy—they feel a kind of alarming energy in it that's somehow not quite decent.

STRICKLAND: *Fearful Symmetries* is an extremely contrapuntal work. Was this premeditated?

ADAMS: Yes. Here I go again criticizing my own work, but . . . one of the things that struck me in *Nixon* was that through the first two acts the orchestra tends to act like a ukelele: the singers sing along and the orchestra strums away. Only in the third act does the orchestra really achieve a contrapuntal complexity with the voices. I was in danger of becoming a composer who functions on one level. So recently I've been working on adding levels of complexity to my music. I'm not talking about making it inaccessible or becoming Elliott Carter but making the experience deeper.

STRICKLAND: Moving from polyphony to harmony, did you see the half-step modulations as a complement to those in *Common Tones in Simple Time*, which as the title suggests were . . .

ADAMS: Smooth. Automatic transmission. I was fascinated by the idea of writing something with chromatic modulations because as far as I know it's never been done by any Minimalist composer.

STRICKLAND: One of the oddest things about *Fearful Symmetries* is the ending a crescendo, pause, and long—what, decrescendo?

ADAMS: Detumescence? That's my West Coast ending.

STRICKLAND: Speaking of anticlimax, I wanted to ask you briefly about *Tromba lontana*. Commissioned as a fanfare, it turned out to be, in your own words, an "incredibly quiet, slowly moving, mysterious, almost ethereal" piece. Is that your idea of a fanfare?

ADAMS: The Houston Symphony had commissioned fanfares from about twenty-five composers. Several of us, independently and unbeknownst to each other, had what we all considered the *outrageously* original idea of writing a quiet fanfare. But the sound of a distant trumpet is very beautiful and appears elsewhere in my work, most recently in *The Wound-Dresser*.

STRICKLAND: I deduce from the liner-note galleys that *The Wound-Dresser*, which precedes *Fearful Symmetries* on the disc, originally followed it.

ADAMS: Yes. That was a tough call, but I think [producer] Bob Hurwitz had the right intuition in putting it first.

STRICKLAND: Otherwise its solemnity is just overshadowed by the rollicking in *Fearful Symmetries*. I can tell you that listening to the two consecutively on the advance tape on the New York to D.C. Amtrak was a real shock to the nervous system.

ADAMS: I guess you can always pull the plug. But honestly, I can only justify this record as the two schizoes of my *phrene*. I was very moved by Sanford Sylvan's portrayal of the almost Lincolnesque figure of Chou En-lai in *Nixon*. For many years I'd had a fantasy of setting *Specimen Days* by Walt Whitman, which has to do with his nursing wounded young men, most of whom died, during the Civil War. Sandy seemed to have the perfect voice for Whitman's feeling. The disparity between Whitman's prose and poetry is dramatic, however, the prose being often totally at odds with my musical ideas, so I chose a fragment of a poem from *Drum-Taps*. It turned out to be in many ways, I think, one of my most important pieces.

I don't disclaim whatever connections may be made with the AIDS crisis—we all know people who have died from or cared for people who have died from AIDS—but what the piece is really about is the relationship of the dying and those who care for them, a relationship that happens every day—I saw it happen between my parents when my father was dying—and is rarely celebrated in art.

STRICKLAND: I think *The Wound-Dresser* is extremely beautiful. And, to be honest, I find it much more successful than the highly praised *Harmonium*, where you set fairly intimate texts chorally, to me incongruously.

ADAMS: I think *The Wound-Dresser* is perhaps my most successful text setting to date. But I think almost all great poetry is intimate. Public poetry just very rarely seems to work somehow. In *Harmonium* the idea of a text setting with no soloist in itself was problematic. And the fragmentation of the Donne poem was a gamble. I think the treatment of the Dickinson poems is perhaps a little more in tune with the texts. "Because I Could Not Stop for Death" satisfies me a great deal. I tried to set *The Wound-Dresser* absolutely simply and used hardly any melisma, since American English does not lend itself to that treatment, as Italian or even German does. The best of American pop and Broadway music by very great composers like Richard Rodgers and George Gershwin had the ability to treat the text in a very direct way, and that's the tack I've taken in this piece.

STRICKLAND: In many of your texts and titles you have a very strong sense of American culture: *Shaker Loops, American Standard, Nixon in China*, texts by Dickinson and Whitman and Burroughs we've mentioned. Is there any conscious effort on your part to—

ADAMS: To be American? With titles like *Harmonielehre*? [*Both laugh.*] I have a very strong affinity to American literature and the American experience. One of my favorite books is *American Renaissance* by F.O. Matthiessen, who somehow managed to encompass the sensibility of a whole era. I also feel there's a real dearth of successful American music drama and the time is absolutely ripe for opera.

STRICKLAND: Was the allusion in the title *Harmonium* to Wallace Stevens?

ADAMS: I was just concerned with harmony—you know, it's a phony word, created by forcing a Latin ending on a Greek root. And it's also the name of a little field organ. It's a coined word for which I coined an additional meaning.

STRICKLAND: My favorite of your works is related in title and chronology and maybe theme. In *Harmonielehre* the third movement, "Meister Eckhardt and Quackie," has your infant daughter whispering a secret, "which also has to do with harmony," according to your album notes, into Meister Eckhardt's ear as she rides through the air on his shoulders. Was this a dream image, like your dream of the tanker rising out of San Francisco Bay that somehow propelled you into beginning the work?

ADAMS: Yes.

STRICKLAND: Are you going to give away the secret?

ADAMS: In that piece harmony was a pun on musical harmony and psychological or spiritual harmony. Hence the second movement refers to the Anfortas wound caused by that mythical king's being out of harmony with both the world and himself. The third movement is definitely a gloss on the conclusion of the Mahler Fourth, a child speaking of heaven, in a purely endowed state of grace, of innocence.

As for the title "Meister Eckhardt and Quackie," it goes back to the image of St. Christopher with the Christ child and Tournier's *The Ogre* and the worm who addresses the old sage from a sack of flour on his shoulder in Günter Grass's *Dog Years*—it's the concept of the homunculus that's important in Medieval alchemy as well as modern psychology. I had a brand-new baby daughter who seemed to impart a sense of grace not only to herself but to the whole household, the grace of a being that had just arrived from nowhere.

STRICKLAND: Why Meister Eckhardt? Was there a connection with the *via negativa* of mysticism?

ADAMS: I was reading Eckhardt at the time, but I think it goes back to John Cage, from whom I first heard of Eckhardt. It's connected to the theme of simplicity that's important in my life and in my art.

STRICKLAND: I bring up mysticism in connection with an article about you in which you criticize Mann's *Doktor Faustus* as a potentially maleficent work for young composers insofar as it promulgates a view of composing as a mystical activity.

ADAMS: No, I really criticized the work for promulgating a view of the composer as—not exactly misanthropic but hermetic, removed.

STRICKLAND: The article contrasts the "mysticism" of waiting for the Muse with the "athleticism" of composing day after day.

ADAMS: The pieces Adrian Leverkühn creates are fiercely complex and inaccessible and are never *heard*: the *Apocalypsis cum figuris* is only performed once—and read poorly by an obscure German orchestra. The image of the great genius Mann creates is of a profoundly diseased albeit brilliant mind. I much prefer mental health.

STRICKLAND: That's connected to the Romanticism of *Harmonielehre*—not just its musical style but the quest motif brought up with the allusion to the Grail-king's wound, which seems connected to your own infertility as a composer at that time. After the "Amfortas Wound" section you have the finale of the flight of Eckhardt and Quackie. The quest ends not with the literal Grail but the liberation of the imagination—as in Harold Bloom's theory of the Romantic internalization of quest romance—in a "grace" that permits creativity.

ADAMS: The arrival of grace is just somehow something you cannot earn. I'm neither a Pelagian nor an anti-Pelagian, but grace seems to be something that either comes or doesn't. You can't earn it. That was my intuition.

STRICKLAND: Would you like to say anything about your relationship to Edo de Waart, who conducted the premiere of *Harmonielehre* and other works of yours?

ADAMS: Edo arrived here as a young Dutch conductor, a very direct and sincere person with a great sense of moral responsibility to among other things American music, about which he acknowledged he then knew virtually nothing. We hit it off very well, and it's proven a very symbiotic relationship. Not only was I able to help him with programming, but he did a great deal to support—morally and materially—the musical imagination he found in me. If it hadn't been for Edo, I don't think I'd have had the rather rapid rise to notoriety I've enjoyed.

STRICKLAND: What about your relationship with Nonesuch, with whom you're now on exclusive contract?

ADAMS: One does not make much money from recordings of contemporary serious music. My records sell well—30,000 for the last few, which must make *Nixon* one of the best-selling operas of all time—but my records are so *extremely* expensive to make. In *Harmonielehre* or *The Chairman Dances* you're out of pocket $30,000 just for the performers. The cost of *Nixon* was staggering. I'm not trying to poor-mouth, and I will say another thing about Nonesuch. It's a wonderful relationship, analogous to the relationship Beethoven and Brahms had to their publishers. Music publishing is no longer the great career promoter that it used to be, while record publishing is. My music is known throughout the world now because of my records, not my publications. Bob is extraordinary because nothing he does is business as usual. He only makes a record if he feels a personal need for it, and he gets *intensely* involved in every aspect of the quality control.

STRICKLAND: Keith Jarrett has spoken to me similarly of Manfred Eicher at ECM.

ADAMS: Bob knows when to leave the engineer and artist alone. Manfred couldn't resist actually getting involved with turning the knobs and making engineering decisions about matters which he knew little about, and I personally think he and I together managed to ruin what could have been a spectacularly beautiful recording of *Harmonium*.

STRICKLAND: I found much of the text inaudible.

ADAMS: Just a mess.

STRICKLAND: What projects are you working on now?

ADAMS: I've recently finished a work called *Eros Piano*. I've been spending a lot of time with the work of Toru Takemitsu. You know, when you reach my—our—age you sometimes feel you'll never have that hit again as you did listening to music when you were younger. But I encountered Takemitsu's *riverrun*, a rather modest piece about fifteen minutes long for piano and orchestra that he wrote for Peter Serkin, who played it in several American cities several years ago, but nobody seemed to have a very strong response. The English performance I found extraordinarily beautiful and listened to it many times and had the response I often do of writing a piece of my own in order to exorcise it. *Eros Piano* is a gloss on *riverrun*, as *Harmonielehre* is a gloss on various Romantic composers. It's a very perfumed, dreamy piece with many influences other than Takemitsu evident: Bill Evans and other American jazz musicians, Ravel . . .

STRICKLAND: What are you composing now?

ADAMS: I've just started another opera with Peter Sellars and Alice Goodman called *The Death of Klinghoffer*, about the 1985 hijacking of the *Achille Lauro* cruise ship, and I think it's . . . *[laughs]* I hope you'll buy it, I hope you'll buy its premise, as you say. I think the historical framework is potentially even more meaningful and interesting than *Nixon* because it has to do with Israel and the struggle over land that's gone on from the Old Testament to the present, as well as the question of the obtuse, uneducated relationship of Americans to world events.

STRICKLAND: Who commissioned it?

ADAMS: Six opera companies—I'll never do this again. It's far too complicated although practical insofar as six companies can pool their resources to pay for the production, which is *far* more expensive than paying for the commission, which allows me to do nothing but compose an opera for the next two years. The premiere is scheduled for March '91 in Brussels, then Lyon, BAM [Brooklyn Academy of Music], Glyndebourne, San Francisco, and Los Angeles.

STRICKLAND: What about recordings?

ADAMS: We have two more albums for Nonesuch that are already made. *Shaker Loops* and *Pianola* should be out in late '90, then one which will have *Eros Piano* and pieces I've conducted: Ives's *Unanswered Question* and some songs of his I've arranged, pieces by Morton Feldman, and early Elliott Carter, and *Fog Tropes* by Ingram Marshall, a composer we both admire. The next album after that will probably be *Klinghoffer*, if we can get the money to get it together. I also intend to do an electronic studio MIDI [Musical Instrument Digital Interface] album—sounds like more boring Technospeak, and with your sensitivity to literature you probably have the same aversion to these acronyms that I do—but MIDI is now a prominent technology whereby you can control any number of synthesizers, drum machines, samplers, etc., with a single computerized pulse. I'll go to work on that once I finish the opera. [*Note: The second disc was released first by Nonesuch in early 1991 as* American Elegies, *without Carter and with David Diamond's* Elegy in Memory of Ravel.]

STRICKLAND: Have you ever thought of or been offered work scoring films?

ADAMS: I frequently get offers, but the working conditions are terrible. Inevitably an agent in Hollywood calls and says, "Money is no object"—money is never an object—"but we need ninety minutes of music in a month." Well, you know, what's the point of killing yourself to make a piece of junk?

STRICKLAND: I guess the money that's no object is the point.

ADAMS: But that's why Hollywood is full of very wealthy film composers who haven't written one single successful piece of music.

Ingram Marshall

Photo by Collette Valli.

Of the myriad American composers utilizing electronic media in the past forty years, no one has been more successful than Ingram Marshall in adapting technology to expressive ends. Rather than the cold and freakish abstraction of many electronic compositions, Marshall has consistently created—in part through a combination of voice and found sounds with acoustic and electronic instruments—works that convey a sense of both grace and haunting.

Marshall was born in Mount Vernon, New York, in 1942. He studied at Lake Forest College and began graduate studies in historical musicology at Columbia University but dedicated much of his time to experimentation at the Columbia-Princeton Electronic Music Center with Vladimir Ussachevsky, Mario Davidovsky, and Ilhan Mimaroglu. He decided to continue in electronic composition, studying with Morton Subotnick at the NYU Composers Workshop. In 1970 Marshall went to the California Institute of the Arts, where he served as Subotnick's teaching assistant and, after earning the M.F.A., as an instructor. At Cal Arts he came under the influence of master Jogjakartan musician K.A.T. Wasitodipura, and he spent the summer of 1971 in Indonesia.

In the mid-'70s Marshall began to combine his interests in Indonesian and electronic music in live-electronic performance works featuring the gambuh (pronounced with short *a* and *u*) flute and analogue synthesizers with complex tape-delay systems. The Indonesian influence is most apparent in his gamelan-inspired piece *Woodstone* but is also evident in the interlocking structure of less overtly Asian-hued works.

Marshall went to Sweden as a Fulbright Senior Researcher in 1976, attracted to the text-sound compositions being explored there. This interest was combined with the aforementioned influences in his breakthrough work, *The Fragility Cycles*, an unsettling anthology of shorter works involving found sounds, gambuh and vocal drones, musical quotation and text-sound—all skillfully united in a vision at once weighty and, as the title indicates, fragile.

In the early '80s Marshall wrote his most frequently performed works, *Fog Tropes* (for brass sextet and tape) and *Gradual Requiem* (for piano, voice, mandolin, and gambuh with tape delay). Both share with *The Fragility Cycles* his distinctive aura of solemnity and mystery and fuse acoustic instruments and electronics with great imagination and craftsmanship. *Voces Resonae* (1984) for the Kronos Quartet combined Sibelius and American hymnody, two abiding presences throughout his work.

In that and other recent works Marshall has turned to more traditional performing ensembles and lyricism. *Sinfonia "Dolce far niente"* (1988) and *A Peaceable Kingdom* (1990) were commissioned respectively by Leonard Slatkin and the St. Louis Symphony and Betty Freeman for the Los Angeles Philharmonic New Music Group. Though Marshall is sometimes called a Minimalist, the *Sinfonia* is perhaps more amenable to the "New Romantic" tag, which is also affixed to his music on occasion. A constant in Marshall's music is a dark Romantic sense of abiding gloom with hints of transcendence, to my ears communicated most originally in his less conventionally scored pieces.

His 1990 Nonesuch album pairs *Three Penitential Visions* and *Hidden Voices*. The first two parts of the penitential triptych derive from an earlier work called *Eberbach*, named after the German monastery, photographs of which by Jim Bengston accompany the music in performance. Marshall also collaborated with Bengston on *Alcatraz* (released by New Albion in 1991), a deleted section of which

now serves as the third of the *Penitential Visions*. *Eberbach* was constructed in
good part of tape loops of the versatile Bengston's saxophone playing in the
church (continuing, apparently without premeditation, the saxophone–tape loop
partnership that goes back a quarter century to Terry Riley's *Dorian Reeds*). They
were combined with Marshall's always evocative *musique concrète* (here of church
bells) and his own voice, a rich bass or falsetto hovering over his sonic landscapes
like a disembodied but mournfully immanent deity who wishes he'd created some
other universe.

Hidden Voices is a masterfully paced work, building up from a soprano invocation based on "Once in Royal David's City," traditionally sung in a Christmas eve
processional by the choristers of King's College, Cambridge, to a dense structure
of digitally sampled voices that seem to rise from some electronic Purgatory rather
than from Eastern Europe and the Soviet Union. The use of the hymn illustrates
Marshall's long-abiding proclivity toward quotation, with the original transformed
at times beyond recognition by his imaginative recontextualizing. As explained below, the piece was not planned as but became a memorial to Marshall's mother a
decade after he began writing *Gradual Requiem* for his father.

Marshall continues to explore an ominous nocturnal realm of haunted spirits
that evokes the starkness of Old English elegies. Whatever stylistic or technical affinities Marshall's music has to Minimalism and New Romanticism, his work represents a revaluation of Impressionism and the *old* Romanticism of Bruckner and
Mahler. With his programmatic, quasi-narrative impulses, combined with his
painterly sonic techniques, Marshall may be our finest exponent of the electronic
Tondichtung.

We met in February 1990 at the studio where he was completing the recording
of *Hidden Voices* with soprano Cheryl Bensman Rowe and taped our conversation
the next afternoon over lunch at his mother-in-law's Westchester home.

STRICKLAND: Where did you study music?

MARSHALL: I went to Lake Forest College near Chicago. I majored in music
    but took a lot of history too. I took piano and voice but gravitated to
    music history. It was a small liberal arts college where you didn't major
    in a particular instrument, you did history and theory. I did some com-
    position too, but I wasn't exactly encouraged.

STRICKLAND: Which area of music history most attracted you?

MARSHALL: I like Baroque music a lot. After Lake Forest I studied musicol-
    ogy at Columbia and got interested in eighteenth-century esthetics, par-
    ticularly the doctrine of "affections," which has to do with how music
    represents emotions. That's something in our age we had forgotten
    about, in terms of our systematization. Everyone says music's emotional,
    but in what way we don't really know. However, in the eighteenth cen-
    tury, as a holdover from the Cartesian philosophy, you really could clas-

sify everything. The big guy was Mattheson. It was all in black and white: this key's good for heroic feeling, this key for sadness, this kind of melody for jealousy.

STRICKLAND: We still have historically based analyses of Bach preludes and fugues in terms of *Affekten*. D-sharp minor represents gloom . . .

MARSHALL: Schweitzer's book on Bach talks a lot about that. In any case, that approach to his music fell out of favor but may be coming back. A musicologist named Marshall—no relation—has recently written a book on the subject. As I drifted away from music history and towards composition, I forgot about these things. But later on in life I've come to realize the portrayal of emotions and feeling in music is very much with us after a period of drought.

STRICKLAND: Where would you locate that drought?

MARSHALL: You *might* say the whole twentieth century has concerned itself less with the emotional side of music and more with the cerebral side, but, more specifically, in the post–World War II period there was a shunning of Romanticism because of the feeling that Romanticism was in a way responsible for the terrors of war. Maybe it was, in the kind of mysticism associated with the rise of nationalism and Nazism. So I think there was a desire to cleanse the art of music of its Romantic trappings. Stockhausen, Boulez—you know, the whole gang . . .

STRICKLAND: Boulez seemed militantly puritanical, espousing "progress" but at times in an almost dictatorial and anal-retentive way.

MARSHALL: The same impulse to purity may account for the beginnings of Minimalism too, in a funny way. In its purest form, like La Monte Young's early work, you're seeing something dealing with purity and absolute relationships that has more to do with Webern than anyone else. La Monte writes a piece that's just an open fifth played for a long time—but it has to be *perfectly* tuned, to symbolize, in his mind, the perfection of the universe. This kind of purity is associated in my mind with a turning away from "affections."

In New York in the mid to late '60s, when I was a graduate student and afterward, there were a number of musicians interested in reducing art to its basics—namely, the composer Charlemagne Palestine, who used to do tremendous improvisations on the carillon in the St. Thomas Church on Fifth Avenue, the film maker Tony Conrad, all the people around La Monte Young, and the Tone Roads people, such as Malcolm Goldstein and Jim Tenney, who were allied with Cage and Feldman.

After World War I there'd been a similar cooling-off period. Just look at Stravinsky—the fire and passion of the early ballets. Then the war comes along, nothing happens for a few years, then you have all these neoclassic works, colder, more austere, though in his case never completely so—he always managed to get a good tune in there somewhere.

STRICKLAND: I think La Monte's aiming at *Affekten* Mattheson never dreamed of. Anyway, he wasn't an influence on you . . .

MARSHALL: No. A work like Terry Riley's *In C* had a certain impact. I heard that about the time I was first exposed to Indonesian gamelan music, with which it shared the steady pulse and metallic quality and the inter-weaving of melodic fragments that could work any which way. I associated the two, even though *In C* doesn't have formally much to do with gamelan.

Steve Reich's *Drumming* is a real masterpiece, and some of the things Steve was doing with rhythm and melody I tried to emulate in my work at that time by doing them with harmony. It didn't work [*laughs*]. I did a piece called *Augmented Triad Ascending*, an augmented triad constantly shifting in different ways with different instruments. Seemed like a good idea, but it just didn't add up to anything. That's one of the big problems with process music in general—the process happens, but that's it. Steve's *Clapping Music* is very simple process music, but it works.

In my music I've tried to modify process music so I don't become a slave to it. The biggest errors I've made are when I've let the process rather than intuition take control. It's more old-fashioned, of course, to let your ear dictate, but it took me a long time to realize that's the way to do it!

STRICKLAND: To what extent are Minimalist elements present in your work?

MARSHALL: The term Minimalism is like sonata-allegro form. No one who practices it uses the term. Mozart wouldn't know what a sonata-allegro was if you hit him over the head with it. To me the real Minimalists are people like Alvin Lucier and Phill Niblock. Feldman was in a way a Minimalist, although he would probably have eschewed the term. It was borrowed by music critics from the art world.

STRICKLAND: Reich says by Michael Nyman, Glass says Tom Johnson.

MARSHALL: H. Wiley Hitchcock says Barbara Rose first used the term in art criticism. If you think of repetition and the gradual unfolding of a process as being Minimalist, to that extent my music is Minimalist. But minimal music has been called "process music," "systemic music," and "repetition music." Once people like Reich start writing more complex works and through-composing rather than using modules, I think you've left pure Minimalism behind. As for my own music, I'm not a pure Minimalist either, as I leave process behind and follow a more intuitive path.

STRICKLAND: I'm really more interested in your relationship to the whole tape tradition. How about Stockhausen, whom we've already mentioned?

MARSHALL: The piece that hit me was *Gesang der Jünglinge*, which almost goes against his esthetic at the time, as reflected in the icy precision of his other electronic work. That piece represents a marriage of French *musique concrète* and German *Elektronische Musik*, the real world and the world of oscillators.

STRICKLAND: You studied with Vladimir Ussachevsky at Columbia, who gave the first American tape concert in October 1953 at the Museum of Modern Art.

MARSHALL: He was my first important composition teacher, though as an undergraduate I received help from Ann Bowen. Then I wasn't sure I wanted to compose. But when I got into graduate school I suddenly saw the light, realizing with electronic music I could compose directly onto tape as an artist paints directly on his canvas. That's the great advantage of tape music, the direct relationship between the head sound and the composer's work—there's no middleman. Now I love to work with ensembles, but that was what gave me the initial impetus back then. Without it I might not have gone into composition. Electronics may have made it possible for me.

Ussachevsky was very encouraging. I always appreciated that. Had he not been . . . who knows? I miss him now that he's gone. I didn't see him much over the years, but a little over a year ago he happened to be out in Olympia for a SEAMUS conference at Evergreen and heard me conduct *Fog Tropes*. I don't know what he thought of it, but I suddenly felt a strong connection to him. He was in fine shape. Then, of course, he got brain cancer and died. After his death I started thinking, "My God, that man really meant a lot to me!" Wish I'd told him.

There were also Davidovsky and Mimaroglu, but their music somehow washed over me. I think technically, much more than stylistically, I learned a lot from the three. After Columbia I got involved with the NYU School of the Arts music studio, a more free-wheeling place—almost anyone could go there if they agreed to the cooperative spirit of the space. Mort Subotnick kept the whole thing going, and there was a great air of convivial collegiality with people like Charlemagne Palestine, Serge Tcherepnin, Rhys Chatham, and Maryanne Amacher. A few years later I went to California Institute of the Arts and became Mort's teaching assistant.

STRICKLAND: Ussachevsky was the first to combine live instruments with tape. I was wondering if that led you in the same direction.

MARSHALL: No, my first works were pure tape pieces. The first piece I ever played in public was called *Transmogrification*, which used a singing and speaking human voice modified through splicing, speed change, filtering. My girlfriend was a dancer, and I had her reciting and singing William Blake's "And did those feet in ancient time."

STRICKLAND: Did Takemitsu's *Vocalism 'I'* have any influence on that or the other vocal/tape pieces?

MARSHALL: No, it impressed me, but I never liked it that much.

STRICKLAND: Did the electronic lyricism of at least some of Subotnick's work influence you?

MARSHALL: Maybe *Touch,* which Columbia recorded. Entirely done on the Buchla synthesizer, it has a ringing, gamelanic quality I liked a lot, which shows my interest in that area when I got to Cal Arts. I was obsessed with it from about '70 to '74 and went to Bali and Java in the summer of '71.

STRICKLAND: How about Varèse?

MARSHALL: I used to think he was the greatest thing to ever come down the pike, though he was misunderstood and poorly performed. The first electronic piece I ever heard was *Poème électronique*, which I heard on the radio as an undergraduate. I turned on the radio as loud as I could and stuck my head right down into it to drink it all in. Another piece that interested me, though it's not as successful, is *Déserts*. There's a great live recording of its premiere in Paris, just as scandalous as *Rite of Spring*. The audience is making all kinds of noises. Hoots and catcalls . . . the French, you know . . . they considered him scandalous even in the late '60s, when I was in Paris. He worked with sound like a sculptor, with sounds as masses. He wasn't interested in whether something was an inversion of an interval that happened in a row some measures back. It was like metallurgy. The Columbia-Princeton types could never figure out what his system was. He didn't *have* any system, or if he did it wasn't important. Like Ives, he wanted to manipulate conglomerates of sound.

STRICKLAND: Varèse calls to mind Pierre Schaeffer and the origin of *musique concrète*. Have you ever done sound installations like Schaeffer or, more recently, Max Neuhaus?

MARSHALL: I did a piece in San Francisco in '78 or '79 called *Water Walk* in which I used recordings of mountain brooks. Four channels of tape were fed to loudspeakers hidden in the ivy of a very formal park. As you'd walk along the path you'd hear the sounds being filtered higher and higher until the water sounded more like wind. My esthetic couldn't deal with the transitory or aleatory aspect of environmental sound, however. Doug Hollis and Bill Fontana do this well, but it wasn't the right path for me to pursue.

STRICKLAND: How about multimedia? Subotnick is known for that.

MARSHALL: Mort was kind of a techno-freak, maybe still is. I've been involved in it, but I've tried to keep it simple. In both *Alcatraz* and *Eberbach* I've collaborated with Jim Bengston. His very beautiful photographs change slowly on the screen, one fading into another, like a very slow movie. In *Alcatraz* you'll see a wall become another wall, then a cell. Very gloomy but beautiful. I composed the music very much to the order of the slides. In *Eberbach,* which is now the first two parts of *Three Penitential Visions,* the subject is a German monastery. I had the photographs but didn't know the order, so Jim ordered them to my music. We're calling them musico-visual operas, the photos being the libretto.

STRICKLAND: What about *Fog Tropes*, which was originally a sound score for performance artist Grace Ferguson's "Don't Sue the Weatherman"?

MARSHALL: First I just gathered the sounds of foghorns, bird cries, and so on for that. Her piece dealt with acting, dancing, and mime. It was a rather amusing narrative about a Fog Woman who sort of controlled the weather in San Francisco, but it didn't have much success.

STRICKLAND: *Fog Tropes* has.

MARSHALL: But *Fog Tropes* was a later development. The original tape piece was about half an hour, then I took one central section of it, changed it a little bit, and played it as a separate piece called *Fog*. Then a year later John Adams was doing a series called New and Unusual in San Francisco and suggested I add brass for that performance. First I thought of just low brass—tubas and trombones—but then realized a balanced brass ensemble would work.

STRICKLAND: How difficult was it to incorporate the brass into the environmental sound?

MARSHALL: It was fairly easy. The foghorns gave the tape a pitched sense—A, C, and D—so I built the brass parts around those pitches.

STRICKLAND: Was that the first time you'd combined tape with more than a single instrument, usually your Balinese gambuh?

MARSHALL: In '75 or '76 I did a piece called *Non Confundar Gambuh* for strings, alto flute, and clarinet, and treated them exactly as I treated oscillators in the piece called *Gambuh*. They went through tape delay and filters. The amplitude of the wind sound would make the filters of the strings go up higher and change the timbre of the strings. John Adams conducted it in San Francisco and later with Steve Reich's ensemble in New York.

STRICKLAND: Did *Fog Tropes* influence his *Light Over Water*?

MARSHALL: If you compared our music after 1973, the year of our acquaintance, you might find similarities. We really got along well. I know he's influenced me, and I may have influenced him. *Shaker Loops,* a great piece, showed me that modular melodic fragmentation could be taken beyond what Reich had done with it and be put in a more composerly, intuitive framework.

STRICKLAND: The influence might be heard in your string quartet, *Voces Resonae*.

MARSHALL: Maybe. And possibly in a trio I've written for piano, violin, and cello that'll be premiered next month. The cellist who commissioned it, Jenny Culp, was in the original group that John wrote *Shaker Loops* for. We were all such good friends I might have subconsciously gone in the direction of *Shaker Loops*.

STRICKLAND: One more question about '60s electronics. Did you feel affected at all by Musica Elettronica Viva—Curran, Rzewski, and Teitelbaum—or the Sonic Arts Union—Mumma, Ashley, Lucier, Behrman?

MARSHALL: It's secondary. I never heard MEV in their heyday—they were in Europe then. My first public concert in New York after Columbia was the WBAI Free Music Store, and MEV were playing too. They were so disorganized. Rzewski would improvise a little on piano, Teitelbaum would throw in some snoots and snorts on synthesizer . . . I think Garrett List was there with a few honks on his trombone. They seemed totally uninterested in the audience and unhappy because things hadn't been set up right. This art is so close to life—you know, "If something happens, great! If not, don't worry about it." I've heard good recordings of theirs, and I hear some of their performances could be electrifying. Rzewski's later composed work I like a lot. I've always liked Lucier's work—*I Am Sitting in a Room* is a real masterpiece.

STRICKLAND: It used to drive my roommate absolutely crazy. She finally refused to let me play it when she was home.

MARSHALL: I also liked Ashley's early work, but he lost me after a few years. Mumma's technical prowess fascinated me—seemed he could do anything with electronics.

STRICKLAND: I'm not a great fan of tape music, but I saw a connection between your work and things like David Behrman's *Figure in a Clearing* or *On the Other Ocean* and Alvin Curran's *Fiori chiari* or *Canti e vedute*—

MARSHALL: Curran's *Magnetic Garden* and my *Fragility Cycles* have something in common. I like David's work—and David too—but I don't think there's an influence. As often happens, you'll have two or three people doing things concurrently that have a similar resonance. Swimming in the same pond.

STRICKLAND: *The Fragility Cycles* was released on IBU . . .

MARSHALL: That was my own label. A lot of people in the '70s just made their own records. New Albion, which released *Fog Tropes* and has been very successful, started in a way as a vanity label. After years of being teased and given the run-around by Manfred Eicher and ECM, I finally suggested to Foster Reed, my friend who'd played mandolin on *Gradual Requiem* and had access to some family money, that we put it out ourselves. If he hadn't come through, I'd probably have had to revive old IBU for a second release.

STRICKLAND: When did you start writing *The Fragility Cycles*?

MARSHALL: In '75 I started doing pieces with the gambuh using tape delay, very simple analogue synthesizer chords. First I developed a piece called *Gambuh*, not very long, an ascending series of chords and some melodic elements from the flute with a series of tape delays. Then I started building things around it. I added the Swedish text-sound piece and the wild *Sibelius in his Radio Corner* piece. Now *that's* multimedia [*laughs*]—in performance I always show this very haunting photo of Sibelius in his easy chair listening to the radio. [*Mimics magisterial voice*] *This*, Edward, is a *truly* Minimalist multimedia piece . . . especially since I don't do anything during that section except sit in a chair myself and wait out the tape.

STRICKLAND: Another interesting section is the opening "Cries on the Mountain" with the herding calls. What's that very strange thin melody that opens with a sixth?

MARSHALL: Those are old recordings made before the war, released by Swedish Radio. They went up to northern Sweden and sent them back to the station in Stockholm by telephone lines—isn't that weird? The cries go [*does herding call; interviewer shakes head, sings melody*]. Oh, *yes*, you're right! There's a children's song in there—I forgot. It's not mentioned in the liner notes. I recorded that off the radio in Norway, actually. The whole section is a strange collage. I also have a part where I let a microphone hang down as I walked on skis through the snow.

I did a piece called *Weather Report* on tape—a weather report by Danish radio but emanating from Greenland, I think. A very lilting Danish voice telling what the weather's like in various places from Greenland through northern Europe, the Mediterranean, North Africa, and out to the Azores. Like a little tour of the whole area.

STRICKLAND: *The Fragility Cycles* may still be my favorite piece of yours, but also in the running is *Gradual Requiem*. I've already confessed my technological ignorance, so could you explain to me how Part V "begins with infinite delay regressing to simple four-channel echo"?

MARSHALL: In *Gradual Requiem* I used a fairly complex tape-delay system. I would take two four-channel tape recorders—that is, they have four distinct channels of sound, like quadraphonic—and I would run the tape from one machine to the other so that the tape starts on machine one, passes over the heads of that machine, and then instead of being taken up on the same machine goes over to machine two and is taken up there. Needless to say, the machines have to run at exactly the same speed. What's recorded on machine one is played back on machine two. I can then take the sound on machine two and send it back to machine one on another channel.

I get increasing longer delays—I can get eight different channels of super-reverberated sound. At its most complex it's very rich and resonant to the point that it's hard to tell what's going on for the reverberance. The section starts off with that very rich array of delays and slowly comes back to what I call a simple four-channel delay, which sounds more like an echo than a long noticeable delay. In *Gradual Requiem* and elsewhere I've used delays as a structural element, not just an "effect" to make it sound juicier or warmer or wetter, as they say in the trade.

STRICKLAND: You mentioned you weren't thrilled about this week's premiere of another tape/ensemble piece, *A Peaceable Kingdom*, in L.A.

MARSHALL: It was a real crowd pleaser, but I wasn't happy about the balance between the eight woodwinds, nine string players, and keyboard with the tape. If one had time, one could work on that, but one [*glumly*] never has it.

STRICKLAND: I realize rehearsal is limited whether it's the Beethoven Fifth or an unknown work. How many hours of rehearsal do you have?

MARSHALL: The first rehearsal was about an hour, the second maybe forty-five minutes, the third maybe an hour. I would have liked to work a little on tuning and intonation: "Look, here the tape is actually a little flat, so I'll ask you to tune down a little bit." They could do that, though it's very subtle. But there just wasn't time. Or "Here the violins and violas are marked *mf*, but I can't really hear you properly, so play a little louder." All these things you could normally do in an orchestra rehearsal are harder to do with a tape because you have to listen to it, stop, rewind . . . that's one of the problems with tape/ensemble pieces—you really need more time. The perfect performance of this would be put together in a recording studio.

STRICKLAND: Glenn Gould was ahead of his time.

MARSHALL: The audience enjoyed it a lot, but I was sort of writhing in pain and felt really surprised they seemed to like it. Maybe they found the rest of the program pretty dull. Taken by themselves, the ensemble parts are not difficult. The conductor told me over the phone, "Look, this is a piece of cake." I said, "Yes, but coordinating it with the tape is going to be tricky." He said, "Maybe so, but the players won't have any trouble with this, they'll play it right off the bat." But there were still some intonation problems. It's hard for them to play in tune with all those bells ringing on the tape. Bells sound out of tune even when they're *in* tune.

So you come to the first rehearsal with your tape. The musicians come with their parts, some of them looking at them for the first time . . .

STRICKLAND: Is your tape adjustable or played intermittently?

MARSHALL: It's an eighteen-minute tape played straight through, even though there are times when there is only silence on the tape. Another problem with tape is that you never know until you get into the hall what the actual acoustical balance will be like.

STRICKLAND: But the band ultimately has to keep up with—or down with—the tape or we're in trouble. Another technical question about this work is how you created a mini-waltz from a funeral song through digital sampling.

MARSHALL: The Yugoslavian village band is playing this march [*sings*]. I took that opening phrase [*sings*], got it into my digital sampler, so that when I play middle C on the keyboard you hear [*sings same phrase*]. I play B-flat, and it goes [*sings phrase a tone lower*]—whatever note you play it shifts the pitch of the phrase—*and* its tempo, slower as you go down, faster as you go up. So on the tape I created this rocking thing back and forth, slow-fast-slow . . . all the way down finally to G—kind of like a very *rubato* waltz. The ensemble has to play along, so they have to watch the tempo very carefully.

This piece and *Hidden Voices* both use digital sampling technique. A lot of my earlier works use tape loops. So I've gone from analogue technology to the more advanced technology of digital samplers—*just* to let you know that I'm *completely* up-to-date [*both laugh*]. Let me just check the noodles—hey, don't eat any more of that bread! I don't care if you're Irish, I'm making some pasta now.

STRICKLAND: Our cuisine may be impoverished, but we're rich in the preternatural. Did you know Randall Thompson did a piece in '36 called *The Peaceable Kingdom?*

STRICKLAND [*from the kitchen*]: Is it a choral piece?

STRICKLAND: Yeah, mixed and *a cappella*, eight choruses from Isaiah. Where'd you get your title, Edward Hicks?

MARSHALL: Well, it's complicated. I started writing the piece last summer in Vermont. The very beautiful place where my wife and son and I were staying is on the side of a mountain—it's very peaceful and the people who have been going in the summer for forty years have always called their property The Peaceable Kingdom. They're very much involved with children's books. Clement Hurd was an illustrator of children's books, and his son Thacher is also. There's a famous series of paintings by the American Edward Hicks, and there's a painting by Rousseau often called *The Peaceable Kingdom*, but I don't think that's its real name. Anyway, it's the idea of the lamb lying down with the lion, the white man and Indian trading. I was living in The Peaceable Kingdom thinking about funerals and the passage from this world to the next as a peaceable kingdom. Many people conceive of heaven as a peaceable kingdom. I wasn't trying to be funereal, but I was thinking about the transition from life to death, which is so natural and communal in this Yugoslavian village. People mourn, of course—it's a very sad event, but as in most traditional cultures the transition from life to death is not viewed with the cold distance with which we tend to view it. Anyone who dies there gets a proper funeral—the whole town is there, as in Bali, where they cremate them.

STRICKLAND: "The Peaceable Kingdom" is really heaven, the afterlife, as well as the site of composition.

MARSHALL: Yes, but the title is *A Peaceable Kingdom*, not *The Peaceable Kingdom*, because we all have our own.

STRICKLAND: An interesting feature of your ensemble and orchestral work is that although the harmony seems more conservative you tend to evade traditional harmonic resolution—in both movements of the string quartet and *Sinfonia*.

MARSHALL: Just because you're working with traditional tonality doesn't mean you're bound by the dictates of standard harmonic theory. You can play off the expectations and thus create a dramatic situation. Starting in C major doesn't mean you have to end in C major. At the end of *Sinfonia* there's a sudden shifting of gears into the relative minor of the dominant. It *has* bothered others, who felt it was so tonal as to require the tonic, but I wanted to leave a question at the end.

STRICKLAND: Your work has been described as New Romantic, and if any of it fills the bill it's the sinfonia and the quartet. But after a largely diatonic two movements, the quartet just—it's as if Del Tredici just left us hanging.

MARSHALL: As for the quartet tape, it doesn't resolve but peters out. That's because only the first two movements of three were performed and re-corded on the tape you have. I sent the piece to Kronos as I wrote it. I was late with the last movement and they felt they didn't have enough time to rehearse it. I told them they'd have it in March but gave it to them in April.

STRICKLAND: How do you find working with others as opposed to alone, as you did in *The Fragility Cycles* and elsewhere?

MARSHALL: I've done that so much that for now I'm more interested in working with good musicians. Who knows? I may go back to that. When I was performing, like everyone else, I experienced a case of nerves be-forehand. But once the performance got going I often felt a wonderful sense of well-being, a great sense of satisfaction. I think any musician would know that feeling. The one advantage of solo work is the sense of control, although with live electronics and open mikes the acoustics can be out of your control. I was once completely thwarted by the acoustics of a hall in Berlin, which apparently wanted to play Stockhausen.

STRICKLAND: Are there other composers labeled Minimalist or New Roman-tic—or nothing—you admire?

MARSHALL: I've always admired John's work, though I've had trouble getting into his magnum opus, *Nixon in China*. I just don't like opera that much. His recent work, like *The Wound-Dresser,* is beautiful. I think Steve's recent *Different Trains* is also very good. I liked Glass's *Satya-graha*—the simplicity of its scoring for just strings and winds, its static and ritualistic quality—and saw it twice, but I liked it more the first time and I haven't liked what I've heard since. La Monte is a wonderful per-son and in a way the mother of us all, but also full of it in a way, concocting these theories and playing to invented intervals nobody's ever heard before in the universe. *Strange.* I like some of Riley's string quartets and *In C.* I like Arvo Pärt a lot, and recently I heard the Pole Górecki's Third Symphony and was strongly attracted to it. I see flashes of very interesting stuff in some people sometimes called New Roman-tics who compose very directly and skillfully for orchestra: Christopher Rouse, Stephen Albert, Bob Beazer, Joan Tower, Stephen Stuckey. Stylis-tically they're very different but write for the orchestra very naturally, very intuitively, more concerned with sound *per se* than with any formal system. Michael Torke and Aaron Kernis also seem quite original among the younger symphonists.

STRICKLAND: What about the latest New York avant-garde?

MARSHALL: I have no interest whatsoever in that school. Leaves me cold. I just don't know what to make of it, don't quite see the point—like graffiti art. I'm not saying they're not important. I'm just out of sympa-thy. Fred Frith was performing the same day I was at BAM [Brooklyn Academy of Music], and I could see the skill involved, but it seemed kind of silly. I don't like Zorn's music, and though I don't know him person-ally, in his published statements he seems like a loudmouth. I think a lot of them don't understand their own tradition—the Cageians of the '40s and '50s—maybe because they're a little young.

STRICKLAND: Not to play New York Avenger, but I don't care too much for the final section of *Three Penitential Visions*, which I feel introduces a note of levity I don't find congruent with the rest, which is weightier and lovely.

MARSHALL: That section was composed for *Alcatraz*, but I felt it wasn't right for the piece.

STRICKLAND: I don't think it's right for *Three Penitential Visions*.

MARSHALL: I always liked the section, and the reason I think it's right for *Three Penitential Visions* is that it provides an escape, a release of tension.

STRICKLAND: It's a release of tension, but I feel it's kind of disjunct, imposed, as if you played the Italian Concerto after the *Art of Fugue*. I guess I didn't find it very penitential.

MARSHALL: Maybe you should [*laughs*] think of it as a different piece. I'll be [*demi-sec*] sure to put an index-point before it on the CD, so people can hear the work without it.

STRICKLAND: What I found odd about *Three Penitential Visions* is the equation of the penitentiary and the monastery. I find that a problematic association. I've spent weeks or weekends in monasteries—not in prisons, yet—from time to time, and I've never seen it as an incarceration but a liberation.

MARSHALL: I'd have to say it's an ironic association. Men go willingly to a monastery to spend lives of work and meditation. However, it does represent a kind of imprisonment, the traditional walled monastery. And a prisoner should also be a penitent—thus the word penitentiary—just as monks traditionally do penance for their sins.

STRICKLAND: And ours. It may be just a difference in our sensibilities. When did you record the ethnic vocals for *Hidden Voices*, a great piece which follows on the CD? The concatenation of voices in the section named "A Gathering" is magnificent.

MARSHALL: That was a commission from Nonesuch. I had recorded things in Serbian Orthodox churches—the singing there is wonderful—and in 1987 I was sort of on the prowl, recording all over the place, but nothing really seemed right for that piece. I finally went back to some wonderful old ethnic recordings I had found, done in the '30s or '40s in northern Russia, of a bridal dirge, plus some stuff from Hungary and Romania and central Russia—they're all laments sung by women.

STRICKLAND: Bridal *dirge*?

MARSHALL: Yes, there's a tradition in Eastern Europe of a bridal lament or dirge.

STRICKLAND: For what? Her virginity?

MARSHALL: No, it's a patriarchal society and the tradition says that when a bride goes to her husband's family it's a kind of death. She's losing her freedom, it's something to be lamented. In the traditional Dinaric society in Yugoslavia women are treated as possessions, though not so much in the postwar years. In fact, in Stravinsky's *Les Noces* there's a bridal dirge by the bride's mother.

STRICKLAND: What about the Corsican singing in *Gradual Requiem*?

MARSHALL: Again, it came off an old ethnic recording. It was a glee club chorus of men singing the Mass in church. Corsica maintained a very old liturgical tradition of laymen singing the Latin Requiem Mass.

STRICKLAND: Let's go from Corsica back to Bali. What took you there in '71?

MARSHALL: I went to Cal Arts to study composition and work with Morton Subotnick with a specialization in electronic music. But what instantly grabbed me was that they had an entire gamelan there led by a wonderful man named K.A.T. Wasitodipura.

STRICKLAND: What did he play?

MARSHALL: Everything. When you're a musician in Indonesia you play everything: drums, a little fiddle called the rebab . . . he had a lot of influence on me because of his quiet presence and the way he approached making music. When we write our résumés we put down various composers, but it occurs to me that I really never got that much from the others compositionally, but I got worlds from him, as if by osmosis. Bali was a very unique culture, Hindu amid an Islamic culture, albeit a very peculiar form of Islam.

STRICKLAND: Not Shiite or Sunni.

MARSHALL: Javanese basically worship rocks. They are very spiritual people, and down deep animists, with a Hindu, then a Buddhist layer, and a relatively recent Islamic layer with some Christian elements that have gotten in there. Bali is Hindu. Javanese gamelan music is more deep, ponderous, slow-moving—some Javanese pieces will go on for twenty-five or thirty minutes. In the West we're used to that with our symphonies, but outside of music drama like Chinese opera or Japanese Noh plays and others there aren't many forms in the Orient that last that long. Their structure is quite wonderful. I like that slow-moving, slowly evolving sense of music.

STRICKLAND: Does *Woodstone*, the piece you wrote for American Gamelan, resemble more the Balinese or the Javanese style?

MARSHALL: I didn't try to write a piece specifically in either style. I just tried to write something that was me. I don't think a Balinese or a Javanese would recognize *Woodstone* as gamelan. I've used Javanese formal elements in some of my other music; the *Sinfonia "Dolce far niente"* has a Javanese gong structure and a section deliberately modeled after the Balinese gamelan sound, much to many people's disappointment, I think. If I'd wanted *Woodstone* to sound Indonesian I wouldn't have fooled around with the theme from the Beethoven *Waldstein* Sonata that gave me the title [*sings theme*]. Just happened to fit in with the notes of a gamelan, and I got carried away.

STRICKLAND: What brought you to Sweden a few years after Indonesia?

MARSHALL: At Cal Arts I was doing a lot of electronic and tape music and was very much taken by working with texts involving the human voice. I met a composer from Sweden, named Lars-Gunnar Bodin, who liked what I was doing, as I did what he was doing. In fact the Swedes had invented this term "text-sound composition" to indicate a hybrid art that could be practiced by composers or poets without musical training who wanted to manipulate sound. I applied for a Fulbright to go to Sweden—it proved a bit of a scam insofar as by the time I got there I found I wasn't so interested in text-sound composition anymore, although I did do some pieces using Swedish texts which I still like a lot—one of them in *The Fragility Cycles*, the setting of the poem "IKON: Ayiasma," which still haunts me. I think the Swede Gunnar Ekelöf is one of the great twentieth-century poets.

It was after that year in Sweden that I began doing live concerts of my work, building up the "Gambuh" piece from *The Fragility Cycles*.

STRICKLAND: The gambuh almost became your trademark. What fascinated you about it?

MARSHALL: It's almost impossible to play. It's a meter long and the finger holes are so far apart you can only cover them using your thumbs. I studied a little in Bali with a master gambuh player, but [*laughs*] it didn't do any good. I very slowly developed a way of playing one tone at a time along with the strange harmonics I could make by manipulating my mouth and fingers. I loved the tone of it, very much like a shakuhachi in its depth.

STRICKLAND: The gambuh adds a beautiful presence to your tape and vocals in *The Fragility Cycles*. Those live/tape concerts were your main activity in the late '70s. How much room for improvisation did you leave yourself?

MARSHALL: There was a good deal. A performance of *Gambuh* or *Gradual Requiem* would never be the same. The timing would be the same, the structure would be the same, and certain parts would be the same—the very tight coordination between mandolin and piano would almost always be the same—but the rest would be more loosely structured, improvising within certain constraints, as in Indian music. In *Fog Tropes* the instruments actually have melodic fragments written out as modules, which permits improvisation, though the musicians usually figure out in advance how they're going to play it. I was even thinking of doing this for the strings in *A Peaceable Kingdom*—"Repeat this module two or three times and move on to the next." But giving the musicians that freedom creates new problems of synchronization and coordination—again, you need more time to rehearse and work it out, and that time isn't available. In the prelude of the string quartet there was something of an improvised repeating of figures which go into a digital delay.

STRICKLAND: Basically improvisation is restricted to your solo performances. I'm still unclear about the mechanics of the live/tape performances of

The Fragility Cycles. You'd roll a tape and play and sing over it without adjusting the tape itself?

MARSHALL: There are actually two tapes. One tape has the sound of the skis and the mountain cries and so on. The other tape has nothing on it. I'm recording on it. Whatever I play or sing into the microphone or whatever comes out of the synthesizer goes through that tape and is spun around the room through the speakers. So that second tape recorder is used to create a *live* tape delay. Sometimes the recorded sounds also go through the second machine, as in the Sibelius radio section.

STRICKLAND: Sibelius is a strong presence in your work. The Sixth Symphony in *Fragility Cycles*, the Seventh influencing the structure of your *Sinfonia.*

MARSHALL: In the sense that it's a one-movement work. I thought the Javanese influence was more important. But there's the Sibelius Fifth in the first movement of the quartet [*sings*].

STRICKLAND: That's astonishing! I've heard it three times and never recognized it. I can't *believe* I didn't catch it.

MARSHALL: No one ever does. I can't believe it either, unless it's because the context is so different.

STRICKLAND: We're back to Finland after a world tour. Now let's go home. Are there any important American influences on your work?

MARSHALL: I've just been going back to Ives again after a long time away. His concept of simultaneity interests me. The amplification of rock might have a strong subconscious influence on us all. Jazz I've always admired from afar.

More important might be American hymnody. I grew up singing in the Congregational choir. My mother—I swear to God she used to play two hymns at once sometimes, one with each hand—either that or she was playing in different keys with each hand. I'm not sure why she did it, maybe just the second drink of the evening. But I've always thought she played "Watchman, Tell Us of the Night" with one hand and "Nearer My God to Thee" with the other. She used to play piano for the Sunday school and had an incredible way of playing. "Full pedal down and damn the torpedoes!" Maybe there's a subtle influence of that. But I've always liked old hymns, and I'm always sticking them in my music.

STRICKLAND: One of the most impressive qualities in your music is its sense of solemnity, of gravity. Maybe that derives from your exposure to spirituals.

MARSHALL: I think music of all the arts has the absolutely unique capacity of delving deepest into the human psyche and soul. As you say, it has gravity, it can get down deep, plumb the depths. If that's what music can do, I feel that's what *I* should do. So [*speaking more slowly and softly*] my music does take a dark, somber path, it's true, but I find that leads to its profoundest moments, and so I'm attracted. [*Raising voice*] I'm not a grave *person*!

STRICKLAND: I was really expecting someone quite different, almost grim, Teutonic-existential maybe.

MARSHALL: Arvo Pärt always strikes me as the kind of person I ought to be [*laughs*] . . . hang a lot of icons around the house . . .

STRICKLAND: He's got that wonderful Dostoevskian face, but in a way you don't have any. You have your back to the camera on two album covers—[*laughs*] can I include this in my introduction under jazz influences/Miles Davis?—and distorted images in other photos.

MARSHALL: I did a concert once at The Kitchen in the '70s and erected a barricade between me and the audience. I got all these potted plants, big speakers. I realized I was in a way hiding from my audience. I wanted to be in the same room with them, but I didn't want them to see me—like a priest in the Orthodox church who spends most of his time behind the iconostasis. A good deal of the service is done in secret—you hear him but you don't see him. It's not shyness—I need to do it in front of people, but not *quite*.

STRICKLAND [*warily*]: This affects the album pictures too?

MARSHALL: Maybe subconsciously. It wasn't part of a plan.

STRICKLAND: To get back to more important matters, John Adams talks of the elegiac quality of your music. Two works relate directly to your parents' deaths, *Gradual Requiem* and *Hidden Voices*, dedicated to your father and mother respectively.

MARSHALL: *Gradual Requiem* was deliberately created as a memorial to my father and speaks very strongly about his loss, my loss. That wasn't the way with *Hidden Voices*. I didn't set out to create a musical memorial to my mother. It just turned out—in the end I realized it was because I actually heard her voice in that piece. At the end I heard, I *heard* her voice. It was almost as if she was coming back and saying to me, "Now don't *forget* about me!" [*Laughs.*] It just *happened* to be that I heard her voice in that female lamentation, though what she has to do with East European wedding dirges I don't know. I'm trying to talk about the personal elements, unlike some composers who simply won't, but it's hard.

STRICKLAND: The elegiac element is less directly personal in the second movement of the string quartet, which is variations on "Shall We Gather at the River?" Then you have a funeral procession in *A Peaceable Kingdom*. And in *Alcatraz* and elsewhere your singing strikes me as a Celtic keening—or almost a banshee sound at times. Even *Sinfonia "Dolce far niente"* sounds more like *niente* than *dolce*, as you acknowledge. I'm not here from *People* or *Psychology Today*, but what does all this reflect about the composer?

MARSHALL: As I said, what interests me in music is its profundity. The elegiac mode seems to be what I do best as a composer, and that's where my music gravitates—even the word "gravitates" suggests downward movement. I love Bruckner—his harmony, his music is *about* gravity, about being brought back to where you came from. I hope I've imbued my own music with a distinct personality, so that people will be able to say, "Yes, that's Ingram Marshall, that's his music." I think any artist wants his work to be in some sense an extension of his personality, though not the superficial aspects of it. I'm an outgoing, gregarious person, sure, but down deep I'm not that way. Down deep I'm more like what you hear in the music.

That might explain it.

Index

EDWARD STRICKLAND is a Contributing Editor of *Fanfare* magazine. His writings on music have appeared in *Atlantic Monthly*, the *New York Times*, and other publications in the United States, Europe, and Japan. In 1990–91 he lectured on music and literature across Southeast Asia as a Fulbright Professor in American Studies.